Parables for Our Time

AMERICAN ACADEMY OF RELIGION

CULTURAL CRITICISM SERIES

SERIES EDITOR
Bjorn Krondorfer, St. Mary's College of Maryland

A Publication Series of
The American Academy of Religion
and
Oxford University Press

ANTI-JUDAISM IN FEMINIST RELIGIOUS WRITINGS
Katharina von Kellenbach

THE GREAT WHITE FLOOD
Racism in Australia
Anne Pattel-Gray

ON DECONSTRUCTING LIFE-WORLDS
Buddhism, Christianity, Culture
Robert Magliola

CULTURAL OTHERNESS
Correspondence with Richard Rorty, Second Edition
Anindita Niyogi Balslev

CROSS CULTURAL CONVERSATION
(Initiation)
Edited by Anindita Niyogi Balslev

IMAG(IN)ING OTHERNESS
Filmic Visions of Living Together
Edited by S. Brent Plate and David Jasper

PARABLES FOR OUR TIME
Rereading New Testament Scholarship after the Holocaust
Tania Oldenhage

Parables for Our Time

*Rereading New Testament Scholarship
after the Holocaust*

TANIA OLDENHAGE

OXFORD
UNIVERSITY PRESS

2002

OXFORD
UNIVERSITY PRESS
Oxford   New York

Auckland   Bangkok   Buenos Aires   Cape Town   Chennai
Dar es Salaam   Delhi   Hong Kong   Istanbul   Karachi   Kolkata
Kuala Lumpur   Madrid   Melbourne   Mexico City   Mumbai   Nairobi
São Paulo   Shanghai   Singapore   Taipei   Tokyo   Toronto

and an associated company in Berlin

Published by Oxford University Press, Inc.,
198 Madison Avenue, New York, New York 10016

www.oup.com

Oxford is a registered trademark of Oxford University Press

Scripture quotations are from the New Revised Standard Version of the Bible,
copyright © 1989 by the Division of Christian Education of the National Council
of the Churches of Christ in the USA. Used by permission. All rights reserved.

Franz Kafka's short story "Give it Up!" is reprinted by permission of Random House, Inc.
from *Franz Kafka: The Complete Stories* by Franz Kafka,
edited by Nahum N. Glatzer, copyright © 1946, 1947, 1948, 1949, 1954, 1958. 1971
by Schocken Books. Used by permission of Schocken Books, a division of Random House, Inc.

Passages from Paul Ricoeur's essay "Biblical Hermeneutics" in *Semeia 4* are reprinted
by permission of the Society of Biblical Literature.

Parts of Chapters 5 and 9 are revised versions of an article published in *Semeia* 77.
Used by permission of the Society of Biblical Literature.

Library of Congress Cataloging-in-Publication Data
Oldenhage, Tania.
Parables for our time: rereading New Testament scholarship after the Holocaust / Tania Oldenhage.
p. cm.–(American Academy of Religion cultural criticism series)
Includes bibliographical references.
ISBN 0-19-515052-X
1. Jesus Christ–Parables.   2. Holocaust (Christian theology)   3. Bible. N.T.
Gospels–Hermeneutics–History–20th century.   4. Harnisch, Wolfgang.
Gleichniserzählungen Jesu.   5. Jeremias, Joachim, 1900– Gleichnisse Jesu.
6. Crossan, John Dominic. Raid on the articulate.   7. Ricoeur, Paul–
Contributions in Biblical hermeneutics.   I. Title.   II. Series.
BT375.3 .O43 2002
226.8'06'09045–dc21   2001036518

1 3 5 7 9 8 6 4 2

Printed in the United States of America
on acid-free paper

In memory of my father
Hans-Otto Oldenhage
1939–1993

Acknowledgments

This study is the result of many years of writing and rewriting. I would like to thank the people who supported me in this process. Above all, I am indebted to Laura Levitt who encouraged me to follow my intuitions and opened up for me the interdisciplinary space I needed to carry out this project. For her passion, her genius, her incredible scholarly energies, I thank her with all my heart. Markus Felß in Germany and Michelle Fried-man in the United States were my two first readers who patiently took it upon them-selves to discuss with me my rough drafts and my not-quite-processed arguments. With-out them, writing would have been a much lonelier process. For their care and refusal to let me get away with vagueness, I am deeply grateful. Björn Krondorfer read the entire manuscript and made invaluable suggestions to refine my arguments and my rhetoric. I also would like to thank my friends and teachers for their engagement with my work, particularly Henning Backhauß, Liora Gubkin, Vasiliki Limberis, Ruth Ost, Cindy Patton, Marian Ronan, Claudia Schippert, Sandra Schleimer, Tim Schramm, Geling Shang, Gibson Winter, and Simon Wood. Special thanks to my brother Frieder Oldenhage for his humor and his tireless efforts to provide me with German literary references, to my sister Marijke Oldenhage for her great friendship, to Claudia Schippert for her gen-erous help with so many things and for offering me a home in Philadelphia whenever I needed it. I am grateful, too, to my mother Rosmarie Oldenhage, to Annemarie Mattenberger, and to Heiner Krone for their love. I gratefully acknowledge permission for use of the following. Marie Luise Kaschnitz's poem "Zoon Politikon I" is reprinted and translated into English by permission of Claasen Verlag. © Claassen Verlag 1965; passages from *Raid on the Articulate* are reprinted by permission of the author, John Dominic Crossan; and parts of Chapter 12 are excerpted from my article "How to Read a Tainted Text? The Wicked Husbandmen in a Post-Holocaust Context," published in *Postmodern Interpretations of the Bible*. Copyright 2001 Chalice Press. Used by permis-sion of Chalice Press.

Contents

Parables for Our Time

1

Introduction

Reading the Bible in America

> What makes biblical interpretation possible is radical detachment, emotional, intellectual, and political distanciation. Disinterested and dispassionate scholarship enables biblical critics to enter the minds and world of historical people, to step out of their own time and to study history on its own terms, unencumbered by contemporary questions, values, and interests.

With these words Elisabeth Schüssler Fiorenza critically summarized the dominant "ethos" of biblical scholarship in America since World War II.[1] Her audience was the Society of Biblical Literature, the year was 1987, the place was the annual meeting of this academic society in Boston.[2] Schüssler Fiorenza spoke as the first woman president. Her address was a passionate call for a "rhetorical-ethical turn" (4) and a strong appeal against the posture of value-free detachment in biblical studies: "Biblical interpretation, like all scholarly inquiry, is a communicative practice that involves interests, values, and visions" (4).

Schüssler Fiorenza enacted this shift in her address. In an effort to clarify her own rhetorical situation as presidential speaker, she recapitulated the history of the organization in two steps. First, she described the conflicting participation of women in the Society. She pointed to the first presentations and publications by women in the beginning of the century, to the decline of women's membership until 1970, and to the gradual increase in the representation of female members on the Society's boards, councils, and committees that led to her own appointment as president in 1987.[3] However, Schüssler Fiorenza emphasized that she was speaking not simply as the first female president but as a feminist scholar committed to promoting work "in the interest of women" (8). Feminist scholarship on the Bible, according to Schüssler Fiorenza, went beyond the focus on women-related issues in biblical interpretation. It sought "to change our methods of reading and reconstruction, as well as our hermeneutical perspectives and scholarly assumptions" (8). At stake in feminist biblical scholarship, for Schüssler Fiorenza, was a new paradigm.

In a second step, Schüssler Fiorenza described the scholarly ethos that had dominated the Society up to that time. To do so, she examined the rhetoric of the presidential addresses given by her (male) predecessors in the twentieth century. She pointed

out that these addresses propagated biblical scholarship that was far removed from contemporary history and politics. Even after the Second World War the presidents of the
Society did not discuss how and in what ways biblical scholars should take account of
the period's devastating events.

> Since 1947 no presidential address has explicitly reflected on world politics, global crises,
> human sufferings, or movements for change. Neither the civil rights movement nor the
> various liberation struggles of the so-called Third World, neither the assassination of Martin
> Luther King nor the Holocaust has become the rhetorical context for biblical studies. (9)

This failure of the Society's presidents, according to Schüssler Fiorenza, was reflective of a widely shared attitude. Biblical scholars after the war by and large pursued
their studies in a "political vacuum" (9), as she described it. She also pointed to a series
of shifts toward a new paradigm that, she hoped, would undermine this approach: "The
decentering of this rhetoric of disinterestedness and presupposition-free exegesis seeks
to recover the political context of biblical scholarship and its public responsibility" (11).
According to Schüssler Fiorenza, efforts toward such recovery were already underway.[4]
She ended her address by asking the members of the Society more broadly to become
aware of their own work's situatedness in the twentieth century, to engage in what she
called an "ethics of accountability," and to attend to the material consequences of biblical interpretation in the present.[5]

In 1988, Schüssler Fiorenza's address was published in the *Journal of Biblical Literature* under the title "The Ethics of Biblical Interpretation: Decentering Biblical Scholarship." I encountered this text in 1992, shortly after I left Germany. Schüssler Fiorenza's
essay was my first introduction to contemporary American biblical studies, and it made
an impression on me. Its critical description of the dominant ethos in biblical scholarship poignantly captured the scholarly atmosphere with which I was familiar. The "rhetoric
of disinterestedness and presupposition-free exegesis" had been the standard mode of
discourse during my study of the Bible at German universities. Schüssler Fiorenza's
insistence that scholarship happens in a sociopolitical context, that there is a certain
"rhetoric" to every scholarly practice, and that scholars are ethically accountable for their
work opened up for me an entirely new way of thinking about what it means to do
biblical scholarship.[6]

During the 1990s biblical scholars began to take up Schüssler Fiorenza's challenge
to "decenter biblical scholarship."[7] Scholars of various trainings are now discussing the
embeddedness of interpretation within contemporary contexts and are theorizing the
ethics of reading biblical texts. These discussions are quite diverse.[8] Their participants
make use of different, sometimes opposing, strategies with often contradicting results.
Schüssler Fiorenza's presidential address, for example, links the ethics of accountability
to an "ethics of historical reading" that does "justice to the text in its historical context"
(14). Ethically responsible scholarship, according to Schüssler Fiorenza, continues the
project of historical inquiry, albeit with different presuppositions. In other corners of
biblical studies, scepticism about the possibility of unearthing a text's historical meaning prevails. Informed by a variety of critical theories, biblical scholars have begun to
emphasize the contingency of meaning and think through the radical implications of
this insight for their discipline.[9] The 1995 publication of *The Postmodern Bible*, written
by ten scholars who call themselves "The Bible and Culture Collective," is a landmark

in these endeavors. The book presents and discusses a range of "postmodernist" reading strategies, which

> share a suspicion of the claim to mastery that characterizes traditional readings of texts, including modern biblical scholarship. . . . [B]y sweeping away secure notions of meaning, by radically calling into question the apparently stable foundations of meaning on which traditional interpretation is situated, by raising doubts about the capacity to achieve ultimate clarity about the meaning of a text, postmodern readings lay bare the contingent and constructed character of meaning itself. (2–3)

This agenda conflicts with the work of Schüssler Fiorenza, who is wary of postmodernist discourses because of what she considers to be postmodernism's lack of political accountability and vigor, an assessment not shared by the Bible and Culture Collective.[10] However, Schüssler Fiorenza's presidential address and *The Postmodern Bible*, despite all their differences and disagreements, participate in a similar effort: they both develop a critique of the "disinterested and dispassionate" scholarship and, in one way or another, try "to make sense of the Bible in relation to contemporary culture" (*Postmodern Bible* 8).[11]

From Germany to America

During my years in the United States, the research topic I had brought with me from Germany was affected by the challenges posed by Schüssler Fiorenza and *The Postmodern Bible*. In Germany I had become interested in the hermeneutical discussions around the parables of Jesus. In the center of these discussions stood the conflict between historical criticism, dominant in German biblical studies generally speaking, and more recent literary approaches to the Bible. In regard to the parables, historical-critical approaches had produced two eminent works by Adolf Jülicher and Joachim Jeremias. These classic works had set the basic rules of discourse and had opened up a research framework in which the parables of Jesus were investigated within their first historical settings. More recently, historical critics in Germany had begun to work against the anti-Jewish trends in the scholarship of Jeremias and others by reconfiguring Jesus' stories as genuinely Jewish parables and by recovering their first-century Jewish horizon of understanding.[12] The historical-critical paradigm was contested, however, by a number of scholars who argued that the meaning of Jesus' parables can be found not in their first-century historical context but in their timeless poetic powers.[13] Appropriating methods and theories from secular literary criticism, these scholars treated the parables of Jesus not as ancient artifacts but as autonomous works of art. To me, the investigation of the parables by means of literary criticism had seemed like an exciting new alternative to historical criticism. I was particularly intrigued by the idea that the parables are metaphorical narratives whose poetic powers can still affect us today.

When I came to the United States in 1992 I intended to deepen my study and was embarrassed to learn that the scholarly movement that I had considered the most progressive strand in New Testament studies was actually already twenty years old. The notion of the parables as metaphors first emerged in American biblical studies in the late 1960s and early 1970s. It grew out of what today is often called the "literary turn" in New Testament studies, a shift that several scholars in the United States initiated away from traditional historical-criticism to a literary approach to the Bible and to the parables in particular.[14] These discussions arrived in Germany with some delay and in the early 1990s could still be considered "new."[15] In America they were dated. Arriving from Germany, I was caught in a time lapse.

In her presidential address, Schüssler Fiorenza described the literary trend in biblical studies:

> In the past fifteen years or so, biblical studies has . . . adopted insights and methods derived from literary studies and philosophical hermeneutics; but it has, to a great extent, refused to relinquish its rhetorical stance of value-free objectivism and scientific methodism. This third literary-hermeneutical paradigm seems presently in the process of decentering into a fourth paradigm that inaugurates a rhetorical-ethical turn. (3-4)

Indeed, as I explored the landscape of biblical studies in the United States I noticed that scholars who in the 1970s had been discussing the literary qualities of biblical texts had quite different concerns now and that these concerns were often precisely the ethical and political implications of scholarship pointed out by Schüssler Fiorenza.[16] Eventually I, too, became involved in an effort to reclaim a "rhetorical context" for my work in biblical studies.

One of my aims in studying in the United States was to deal with the problem of anti-Judaism in my field of research and to deepen my knowledge of rabbinical parables. I had encountered the critical concern with anti-Jewish tendencies in New Testament interpretation in Germany and had learned to look for affinities between the parables of Jesus and those of the Rabbis. When I came to the United States I expected that the Jewish studies program of my department would be an excellent site for me to become familiar with rabbinical literature. But things took a different turn. Jewish studies in America engaged me not in a study of ancient rabbinical texts but in the study of the Holocaust.[17] It gave me an opportunity to struggle with the legacy of the country where I grew up.

The history of the Holocaust was not a new topic for me. But what I encountered now was a way of thinking about "Nazism and the 'Final Solution'"[18] that greatly differed from the historical or theological approaches I had known in Germany. I was introduced to discussions of remembrance and representation, to a growing body of scholarship informed by insights from cultural studies and literary theory.[19] I became aware of the intricacies of memory—the dilemma, for instance, that the construction of Holocaust memorials does not safeguard a population from the processes of forgetting.[20] And I learned about the problem that our knowledge of Auschwitz depends on the language and narratives that are available to us; that a chronological account, a memoir of a survivor, a fictional Holocaust novel, a movie are all particular kinds of representations with different interpretative patterns, which in their turn have different consequences for our understanding of the events.

The debates over these questions, as I read and studied them, provided me with a new lens for looking at my own field of research, for perceiving how the Holocaust was remembered and represented in the context of parable scholarship. In the spring and summer of 1994 I began to reread major texts in parable interpretation and to examine the ways the legacy of the Holocaust echoes in these texts.[21] I embarked on a project to show that New Testament parable scholars during the last five decades worked not in a political vacuum but in situations shaped by memories of the Holocaust.

Outline

This book is divided into four parts. Part I, "Holocaust Remembrance in Germany," introduces questions of Holocaust memory as the broad framework of my project. It is centered around Wolfgang Harnisch's book *Die Gleichniserzählungen Jesu*, published in 1985. Harnisch's work presents an early and original attempt by a German scholar to adopt and integrate into European scholarship the American hermeneutic approaches to the parables. According to Harnisch, the parables of Jesus should be understood as works of art endowed with the power of poetry to reveal new dimensions of reality. I am concerned with one particular place in Harnisch's work. In developing his understanding of "metaphor," Harnisch cites the first segment of Marie Luise Kaschnitz's poetic cycle "Zoon Politikon," written in Germany in the mid-1960s. The poem describes how the forgotten memories of Nazi genocide return to a German home and haunt its inhabitants. The poem's place in Harnisch's book raises important questions about the difficulties of remembering the Holocaust in Germany in the 1980s and 1990s. By situating Harnisch's use of Kaschnitz's poem within a contemporary German context, I also situate my project within what Schüssler Fiorenza would call my own rhetorical situation, which is shaped by my status as a member of the so-called third generation in Germany.

Part II, "Historical Criticism and the Legacy of the Holocaust," turns to the classic work of parable interpretation: Joachim Jeremias's book *The Parables of Jesus*, first published in Germany in 1947. By attending to Jeremias's historical-critical approach, I describe the legacy and common point of departure of the work done by Harnisch and by American literary scholars of the 1970s. I also clarify my own approach to parable interpretation in conversation with historical critics who recently have begun to raise questions about the anti-Jewish tendencies in Jeremias's work. I argue that the current focus on the problem of anti-Judaism fails to historicize Jeremias's book. It is important to take into account the time and place of the book's first publication: Germany in 1947. I show that Jeremias's book, once it is situated two years after the end of the war, becomes symptomatic not so much of Christian anti-Judaism in general but, much more specifically, of the difficulties of responding to the Holocaust in Germany shortly after the events.

My effort to historicize Jeremias's work leads me to an examination of how the difficulties of remembering the Holocaust were transported to the next generation of scholars. To do so, I move to America and to the 1970s where parable scholarship took a hermeneutic turn. Parts III and IV of this book show how scholars in America, working under a new literary paradigm, responded to the legacy of the Holocaust. I focus on two proponents of this literary turn in parable studies. Part III, "Jesus as Poet of Our Time," focuses on the most prolific and perhaps most influential participant of the literary turn in American biblical studies: John Dominic Crossan. I offer a critical reading of Crossan's book *Raid on the Articulate*, published in 1976. I argue that this book is perhaps the first instance of a biblical scholar trying to make Jesus' stories speak to a post-Holocaust situation. The book exemplifies an important side effect of the literary turn: as the parables of Jesus were turned from historical artifacts into literary texts, they were brought into contact with so-called secular literature, or "texts within our own world," to use Crossan's phrase. I am interested in the fact that many of the twentieth-century literary texts cited in *Raid* are charged vis-à-vis the Holocaust. Through close readings of two examples of twentieth-century novels as they appear in Crossan's work, Kurt Vonnegut's *Cat's Cradle* and Elie Wiesel's *Gates of the Forest*, I investigate how memories of recent catastrophes shape Crossan's work without, however, being integrated or explored by Crossan in any way. I also argue that these shapes of memory are typical of American Holocaust culture in the mid-1970s.

Part IV, "The Promise of Metaphor Theory," turns to a second major participant of the literary turn in American biblical studies: Paul Ricoeur. I examine Ricoeur's essay "Biblical Hermeneutics," which was published in the experimental journal *Semeia* in 1975. Although written by a French philosopher, the essay is very much at the heart of American discussions of the parables in the 1970s. In "Biblical Hermeneutics" Ricoeur makes metaphor theory fruitful for parable studies and thereby offers a new interpretive vision of Jesus' stories. Understood as metaphorical narratives, the parables are said to offer a new vision of reality. Ricoeur argues, moreover, that, as limit-expressions, the parables refer to limit-experiences of human life, including death, suffering, guilt, and hatred. I develop a critical reading of what I call the limit-rhetoric in Ricoeur's 1975 essay in light of the fact that the notion of limit was already becoming a crucial trope within Holocaust literary studies.[22] By cross reading the fields of Holocaust studies and New Testament parable studies, I raise questions about Ricoeur's deployment of the charged trope of "limit-experiences" in relation to the parables of Jesus.

My last chapter concludes the book by addressing its implications for future work in New Testament scholarship. Tying together my arguments, I demonstrate what a post-Holocaust reading of a New Testament parable might look like. Focusing on the story of the Wicked Husbandmen, I develop an interpretation that critically and consciously builds on the literary turn in biblical studies while situating itself as thoroughly as possible in its own cultural and rhetorical context.

Autobiographical Interventions

Throughout this book I often deploy an autobiographical voice.[23] I decided to do so for several reasons. By taking account of my own history with parable scholarship I wish to construct a position from which it is possible to talk about the desires that are operative in scholarly discourse as well as the expectations that discourse can provoke. Part of my argument is that the hermeneutic endeavors around the parables bring certain gains to the interpreter and that these gains are significant vis-à-vis the Holocaust. In some ways, this argument follows Schüssler Fiorenza's insight that "biblical interpretation . . . involves interests, values, and visions" (4). This means, for example, that the turn to metaphor theory by parable scholars not only is a quest for the true meaning of biblical texts but also holds promises about reconfiguring and reclaiming Jesus' parables in a particular way at a certain moment in time.

However, these "interests, values, and visions," to speak with Schüssler Fiorenza, are largely contained or hidden in my four texts. It is not the case that certain tendencies in a text can be read as a clear sign of an author's "interests." I argue, for instance, that Jeremias's degradation of Jewish literature is not translatable into Christian anti-Judaism in any straightforward way. Similarly, the meanings of Harnisch's and Crossan's quotation of post-Holocaust literature is not at all obvious or unambiguous. This is why I would speak not so much of "interests, values, and visions" as of motivations, desires, responses, or failures that are mostly inarticulate and less than conscious. I needed a strategy that would allow me to interpret and articulate what in the scholarly texts are only traces, resonances, echoes, gestures, and allusions. It became helpful for me to build a strong "I" in my text, an "I" that is positioned in relation both to the events of the Holocaust and to the hermeneutics of parables, an "I" that picks up, responds to, and interacts with these allusions and echoes.

My autobiographical interventions, finally, intend to make as explicit as possible the rhetorical context of my own project. Granted the impossibility of fully uncovering my own less-than-conscious motivations, I do try to attend to at least some of the reasons that have prompted me to engage in this project. Again, following Schüssler Fiorenza, I want to emphasize that "reclaiming a rhetorical context for biblical studies" is itself a rhetorical practice. Using the autobiographical voice has been a way for me to acknowl-edge how much my work is informed and motivated by my position as a German who sees herself confronted with the legacy of the Holocaust.

This position, however, was never stable. The post-Holocaust reading of parable scholarship that I present here was shaped over several years. It is informed by the dif-ferent encounters I made with each scholarly text and by my varying responses to the legacy of the Holocaust as I found it reflected in parable scholarship. Tracing these changes has become an integral part of my work. This means that my book does not provide a definite reading that puts parable scholarship in its place, so to speak, and thus gives a final answer about its historical meaning. Instead, I offer readings that are multileveled, that take account of my changing perspectives, and that draw attention to my own im-plication in this project.

PART I

HOLOCAUST REMEMBRANCE IN GERMANY

2

"On Sundays the Forgotten Comes"

A Ghost in My Room

The concerns of this book took shape in 1994. They were initiated through a strange deed of mine, something that I did while studying Paul Ricoeur's book *The Rule of Metaphor* and its influence on New Testament hermeneutics. With my eyes fixed on Ricoeur's dense paragraphs and with a growing pile of handwritten excerpts on my desk, I worked my way through Ricoeur's theory. For Ricoeur, metaphors have the potential to lead their recipients to the discovery of new meaning. While numerous scholars over the centuries have looked at metaphors as mere rhetorical devices based on the replacement of one term with another, Ricoeur argues that metaphors are based on a tension between two terms that, according to their lexical usage, are incompatible. Their odd combination releases a creative process in which reality is described in new ways.

I intended to follow Ricoeur into every detail of this argument and soon felt the need to pursue his theoretical journeys with the aid of a concrete example of metaphorical language. I wanted to take recourse to my own sense of poetry in order to check the turns of Ricoeur's discussions—to keep one foot on the ground, so to speak. I needed a German poem. The deed that I suspect was so crucial in initiating my project is this: One day, early on in my reading, I went to my bookshelf, took down a red German paperback, opened it to a page where I knew a particular German poem was cited, copied the poem on a piece of paper, and taped it on my desk. It was a book on the parables of Jesus. The poem was about the forgotten and returning memory of Auschwitz (my translation):

Feiertags	On Sundays
Kommt das Vergessene	The forgotten comes
Auf Hahnenfüßen mit Sporen	On crowsfeet with spurs
Die ritzen mir ins Parkett	They carve in the parquet for me
Ein Schnittmuster, so	A pattern, thus
Wird uns zugeschnitten	It is cut out for us

Das Nesselhemd	The nettle-cloth
Wenn die Wand	When the rose-colored
Rosentapete sich auftut	Wallpaper opens
Und ausstößt die Bettlade voll	And expels the drawer full
Von gemergelten Judenköpfen	Of emaciated Jewish heads
Wenn durch den versiegelten schön	When through the insulated
Glänzenden Estrich hinausdrängt	Clean polished floor penetrates
Nichts. Nur ein Rauch	Nothing. Just the foul smoke
Stinkender. So	Of rotten ones. Thus
Werden wir eingekleidet	We are clothed
In das was uns zukommt	With what we deserve
Wenn die Kinder aufstehen fragen	When the children get up and ask
Wie konntet ihr nur	How could you
In Rauch und Nesseln	In smoke and nettles
Besonders am Feiertag.	Especially on Sundays.

The poem is written from the perspective of Germans who gather together on a Sunday. Their home is tidy and pretty, the wallpaper rose-colored, the floor clean and polished. But the German home has cracks. The past sneaks through the surface, making it impossible for the Germans to enjoy the day. Nazi atrocities fill the room in the terrible form of the victims. "Emaciated Jewish heads" break through the walls; "the foul smoke of rotten ones" poisons the air.

I no longer remember whether or not the poem helped me to understand the intricacies of Ricoeur's metaphor theory. When I eventually finished reading Ricoeur I had forgotten the piece of paper on my desk. The poem jumped into my face a few months later. I was reading through Holocaust testimonies because I was taking a course on the topic. As my eyes turned away from the testimonies they were suddenly caught by the poem. I stared at the familiar German words, and for the first time I was hit by the images. Suddenly the poem had lost any connection to metaphor theory and instead struck old layers in my memory. For a few seconds I was entrapped in the atmosphere of the poem, catapulted back to Germany and back to the places where I grew up. I was a German in a German home where the crimes of genocide loomed like an unspeakable secret, like a drawer full of emaciated Jewish heads shut away behind rose-colored walls.

While the images of the poem entered my mind, an uncanny feeling overwhelmed me. I felt caught, attacked from behind, as I realized what kind of text it was that I had kept in front of myself for months. I knew, of course, that I was the one who had taped the poem on the desk, but it seemed as though the poem had come from someplace else, forcing me to look at something important that I had failed to recognize. At the same time I was shocked as I remembered my own previous use of the poem, which now seemed to me a blind and sterile misreading. How could I possibly have treated a poem like this as an illustrative device that would lead me through dense Ricoeurian theory?

During these moments, I imagine, a number of different issues became connected in my mind. Ricoeur's metaphor theory, the images of Nazi atrocities evoked by the poem, and the German book on the parables of Jesus where I had found the poem, suddenly imbricated with each other, eventually produced a series of questions that I needed to work through: what precisely was the role of a Holocaust poem in a hermeneutic discourse on New Testament parables? What was its connection to Ricoeur's metaphor theory? And why exactly had I put it on my desk?

Over the years the poem remained pivotal to my project. I have read and reread the poem many times; sometimes empathic, sometimes distanced, critical, and even annoyed. I have translated and retranslated it, browsing through dictionaries, arguing with friends about nuances in meaning and about English words that never seemed to be right. I have contrasted and compared the poem with several other texts, trying to trace its profile, its idiosyncrasies, its historical contours. The poem became a main reference point for my personal and academic thinking about the difficulties of remembering the Holocaust, especially in Germany. Thinking about the poem, about my history with it, became emblematic for what I attempt to do in this book, namely, to read and discuss parts of the Christian hermeneutic discourse on the parables of Jesus as a post-Holocaust phenomenon.

Lately I have started to think about the poem through the trope of the ghost, which has emerged in much recent critical theory. Avery Gordon, for example, in her book *Ghostly Matters*, argues for the importance of paying attention to what haunts us, because "haunting is a very particular way of knowing what has happened or is happening" (8). A ghost, Gordon says, "imports a charged strangeness into the place or sphere that it is haunting, thus unsettling the propriety and property lines that delimit a zone of activity or knowledge" (63). When given heed to, a ghost may lead to an acknowledgment of the past and the present that differs from the established academic ways of studying things. I find it helpful to consider the German poem on my desk along Gordon's lines. Like a ghost, the poem has unsettled my occupation with an academic discipline, New Testament parable studies in particular. It has shocked me out of my own established way of thinking; it did not let go of me until I started to reexamine thoroughly my chosen field of research and my involvement in it.

The vocabulary of ghosts, haunting, and the uncanny proposed by Gordon and others has proven useful also in my actual readings of post-Holocaust scholarly texts on the parables.[1] Especially the notion of the uncanny, originally theorized by Sigmund Freud, has allowed me to focus on the marginal and elusive aspects of parable scholarship, to get a hold on its often unconscious dynamics. The uncanny suggested itself to me as an interpretive means especially because the poem itself is very much about "ghostly matters." A haunted home, strange patterns on the parquet, walls that open, smoke sneaking through floors, a drawer full of severed heads is imagery reminiscent of ghost stories. Using this imagery to address the historical theme of Nazi genocide, the poem anticipated a way of representing, of communicating, of talking about charged and difficult things that not only has been useful to me but in fact has been introduced into Holocaust studies by a number of scholars.[2]

For these reasons I center this first chapter around the poem. By considering its historical context, by critically engaging its language, by discussing and recasting its tropes and phrases, I will start to develop my own language for this project. In chapter 3 I will then address the place where I first came across the poem, a German book on the parables of Jesus.

A Haunted German Home in the 1960s

A Poem and Its Historical Background

The poem that was taped on my desk in 1994 is the first segment of Marie Luise Kaschnitz's poetic cycle "Zoon Politikon," first published in 1964.[3] After I had so immediately and powerfully identified with the scene evoked by Kaschnitz I eventually stepped back and looked at the poem from a distance. I became aware of the fact that there were thirty years between my uncanny encounter with Kaschnitz's text and its first publication. I became interested in the mid-1960s as a specific period in postwar West German history and tried to read Kaschnitz's poem as a testimony of a particular time.

Two texts have strongly shaped my view of these years. The first is Jean Améry's essay "Resentments," which appeared in the spring of 1966. Talking explicitly from the position of a Jewish survivor of several Nazi death camps, Améry gives a sharp and bitter account of the public climate of West Germany in the 1960s. "Sometimes it happens that in the summer I travel through a thriving land" (62)—thus he begins his mocking description of Germany's clean cities and idyllic villages, polite, well-to-do citizens, air of sophistication and tolerance, political stability and moderation. Améry feels uncomfortable in this country. He holds resentments against rehabilitated Germany because its rehabilitation went hand in hand with a general silence and repression in regard to the Nazi crimes. The serene and peaceful public life rests, he points out, on the assumption that time heals wounds and that the wounds of survivors such as Améry should be healed by now, forgiven and forgotten. Améry calls this assumption immoral (72). For him, who once was beaten by an SS man with a shovel handle whenever he didn't work fast enough and two decades later still feels these blows roaring in his skull (70), the past is alive and ought not to be forgotten in Germany just because a natural time sense makes the future appear to be more important.[4]

A similar argument about Germany in the 1960s is made by Alexander and Margarete Mitscherlichs' book *The Inability to Mourn*, which was published one year after Améry's essay and became one of the most well-known studies of the German way of dealing with the Nazi era.[5] Employing the interpretive tools of Freudian psychoanalysis, the Mitscherlichs "diagnose" a general German failure to mourn the losses of the war and consequently a failure to mourn the millions of dead, the countless lives destroyed by the Nazis. The Germans, according to the Mitscherlichs, are characterized by a striking lack of concern in regard not only to their past but also to their present. Not only are they indifferent toward the fate of Nazi victims, they are also apathetic when it comes to their own political culture. The Mitscherlichs describe that apathy as "a sluggishness of reaction discernible throughout Germany's whole political and social organism" (7). The only exception of this "psychological immobilism" is the economy. The Germans "concentrated all their energies on the restoration of what had been destroyed, and on the extension and modernization of their industrial potential—down to, and including, their kitchen utensils" (9). Like Améry, the Mitscherlichs problematize the astonishing economic growth of West Germany after the war in light of the simultaneous denial of Germany's horrific crimes.

Améry and the Mitscherlichs, though from very different angles, produce a picture according to which the Germans during the postwar decades, by and large, were preoccupied with rebuilding their country and refused to deal with the past. "Silence," "repression," "the inability to mourn," "denial" are terms that have shaped the common view about the first postwar decades in West Germany as well as my own understanding of this time. However, when I look into historical works that are concerned specifically with the mid-1960s I gain the impression that things were a bit more complicated than the notion of a "general silence" suggests.

The mid-1960s—the time when Kaschnitz wrote her poem—was actually characterized by the slow emergence of a discernible public discussion about the Nazi past. In 1963, for instance, Rolf Hochhuth's play The Deputy was shown for the first time and provoked a heated discussion about the role of the Catholic Church in the destruction of European Jewry. A year later the debate over the statute of limitation was sparked off in view of the approaching twenty-year anniversary of the end of the war: twenty years was the time period after which murder became statute barred, and while there were many who argued for the limitation's enforcement also in regard to Nazi genocide— much to Améry's horror (71)—there were also a number of German politicians and other public figures who wanted the limitation period to be extended. In any case, these issues brought a discussion to life, which in some corners of Germany significantly disturbed the silence that had been kept over the past.

The perhaps most palpable factor in this rising awareness were the Auschwitz trials, which took place in Frankfurt between 1963 and 1965. These trials were West Germany's biggest criminal procedure against former Nazis. Accused were twenty persons who had worked as guards in the camp in Auschwitz. Widely covered by the media, the trials brought the crimes of the past into a public arena, not only in abstract legal terms but also in concrete detail. The perpetrators' deeds, the testimonies of survivors and witnesses, the photographs of the victims, became part of daily press reports. The trials confronted a general public with the facts and figures of Nazi mass murder and initiated numerous projects of working up what so far had been repressed. As one historian puts it, Verdrängung (repression) turned into Aufarbeitung (working through), at least for some (Thrähnhardt 165). Améry's "Resentments" could count as one example of such Aufarbeitung: it was first broadcast by a West German radio station as part of a whole series featuring Améry's experiences during the Nazi era, a project that was inspired by the trials (Meier 49–50).

Still, I keep wondering: what did "confrontation with the past" mean exactly? How, for example, did people respond to Améry's angry radio-voice? What did Germans make of the terrible details revealed during the trials? How many people did closely follow and actually contemplate them? How much did such engagement remain the business of marginal groups? How much did the taboo around the past, observed by Améry and the Mitscherlichs, continue to regulate daily discourse? According to one of Améry's commentators, "Resentments" was more or less ignored by German critics until very recently (Meier 50–52). And the Mitscherlichs claim: "When this period [the twelve years of Nazi rule] in all its crude brutality is again brought to mind—by the trial of a Nazi war criminal, for instance—the avoidance is continued, and the page of the newspaper carrying the report is quickly turned" (20).

All these conflicting texts, viewpoints, bits and pieces of information make it impossible to gain a clear, unequivocal picture of the mid-1960s. Rather than providing me with a coherent "historical background" against which to read Kaschnitz's poem, they have shaped the questions I bring to my reading. What happens when the forgotten past reappears on the scene? How were the crimes of Auschwitz perceived two decades after the war? How did people respond to them?

Kaschnitz not only read the reports of the Auschwitz trials in Frankfurt carefully, she attended the proceedings. "Zoon Politikon" is a result of what she saw and heard during the trials (von Gersdorff 297). According to one critic, the poem is Kaschnitz's most significant attempt to deal with the experience of the Third Reich (Pulver, "Tänzerin" 114; *Kaschnitz* 87). Kaschnitz had lived through the Nazi period by withdrawing into what has been termed *Innere Emigration*—a state she self-critically describes as a passive, interiorized, and therefore utterly inadequate resistance against National Socialism. She was opposed to the regime, but she stayed and continued to work in Germany. She was able to do so because she was not Jewish. During the war she listened to foreign radio stations and anticipated Hitler's defeat but did not get involved in any political and possibly life-threatening activity.[6]

"Zoon Politikon," particularly the segment of the poem with which I am concerned, is not so much about the past as about its return in the present:

Feiertags	On Sundays
Kommt das Vergessene	The forgotten comes
Auf Hahnenfüßen mit Sporen	On crowsfeet with spurs
Die ritzen mir ins Parkett	They carve in the parquet for me
Ein Schnittmuster	A pattern

What happens when the forgotten past reappears on the scene? "The scene" in Kaschnitz's poem is not the public sphere but the privacy of a home. Unlike Améry, who travels through Germany as a critical observer, and unlike the Mitscherlichs, who elaborate an objective view of contemporary German life in general, Kaschnitz's poem speaks from "the inside," from the perspective of Germans who gather together within their own four walls on a Sunday. Nevertheless, the home as it is painted by Kaschnitz shows signs of the same economic growth that Améry and the Mitscherlichs refer to. The home is equipped with a "parquet," a "rose-colored wall paper," a "clean polished floor." These are markers of bourgeois prosperity. And just as Améry and the Mitscherlichs thought that there was something very wrong with the results of Germany's "economic miracle," there is something dubious, something uncanny about the clean domestic setting as it is described by Kaschnitz.

Uncanny Images and Their Effects

Wenn die Wand	When the rose-colored
Rosentapete sich auftut	Wallpaper opens
Und ausstößt die Bettlade voll	And expels the drawer full
Von gemergelten Judenköpfen	Of emaciated Jewish heads
Wenn durch den versiegelten schön	When through the insulated
Glänzenden Estrich hinausdrängt	Clean polished floor penetrates
Nichts. Nur ein Rauch	Nothing. Just the foul smoke
Stinkender.	Of rotten ones.

As it turns out, the rose-colored wallpaper and the clean polished floor are also part of a facade, a cover-up. Freud's notion of the uncanny, das Unheimliche, can capture the ambiguity of Kaschnitz's home.[7] Freud points to the odd use of the German word *heimlich*, the apparent opposite of *unheimlich*, uncanny. According to one meaning, almost lost today but still remembered by Freud, *heimlich* refers to a cozy, pleasant environment. The word belongs to the etymological field of home (*Heim*) and homeland (*Heimat*) and is synonymous with "belonging to the house, not strange, familiar" (222). But *heimlich* has a second and better known meaning. Most people use the term *heimlich* to refer to something secret, hidden, or concealed.

This ambiguity, which Freud finds in the German word *heimlich*, can be found also in Kaschnitz's home. The markers of bourgeois prosperity—parquets, rose-colored wallpapers, a clean polished floor—for many people are markers of heimlich/homey places, "arousing a sense of agreeable restfulness and security" (Freud 222). But these markers are also supposed to keep something out of sight. The floor is not only clean and polished, it is also insulated (*versiegelt*), sealed: something is supposed to be kept from coming in.[8] Freud emphasizes that *heimlich* and *unheimlich* are not opposites as one would assume. The two words are closely related to each other and as such they can illuminate what happens in Kaschnitz's home: when the rose-colored wallpaper and the clean polished floor fail to hold back what is supposed to be hidden, the heimlich/homey atmosphere turns unheimlich.

Freud quotes from a dictionary: "'*Unheimlich*' is the name for everything that ought to have remained . . . secret and hidden but has come to light" (224). Translated into Freud's psychoanalytic language: The "uncanny is in reality nothing new or alien, but something which is familiar and old-established in the mind and which has become alienated from it only through the process of repression" (241). Things are unheimlich not because they are totally strange to us (un-heimlich) but, on the contrary, because they were once quite familiar and then were banished into secrecy. Kaschnitz calls them "the forgotten."

The concrete shapes of "the forgotten" are dreadful: a "drawer full of emaciated Jewish heads," "the foul smoke of rotten ones." Freud's notion of the uncanny would suggest that once upon a time the smoke and the emaciated Jewish heads were well known and familiar to the people in the German home. I want to hold on to this thought but I want to historicize it. These images once were familiar not because, as Freud's theory would imply, they refer back to an individual or collective psychic past, but because they refer back to historical events that spread among the German public twenty years ago. In 1945 Germans were forced to familiarize themselves with the details of Nazi genocide, the systematic murder of millions of Jews.

I have in mind here an exhibition on the liberation of the camps that was mounted by the Washington Holocaust Memorial Museum several years ago.[9] Under the rubric "Confrontation," the exhibition showed Germans being dragged from their homes into nearby camps, where they were forced to walk through the barracks and to look at the terrible conditions, the emaciated survivors and the heaps of dead bodies. In her book *Germany 1945*, Dagmar Barnouw analyzes these photographs in the context of what she argues was a systematic Allied policy of confronting the German population with the atrocities committed under its name. She writes:

The vast majority of Germans did not live close enough to a camp to have a shocking and sobering look at the physical evidence of terror in Nazi Germany. For them, photographs of atrocities were published in newspapers or posted on billboards, or they were marched to an army cinema to watch films about Buchenwald and Belsen. (7)

Whether they saw it through posters and films or with their own eyes, numerous Germans shortly after the end of the war were confronted with the sight of liberated death camps.[10]

In the eyes of the Allies, according to Barnouw, the images from the camps carried an obvious meaning: There could be no clearer evidence of the Germans' collective guilt and responsibility and the necessity for remorse and atonement. However, Barnouw argues that images of dead bodies don't speak for themselves. Despite their visual clarity, the meaning of the 1945 photographs was and still is obscure (x). Barnouw points out the difficulty of looking at and making sense of pictures of atrocity. The Allies, she says, wanted to make the Germans see. But how were Germans to react to the piles of dead bodies? How were they to interpret them? What could it possibly mean to take responsibility for what they saw? What could it mean to atone for murder on such an incomprehensible scale?[11] According to Barnouw, these questions are crucial but were immediately muted by the seeming self-evidence of the images of the dead.

These very images reappeared twenty years later in the course of the Auschwitz trials, this time not as evidence employed by the Allies against the Germans but as part of the coverage of inner-German legal proceedings against ex-Nazis. By and large forgotten over the postwar years, the photographs taken in the camps in 1945 once more circulated in the media and stared in the face of everyone who read the newspaper. This documentation with its reappearing photographs and accounts I take to be the frame of reference for Kaschnitz's poem. Banished from everyday life, the poem suggests, the images from the camps reemerge from behind walls and bring back forgotten knowledge about gas chambers and crematoria: "Die Bettlade voll / Von gemergelten Judenköpfen," "ein Rauch / Stinkender."[12] In light of Barnouw's considerations I would like to repeat and rephrase a question I raised earlier: What did "confrontation with the past" mean in the 1960s? How did it take place, according to Kaschnitz's poem? How did Germans respond to what they, once again, were faced with?

So	
Wird uns zugeschnitten	It is cut out for us
Das Nesselhemd	The nettle-cloth
. . .	. . .
So	Thus
Werden wir eingekleidet	We are clothed
In das was uns zukommt	With what we deserve
. . .	. . .
In Rauch und Nesseln	In smoke and nettles
Besonders am Feiertag	Especially on Sundays

For a while I did in fact assume that the language of the poem implies notions of guilt and atonement: "nettle-cloth," "nettles," "in smoke and nettles." Someone wears a nettle-cloth who has found herself guilty and wants to atone for her sins. Clothed in nettles, the occupants of the German home seem to be marked as responsible for the crimes revealed in 1945. Strikingly, however, the clothing occurs without any agency on part of the Germans. Each time "the forgotten" arrives, something happens *to them*: "They carve in the parquet for me"; "It is cut out for us"; "We are clothed / With". . .[13]

The Germans don't *put on* the nettle-cloth. They endure whatever comes over them. This lack of agency is paired with a lack of affect. The people in the home do not show any signs of emotion, apart perhaps from the acknowledgment that the nettle-cloth is deserved. "We are clothed / With what we deserve." But even this acknowledgment sounds almost mechanical to me, like a well-rehearsed confessional performance. In any case, it remains unclear how the people react to "the forgotten." What is going on in their minds while they are being confronted with "the drawer full of emaciated Jewish heads," "the foul smoke of rotten ones"? Does the sight of the drawer cause grief, remorse, shame, pity? Or disgust? Or are the people in nettle-cloths in a state similar to the one described by the Mitscherlichs: in a state of apathy? Numb and indifferent?

More than anything else the poem evokes, I think, an eerie sense of devastation, most visible in the peculiar expression "in smoke and nettles" toward the end of the poem. Unlike the well-known phrase "sackcloth and ashes" (in *Sack und Asche*), "smoke and nettles" does not necessarily carry connotations of guilt and atonement. Smoke makes one's eyes burn, pollutes the air, and makes it difficult for people to breathe. Nettles sting; they cause pain and an infection of the skin. The forgotten images from 1945 befall the German home like an affliction (*Heimsuchung*—another word related to *heimlich* and *unheimlich*).

From a certain angle, Kaschnitz's poem expresses a notion of time that is not unlike what Jean Améry ironically calls his "madly twisted time-sense" (69). In contradiction to what he perceives as a prevalent readiness to lay the past to rest, Améry insists that the crimes of mass murder ought not to be forgotten as time goes by. As Kaschnitz suggests, the crimes and their victims *cannot* be forgotten, because regardless of whether she wants it or not, they are haunting the present. The dead are coming to life in her home and she has no control over them.

However, this passivity and lack of control stands in contrast to what Améry wants to see, and that is not an internalizing of the images of Auschwitz within the walls of a home but an active confrontation and settlement between victims and slaughterers: "The piles of corpses that lie between them and me cannot be removed in the process of internalization, so it seems to me, but, on the contrary, through actualization, or, more strongly stated, by actively settling the unresolved conflict in the field of historical practice" (69). What exactly this would entail is an open question that "every German may picture for himself" (78).[14] I doubt that this question even occurs to the Germans in Kaschnitz's poem. The uncanny events described by Kaschnitz do not seem to lead beyond the boundaries of the home. Its occupants seem paralyzed, unable to move.[15] It is not even clear whether the return of forgotten images leads to an act of remembrance, since remembering itself requires a certain degree of initiative.

The Second and Third Generations

The only ones who do move are the children. They rise and express the only affect that can be found in the poem: outrage: "When the children get up and ask / How could you." For a long time this last part of the poem irritated me. While I responded easily to the uncanny atmosphere described by Kaschnitz, I was unable to make sense of the children. On the one hand, the children play a decisive role in the affliction that befalls their parents because it is their indignant question, so it seems, that triggers the opening of the wallpaper and the return of forgotten images.[16] On the other hand, the children are strangely disconnected from the events. Do they see what comes through the walls and the floors? Do they see their parents being wrapped in nettle-cloths? Are they themselves free of "smoke and nettles"? Who are these children?

In my memories of German homes there were never any children who stood up to accuse their parents this directly and vehemently. I certainly never raised my voice against anybody in this way, and I do not know anyone my age who did. Kaschnitz's children, in some sense, were the stumbling block that prevented me from fully identifying with the poem. They were also the reason I eventually started to ask questions about the poem's specific historical context. At what moment in the history of postwar Germany could such a conflict between children and parents be imagined? The poem's last part began to make sense when I thought of the "rebellious youth," the students of the 1960s. "The children" who "get up and ask / How could you" are a trope, I believe, for the young generation after the war who confronted not only their parents but the older generation in general about the crimes of the past, a conflict that expressed itself on a broad scale in the course of the so-called student movement, just a few years after Kaschnitz wrote her poem.[17]

This "protest generation" was the generation of my parents. I was born in 1969, a few months after the height of the student movement. I grew up in the 1970s and 1980s. I was twenty-one years old when I first came across Kaschnitz's poem. That was in 1990. I make these simple temporal distinctions in order to illustrate the relatively large time gap that separates Kaschnitz's writing of the poem from my reading of it. Whereas Kaschnitz lived through the war and through the first three postwar decades, I have no personal memories of these times. In relation to Kaschnitz I understand myself as a member of the "third generation." I am a grandchild of people who were adults during the war. Like Kaschnitz, my grandparents were grownup witnesses (*Zeitzeugen*) of the Nazi regime.[18] My own struggle with the Holocaust began to take place five decades after the end of the war and three decades after the Nazi crimes led to the conflict between the generations of my parents and grandparents that is dramatized in Kaschnitz's 1964 poem.

As I now narrate my encounter with Kaschnitz's poem, I want to be aware of the fact that this encounter took place in a historical moment different from the 1960s. I will assume that things are not the same as they used to be in Kaschnitz's time, that "the uncanny return of the past in the present" has a different meaning and different implications from thirty years ago. What does confrontation with the past mean forty, fifty years after the war? What does it mean for my own generation? These questions became pivotal in my efforts to understand the place of Kaschnitz's poem in a book on New Testament parables.

3

The Forgotten Comes to Parable Studies

A Holocaust Poem in a Book on Parables

A Piece of Parable Hermeneutics

I first encountered Kaschnitz's poem while taking a seminar at the University of Marburg in the spring of 1990. The topic of the seminar was "New Approaches in Parable Interpretation," and it was offered by Wolfgang Harnisch, professor for New Testament. The seminar was the most challenging and interesting course I had taken since I had started my theological studies. Harnisch not only introduced me to the century-old history of parable interpretation—the hermeneutic debates over how to read the stories of Jesus—but also managed to convey to me that parable hermeneutics currently was one of the cutting edges of biblical scholarship, the avant-garde of exegesis and theology, to use Edmund Arens's words (52), where interdisciplinary work was at its best. In addition to the works of German theologians such as Ernst Fuchs and Eberhard Jüngel we studied a whole range of texts that had been published in the United States. We read John Dominic Crossan, Robert Funk, James Breech, Dan Otto Via, and Paul Ricoeur, authors who investigate the parables in fruitful interaction with literary criticism and the philosophy of language. For the first time, I heard of things such as "language code," "discourse as event," "poetic function," "referentiality of language," and so on. I was being introduced into what Americans call the "linguistic turn": I learned that language does not simply correspond to a reality out there but that, instead, the reality we know is dependent on the language we have.

I was fascinated. Opening up in front of me was a new and intensely attractive way of being in conversation with biblical texts. In contrast to what I had learned so far, the American authors treated the parables of Jesus not as ancient artifacts to be dissected and dismembered through the dry methods of historical criticism but as something entirely different: as pieces of literature that speak to us in unique ways, and that raise profound questions about the world and ourselves and about the nature of language in general.

Among the many texts I read for Harnisch's seminar, one German-language work especially caught my interest: Harnisch's own book, the red German paperback I referred to earlier. It was published in 1985 with the title *Die Gleichniserzählungen Jesu* (The Parables of Jesus). In this book Harnisch develops the idea that Jesus' parables are autonomous works of art that are independent of their first historical setting and speak for themselves. Like poetic literature in general, the parables break through the parameters of everyday experience and disclose a truth that does not simply reflect reality but refers to the realm of previously unknown possibilities.

At the heart of Harnisch's interpretive theory is an attempt to apply the Ricoeurian concept of "living metaphor" to the parables of Jesus.[1] Probably the most outstanding feature of metaphors, as Ricoeur theorizes them, is the ability to lead their recipients to the discovery of new meaning, to a fresh way of looking at things beyond the well-known views of life. Following Ricoeur, Harnisch argues that the parables of Jesus are metaphorical narratives and therefore share this remarkable ability (141–158). In metaphors, "the semantic innovation," the gain in meaning, is produced by the combination of two words that stand in tension with each other, according to their lexical usage. This tension provokes the recipient to make sense of the odd combination beyond the established meaning of the terms. In parables, the metaphorical tension does not lie between single words or sentences but between two stories that are both planted in the parable's narrative. According to Harnisch, the first story is only indicated in the narrative and lives mainly in the listener's imagination and is about an ordinary, realistic event, which everyone knows from experience. Superimposed on it is the second story, which is extraordinary, unrealistic, even shocking, and undermines the common schemes and themes that the listener expects to hear. The listener then has to cope with the irritating tension between the expected and the unusual story. He or she does this, according to Harnisch, ideally at least, by transferring the tension to his or her own life. When that happens, the known reality, that which is and always has been, is suddenly called into question through a possibility that was unheard-of before.

At this point in his argument, Harnisch states that everything he has said so far about the function of parables may be true for parabolic literature in general (158–159). In a next step, Harnisch tries to define the parables of Jesus as "a religious kind of poetic discourse" and thus to distinguish them from nonreligious parables. Nonreligious poetic discourse, Harnisch says, introduces the listener (or reader) into an illusory world that temporarily may relieve him or her from the pressure of reality but ultimately, has no consequences for his or her life. In contrast to the vague and indefinite possibility suggested by nonreligious literature, the possibility imposed on us through the parables of Jesus, Harnisch argues, is qualified in a specific way and is able to challenge and to change reality: Harnisch describes the possibility disclosed by the parables as a horizon that is defined by absolute love, unlimited freedom, and boundless hope (165). By claiming radical love, freedom, and hope as possible, the parables of Jesus call their listeners to faith in God, and this, according to Harnisch, is the parables' transformative power.[2]

Harnisch embellishes these considerations through several literary references, which help to clarify his points. The following parable by Franz Kafka, "Give it up!" for instance, plays a central role in Harnisch's argument (141–151):

> It was early in the morning, the streets clean and deserted, I was on my way to the station. As I compared the tower clock with my watch I realized it was much later than I had thought and that I had to hurry; the shock of this discovery made me feel uncertain of the

way, I wasn't very well acquainted with the town as yet; fortunately, there was a police-man at hand, I ran to him and breathlessly asked him the way. He smiled and said: "You asking me the way?" "Yes," I said, "since I can't find it myself." "Give it up! Give it up!" said he, and turned with a sudden jerk, like someone who wants to be alone with his laughter. (*Complete Stories* 456)

This "modern narrative" (141), as Harnisch introduces Kafka's text, serves to illustrate the metaphorical tension of parables, the dissonance between an ordinary setting and an extraordinary plot development. At first sight it seems that Kafka talks about an incident that to many readers will be a familiar situation: a person is about to travel, he (or she) can't find the station, time is running out, the person asks a policeman for the way. However, the plausibility of this story is deceptive. When the policeman reacts to the inquiry with a smile and a counterquestion—"You asking me the way?"—the structure of everyday reality breaks down, because in ordinary life policemen don't act this way.[3]

For Harnisch, this ambiguity makes Kafka's story a genuine parable, a narrative that produces for the reader an irritating tension through the strange combination of the probable and the unlikely. Such a tensive combination, Harnisch claims, characterizes the parables of Jesus as well. They, too, create seemingly familiar contours of everyday life that then become strange and unfamiliar. They, too, operate on the basis of an alien-ation effect that causes readers and hearers to struggle with the contrast between their own experiences and those of the story:

A landlord . . . went out early in the morning to hire laborers for his vineyard. After agreeing with the laborers for the usual daily wage, he sent them into his vineyard. When he went out about nine o'clock, he saw others standing idle in the marketplace; and he said to them, "You also go into the vineyard, and I will pay you whatever is right." So they went. When he went out again about noon and about three o'clock, he did the same. And about five o'clock he went out and found others standing around; and he said to them, "Why are you standing here idle all day?" They said to him, "Because no one has hired us." He said to them, "You also go into the vineyard." When evening came, the owner of the vineyard said to his manager, "Call the laborers and give them their pay, beginning with the last and then going to the first." When those hired about five o'clock came, each of them received the usual daily wage. Now when the first came, they thought they would receive more; but each of them also received the usual daily wage. And when they received it, they grumbled against the landowner, saying "These last worked only one hour, and you have made them equal to us who have borne the burden of the day and the scorching heat." But he replied to one of them, "Friend, I am doing you no wrong; did you not agree with me for the usual daily wage? Take what belongs to you and go; I choose to give to this last the same as I give to you. Am I not allowed to do what I choose with what belongs to me? Or are you envious because I am so generous?" (Mat-thew 20:1-15)

This narrative, Harnisch points out, picks up a familiar situation from the world of labor, employment, job seekers, and wages: a man owns a vineyard and hires laborers at different times of the day. Throughout its plot development, the parable plays on the hearer's expectation that payment should correspond with the efficiency of each worker and that thus those who worked the whole day should receive significantly more than those who worked only one hour. What the hearers of the parable, like the workers in the narrative, anticipate then is a pay raise for those who were first employed: "Now when the first came, they thought they would receive more." Provoking and shocking, therefore, is the next statement: "but each of them also received the usual wage." With this unexpected turn the parable creates for the listener a tension between what he or she is used to and an extraordinary course of events. Like Kafka's parable, Jesus' story confronts its audience with the scandalous breakdown and mockery of the usual.

What distinguishes Jesus' story from Kafka's parable, according to Harnisch's hermeneutics, is its referent. The story does not simply end with the distortion of everyday experiences. The owner's last words, "Or are you envious because I am so generous?" specifies the alienation effect in a way that sets Jesus' story worlds apart from Kafka. With this last sentence, Harnisch argues, the narrative breaks through the pattern of wage negotiations and "opens up the possibility to perceive kindness as an irresistible and indisputable good, as something that just cannot be disapproved of" (193, my trans.).[4] Jesus' parable alienates the familiar in order to make something new visible: "a world wonderfully transformed in light of love" (195).[5]

A Poetic Paradigm

Kaschnitz's poem, the first segment of "Zoon Politikon," plays a role in Harnisch's argument similar to that of Kafka's parable. It appears a little earlier in Harnisch's thoughts, where he is concerned not yet with parables but with metaphors, his basic hermeneutic model. Kaschnitz's poem serves as "an example of modern poetry" (131), a "poetic paradigm" (133) that illustrates Paul Ricoeur's notion of "living metaphor."[6] More specifically, the poem helps Harnisch to refute the rhetorical tradition, which defines metaphor as a substitution phenomenon—one word replaces another—and ignores its power to create new meaning. Step by step Harnisch examines Kaschnitz's peculiar language, in order to demonstrate to his readers the strange combination of incompatible words that is typical of metaphors (132–133). For instance, "the forgotten" that comes "on crowsfeet with spurs" is not, as the rhetoricians would say, a compelling figurative expression used in place of literal words. Instead, Kaschnitz's phrase is a creative act through which something that cannot be translated or be said in any other way is disclosed. The innovative strangeness of Kaschnitz's language, according to Harnisch's reading of the poem, increases line by line, from the "pattern" carved "in the parquet" to the peculiar juxtaposition of a clean polished floor on the one hand with crematory smoke on the other.

An illustration of living metaphor—this is how I learned to read Kaschnitz's poem in the spring of 1990 when I studied Harnisch's work. In 1994, the poem must have lain dormant in the back of my mind. When I copied Kaschnitz's text from Harnisch's book onto a piece of paper and taped it to my desk while working through Ricoeur's *Rule of Metaphor*, I was following Harnisch's pedagogical instruction to take the poem as an illustrative device for contemplating the intricacies of poetic language.

A few months later, when Kaschnitz's poem drew me into its uncanny atmosphere, I looked at the lines for the first time independently of Harnisch's commentary. Removed from the context of Harnisch's book, the poem seemed radically transformed. It had changed from "an example of modern poetry" into a piece of Holocaust literature. Kaschnitz's language had ceased to be a strange and artful combination of words and had gained its historical points of reference. And like those ghostly things, which are not what they pretend to be, the poem terrified me to the core.

In the aftermath of this experience, I formulated a number of critical thoughts about Harnisch's treatment of Kaschnitz's poem. It struck me as odd, to say the least, that Harnisch had managed to reduce a text so charged and painful to a phenomenon of form; that he could handle a poem about the returning images of Auschwitz as a compelling "poetic paradigm" and elide its historical significance; that he could possibly suggest that what mattered about the poem was its linguistic features, not its historical theme.[7] The more I thought about it, the more disturbing I found Harnisch's quotation of Kaschnitz. It seemed to me that there is something almost obscene about taking a poem about mass annihilation to illustrate the creative potential of language; about the thought that "the drawer full of emaciated Jewish heads" could be a case of "living metaphor."

Similarly, I became increasingly angry about Harnisch's subsequent attempt to draw a line between religious and nonreligious poetic language. How could he, after citing a poem like this, claim that poetic language of the nonreligious kind was opening up a world of illusion with no consequence for one's life, whereas the parables of Jesus, in contrast, had the power to change reality by disclosing possibilities of "absolute love," "unlimited freedom," and "boundless hope"? What was "the real" for Harnisch? How did his abstract language relate to the language of the poem? Was he implying that the "possibility" suggested in the parables of Jesus could transform or transcend the "reality" of the Nazi death camps? Had he been blind to what he wrote when he quoted Kaschnitz's lines?[8]

Harnisch's book, with which I had spent so much time and which I thought I knew intimately, became uncanny to me, un-heimlich, and I started to see parallels between the haunted German home described by Kaschnitz and Harnisch's red German paperback. Just like the clean rooms of Kaschnitz's home, Harnisch's interpretive theory had been heimlich for me, in the twofold sense of the word; his discourse, the investigation into the nature of language and metaphor had been, for a long time, the thought system in which I felt comfortable, felt "at home" (heimlich-heimisch), I knew my way around. Yet this very discourse had blocked my view of the images of genocide. In the word's second sense, Harnisch's formal reduction had a heimlich effect because it had concealed (*verheimlicht*) the poem's historical content, as the walls and floors in the German home pushed the past out of sight.

On a more general level and perhaps a little flippantly, I imagined that the tropes of absolute love, freedom, and hope, for many readers, must have the coziness and familiarity of a "polished clean floor." At the same time, I pondered, these very tropes were like a thick heavy veil hiding the reality that Kaschnitz's poem was about. Harnisch's pages were, I thought grimly, like the insulated floor, a shield against history, and Harnisch himself was like someone who pastes a rose-colored wallpaper over a closet full of dead Jews.

Today I cannot fail to notice that my grim and critical thoughts were not entirely unlike the children's outrage in Kaschnitz's poem. "How could you?" they ask in regard to the crimes of the older generation; "How could he?" I asked in regard to what I perceived to be Harnisch's mistreatment of a text dealing with these crimes. If the children of the 1960s were concerned with the Nazi era and the events of the Holocaust, I was more concerned with a postwar phenomenon, with what in contemporary critical language would be called an instance of Holocaust representation and its reception. What enraged me about "the older generation"—that is, Harnisch—were not the committed acts of genocide but a neglected act of remembrance or acknowledgment.

My reaction to Harnisch could perhaps be paraphrased with the words of Eric Santner, as an example of "the third generation's grief and outrage over the effacement of the traces of historical suffering by the comforts of the *Heimat*—of a concrete historical *Unheimlich* within the *Heimisch*" (*Stranded Objects* 45). Heimat and the Heimisch, in my case, were parable hermeneutics; the effaced "traces of historical suffering," the Unheimlich, were the "concrete historical" theme of Kaschnitz's poem. What perhaps fueled my strong reactions was my knowledge that I was implicated in whatever I accused Harnisch of since I had perpetuated his use of the poem by putting it on my table while studying metaphor theory. The moment when the poem's reference point caught me, so to speak, I had feelings not only of uncanniness but also feelings of shame. I was ashamed of what I had done with Kaschnitz's piece. My question was not only "How could he?" but also "How could I have done the same?"

The Ambiguities of Holocaust Remembrance

Second Thoughts

Life is complicated, however, and some of our encounters are open to multiple interpretations.[9] As my shock and rage grew dimmer, I gained a new perspective on things. On closer look, or perhaps from a different angle, the parallel between Kaschnitz's German home and Harnisch's red German paperback, which I had posited so readily, is inconsistent. In the German home, the images of Auschwitz are *concealed* behind walls and floors—they are *kept out of sight* until they *break into* the room. While it had seemed to me that in Harnisch's work, too, the historical theme of Kaschnitz's poem had been *concealed* and *kept out of sight*, until it *broke into* my consciousness, the analogy is inaccurate if I take these phrases literally. In Harnisch's text, strictly speaking, the images of Auschwitz were never really kept out of sight. "The drawer full of emaciated Jewish heads" and "the foul smoke of rotten ones" are not concealed behind any wall but are always there for anyone to see and read. The metaphors of concealment, keeping out of sight, and breaking into do not adequately capture the complexity of Harnisch's quotation and employment of Kaschnitz's poem.

What I found more and more important to take into account is the following: it is true that Harnisch quotes Kaschnitz in order to illustrate the poetic function of metaphor. But in spite of his explicit interest in the formal quality of the poem, Harnisch offers a detailed reading, which also addresses the poem's content. In three paragraphs Harnisch explores Kaschnitz's lines—and mid way loses his focus. I translate the middle paragraph:

> The middle segment of the poem conjures up the ambiance of bourgeois security: "the rose-colored wallpaper" and the "insulated clean polished floor." In the context of the poem, however, both wall and floor appear to be a brittle facade, which cannot hide the horrors of the past and cannot keep out the unease rushing in from the outside. For what comes from the flowered walls and the shiny parquet, those markers of private happiness, are skulls and crematory smoke. This combination of the familiar with the improper and inappropriate is the basis of the deep irony of the message: the space of a cozy Sunday atmosphere turns into a place of terror, filled with the signs of an unthinkable crime. The scene culminates in the act of clothing (*Bekleidung*), carefully planned long beforehand, which is being done to "us," the inhabitants of the home. . . . Can the reference to

a cloth that "we deserve" mean anything other than a death garment (*Totenhemd*)? Then the presence of the repressed robs "us" of the ability to enjoy the present. The victims of Auschwitz accuse the life of the executioners and of every accessory. (133)[10]

In these sentences Harnisch moves entirely within the world of the poem, and it seems as though he has lost track of his investigation into metaphor or that for a little while he has interrupted his task. The only hint at metaphor theory might be Harnisch's remark about the "combination of the familiar with the improper and inappropriate." But even this remark is merely a faint echo of the formal observations Harnisch started out with, since the tension of metaphor, properly speaking, lies not between the familiar and the improper but between two incompatible semantic fields. The poem has taken over. Harnisch's reading is not dictated by the interest in metaphorical language in general but by the specific metaphorical language of Kaschnitz's poem. Like me in my own efforts described earlier, Harnisch addresses the imagery of a bourgeois peaceful home on the one hand and of the Nazi death camps on the other. Like me, he tries to paraphrase Kaschnitz's expressions with more literal, historicizing terms—skulls, crematory smoke—and he wonders about the meaning of the nettle-cloth.[11] But what the nettle-cloth means, whether or not it refers to a "death garment," is irrelevant for understanding how metaphors work.

Another striking aspect of Harnisch's reading of the poem is his footnote right before the quotation. This footnote provides the bibliographical reference to Kaschnitz's poem as well as the following information: "The poem repeats *ex eventu* the horrible vision about the fate of the Jews that Franz Kafka confided with cynical self-irony in one of his letters to Milena. This connection is indicated by the motif of the drawer in Kaschnitz's poem" (131, my trans.).[12]

Whereas Harnisch's main text introduces the poem as an "example of modern poetry" that illustrates the innovative power of metaphors (131), the footnote characterizes the poem in very different terms. Harnisch suggests that the uncanny scenario Kaschnitz evokes has a literary source that she took recourse to, something she read in a letter by Franz Kafka to Milena Jesenska. When I followed this suggestion I was led to a short passage written in 1920:

> I could rather reproach you for having much too good an opinion of the Jews whom you know (including myself)—there are others!—sometimes I'd like to cram them all as Jews (including myself) into the drawer of the laundry chest, then wait, then open the drawer a little, to see whether all have already suffocated, if not, to close the drawer again and go on like this to the end. (*Letters* 59)

"The drawer full of emaciated Jewish heads," according to Harnisch, has its source in Kafka's fantasy of a drawer with which to suffocate his fellow Jews. This is not the place to discuss Kafka's highly charged passage or to problematize Harnisch's reading of it, a task that I take on in chapter 9. At the moment I am offering this passage, together with Harnisch's footnote, in order to indicate the complex literary and historical texture that accompanies Harnisch's hermeneutic discourse. At the margins of this discourse, disconnected from his actual topic, Harnisch offers an interpretation of the most jarring image in Kaschnitz's poem by tracing it back to Kafka.

Again, wherever the motif of the drawer (*Bettlade*) came from, whether Kaschnitz took it from Kafka's letter or whether she thought of the loading device in the camps, as I have suggested in one of my own footnotes, doesn't matter if one is solely interested in the function of metaphor.[13] The footnote shows that, contrary to my initial impression, Harnisch was not blind to what he wrote when he quoted the poem but that he closely looked at and puzzled over its lines and their meaning.[14] Like the paragraph I quoted, Harnisch's footnote deviates from the formal, ahistorical discourse that otherwise characterizes his work. These transgressions of the formal, this excess of content, so to speak, defies my claim that the historical theme of Kaschnitz's poem is effaced, concealed, and pushed out of sight by Harnisch's use of it. Even though the footnote and central paragraph of his reading are only brief instances and even though Harnisch immediately resumes his formal definitions, for a few moments the poem's theme, the returning memory of the annihilation of European Jewry by the Nazis, makes its impact on Harnisch's text and becomes manifest, for everyone to see.[15]

It is not accurate to say that Harnisch's text concealed the content of Kaschnitz's poem, nor is it true that I myself had been entirely blind to it and had seen nothing in the poem but an illustration of living metaphor until my eyes were opened in the spring of 1994 when I took a course on the Holocaust. Things were more complicated than that. In some ways I always knew, of course, that Kaschnitz's poem was about memories of the Holocaust. And it would be wrong to say that these memories did not mean anything to me. The year 1994 was certainly not the first time that I had come in contact with Holocaust material. I had known about the horrible events in Nazi-occupied Europe all my life; I knew the facts and figures behind Kaschnitz's poem.

When I try to remember the day I copied Kaschnitz's poem out of Harnisch's book I am no longer so sure of what went on in my head. Did I really simply need a German poem to check the turns of Ricoeur's discussion? Was I really just following Harnisch's instruction? Or did I take the poem because it was "powerful," because it was a relevant contemporary text? Because it had made an impact in some corner of my mind? In the spring of 1994 it felt as though I saw the poem for the first time. It felt as though the images of Auschwitz broke into my consciousness, but these images, somehow, already must have been in my mind before this experience.

The Difficulty of Seeing

Over the years, I have come to understand Harnisch's and my own use of Kaschnitz's poem in the context of post-Holocaust culture in the 1980s and 1990s. As I want to argue, the poem on my desk exemplifies a problem that is typical for our time: the existence of a vague kind of knowledge, a dim presence of the Holocaust that does not reach a level of attention where it would have effects on the established course of thinking. The reduction of a text like "Zoon Politikon" to an illustration of metaphorical language, I want to argue, is a complicated instance of Holocaust remembrance, emblematic of the difficulties of "confronting the past" four and five decades after the end of World War II.

This became clear to me as I further distinguished between my own context and the context of Kaschnitz's poem, between the "confrontation with the past" as it took place in the 1960s and more recent and current situations. The concealment of the crimes of Auschwitz behind the walls and floors of prospering German homes no longer applies today. The vocabulary of "repression" and "silence," already questionable terms in regard to the complex situation of the mid-1960s, has become obsolete since the mid- or late

1970s. The state of Holocaust remembrance today is ambiguous, as has been argued in a range of recent discussions, some of which I would like to briefly address.

A striking visibility and prevalence of Holocaust memory characterize contemporary German culture, according to many critics. Michael Geyer and Miriam Hansen write: "Today, we can no longer say that the Germans have no memory of the Holocaust or that memory is denied." Instead they detect "a near-obsessive emphasis on both the Holocaust and the Nazi era." "Occasions like Bitburg," the authors suggest, "make it clear that just about everyone documents/historicizes/remembers/recollects/commemorates/memorializes" (176). Andreas Huyssen, in a similar vein, talks about a "memory boom" that manifested itself in Germany in "a never-ending sequence of Nazi related 40th and 50th anniversaries in the 1980s that produced a number of fascinating public debates about German identity as well as the embarrassment of Bitburg" (*Twilight* 5). Rather than being interpreted as a hopeful sign of change, this "obsession with memory" makes many critics skeptical. The 1985 "Bitburg affair," evoked by Huyssen, Geyer, and Hansen, is probably the most blatant and widely quoted example of how an apparent act of commemoration has more to do with a desire to forget than with an attempt to remember. How else to make sense of the day when German chancellor Helmut Kohl together with the American president Ronald Reagan went to visit the former concentration camp Bergen-Belsen and, right afterward, the graves of two thousand German soldiers, including forty-nine SS men, in the cemetery at Bitburg?

The problematic aspect of the recent "memory boom" characterizes not only events as dubious as Bitburg but also those commemorative efforts that seem to be motivated by a genuine concern with the Holocaust. In his work on Holocaust memorials, James Young points out that an intention to remember the Jewish victims of Nazism is not safeguarded from forgetfulness. Young suggests, for instance, that a monument that is meant to keep the memory of a vanished Jewish community alive, as can be seen in countless towns in Germany, easily turns into a placeholder that exempts the population from engaging in the work of recollection by shifting the responsibility to the monument (*Texture* 27–48).

In a German publication, Richard Chaim Schneider writes angrily and eloquently about what he perceives to be a veritable mania, an enthusiasm for the Holocaust in German public discourse, most visible in the debates around Daniel Goldhagen's book *Hitler's Willing Executioners* and the planned national memorial in Berlin. According to Schneider's assessment, this obsession with the Holocaust has little to do with a concern with the victims of Nazism and everything to do with people wanting to make money and win fame: "There is no business like Shoah-business" (*Fetisch* 10). And even though signs of the Holocaust can be seen at any street corner in Germany, Schneider comes to a conclusion that is not all that different from the bitter account given by Jean Améry more than thirty years ago: there is still "a frozen sea" (17) in the souls of many Germans when it comes to the crimes committed under their country's name. The broad public majority in Germany, Schneider observes, continues to find it difficult to face the brutality and the horror of these crimes (52).

Huyssen interprets "the memory boom" in more moderate and theoretical terms. He points out that on a very general level the tendency to forget is already implied in the structure of Holocaust representation, since every representation depends on the temporal gap between the event and the memory of it. It is in the nature of temporality, which characterizes Western culture, that remembering and forgetting cannot be clearly distinguished. Huyssen writes that the "difficulty of the current conjuncture is to think memory and amnesia together rather than simply to oppose them" (7). Given that there is no such thing as a clear divide between forgetting and remembering, the question of how the Holocaust has become part of contemporary German culture turns out to be more complicated: "The issue . . . is not whether to forget or to remember, but rather how to remember and how to handle representations of the remembered past at a time when most of us, over forty years after the war, only know that past through images, films, photographs, representations" (214).

In this last quotation Huyssen indicates a current state of affairs that I think is relevant to my encounter with Kaschnitz's poem. "Zoon Politikon," one could say, is an instance of the many "representations of the remembered past" through which my generation knows about the Holocaust. In 1964, Kaschnitz's poem was already one of many literary responses to the Holocaust. In the 1980s and 1990s, the poem, together with numerous other texts, films, photographs, entered the German cultural reservoir. They have been circulating, have been printed and quoted, in places sometimes as unrelated as New Testament parable hermeneutics—and in the process they also have become normalized (*eingebürgert*) to a certain degree. Huyssen writes: "the problem for Holocaust memory in the 1980s and 1990s is not forgetting, but rather the ubiquitousness, even the excess of Holocaust imagery in our culture" (255). I would like to paraphrase this problem in terms of a "difficulty of seeing." In regard to the situation in 1945, Dagmar Barnouw has argued, and I refer to that argument in chapter 2, that the photographs of Dachau, Bergen-Belsen, and other camps, despite their visual clarity, were obscure. Seeing them did not necessarily entail an understanding, acknowledgment, or adequate interpretation of them. Building on Barnouw, I suggested that the situation in the mid-1960s, the time of the Auschwitz trials and the time when Kaschnitz wrote her poem, was characterized by a similar problem. How were Germans to respond to the returning evidence of mass murder that by and large had been shut away for twenty years? I would like to further argue, however, that the situation in the 1980s and 1990s is significantly different.

Strictly speaking, I and many Germans my age were never really confronted with the crimes of genocide. Instead, we grew up with the knowledge of it. I cannot remember anyone presenting me with the facts and the images and saying, "look at this, this is what happened." I cannot remember a time in my life when I did not know that these things happened. What characterizes my generation, I think, is a strange kind of familiarity with the Holocaust and the dilemma that necessarily arises from such familiarity. For how can the systematic murder of six million Jews be something with which one is familiar? How can one be familiar with events that, according to Eric Santner, "need to be theorized under the sign of massive trauma, meaning that these events must be confronted and analyzed in their capacity to endanger and overwhelm the composition and coherence of individual and collective identities that enter into their deadly field of force" ("History" 151)?

Of course, in a way, this dilemma existed as well for the Germans in 1945, who, according to Barnouw, were forced to *familiarize* themselves with the sight of liberated death camps. As Barnouw writes, "their shock was the result of the utter alienness of the horrible, its core dimension was 'unbelievable,' 'unimaginable'—the extreme opposite of *familiarity*" (29, emphasis added). Unlike the Germans in 1945, the Germans who grew up in the 1970s and 1980s have not necessarily gone through an experience of shock because their eyes have always been used to the images of the piles of corpses.[16] Today, when Holocaust imagery is so prevalent in our culture, when just about everyone remembers and memorializes, when signs of the Holocaust are at every street corner, when "Auschwitz and Buchenwald" has become a standard phrase, and when Holocaust literature is quoted in passing, the "difficulty of seeing" is of a special kind.

Seeing, today, does not so much involve the struggle with feelings of guilt or remorse. The difficulty is rather to see and really pay attention. It belongs in the gray area between memory and amnesia about which Huyssen writes. Its effects are neither remembering nor forgetting but something less easy to grasp: namely, that it is possible to be knowledgeable about the historical facts without ever experiencing "their deadly field of force"; to look at the photographs of the dead with "a frozen sea" in one's soul; to sometimes have a vague sense of horror without really finding the energy to deal with these horrible things in any way;[17] to live right next to a Holocaust memorial without ever standing in front of it and thinking about concrete events or specific people; to quote a text such as "Zoon Politikon" in a book on the parables of Jesus; or to have the same text in front of one's eyes without letting oneself get distracted from Paul Ricoeur's metaphor theory.

Recognizing the Uncanny

It seems to me that in a situation characterized by a "difficulty of seeing," as just described, my uncanny encounter with the piece of paper on my desk in the spring of 1994 has a certain significance and value. In order to make this case I would like to elaborate on something I already mentioned at the end of chapter 2: the contrast between the scenario evoked by Kaschnitz in 1964 and my own experience with the poem thirty years later. I have called both instances unheimlich, uncanny. However, what I would like to point out now are the different ways this uncanniness expressed itself or made itself noticeable.

In the poem, the uncanny atmosphere is produced by forgotten images that are usually pushed away behind walls and beneath floors but inevitably reappear on a regular basis, "especially on Sundays." I have also suggested that these reappearing images, the "emaciated Jewish heads," "the foul smoke of rotten ones," are uncanny in the Freudian sense of a return of the repressed. To summarize it a bit schematically: the images in Kaschnitz's poem represent the horrific crimes with which, shortly after the end of the war, a general population in Germany had to familiarize itself. During the postwar years these images were banished into secrecy, and twenty years after the war they came back to light.

To call Kaschnitz's poem on my desk an uncanny return of the repressed may not be inaccurate because there must have been an instance in my mind that for a while blocked off or "repressed" the poem's impact. However, this parallel misses an important aspect of my experience. As I pointed out, I have never been blind to the historical theme of Nazi genocide. Its images were never really concealed by Harnisch's formal discourse. Quite the opposite; they were always in the open and for everyone to see. I want to stress the fact that for a long time it was possible for me to read Harnisch's book, including its uncanny moment, the poem, without ever perceiving the Kaschnitz quotation as uncanny; it was possible for me to have the poem on my desk without finding anything strange about it.[18] This failure to perceive "the uncanny" is one facet of "the difficulty of seeing" I mentioned earlier. To find nothing odd about the quotation of a piece of post-Holocaust poetry in a book on the parables of Jesus is one result of what Huyssen calls "the ubiquitousness, even the excess of Holocaust imagery in our culture." Today "the drawer full of emaciated Jewish heads" does not break into the nice clean home to diffuse an uncanny atmosphere. Rather the Jewish heads lie all over the place, and our eyes have become used to them.[19]

In this situation my encounter with Kaschnitz's poem in the spring of 1994 had a remarkable effect: it woke me up from that strange kind of familiarity with the Holocaust that is typical for my generation. "Zoon Politikon," "the ghost in my room," managed to do something that no history book or documentary film was able to do: it monopolized all my attention and forced my eyes to look closely. It struck me beyond rational discourse and intellectual understanding, involved my affect, interrupted my usual lines of thought, and roused me from my distanced position. And here lies another crucial difference between Kaschnitz's German home in 1964 and my experience with her text in 1994. A striking aspect of Kaschnitz's scenario, as I emphasized in my reading of the poem, is the passivity, even the paralysis, with which the inhabitants endure the affliction that befalls them and their home. I found the lack of affect with which the inhabitants receive the returning memory of the past similarly striking. It was impossible to tell what kind of feelings or reactions or consequences, if any, are provoked by the uncanny arrival of "the forgotten."

When the poem "jumped into my face" in the spring of 1994, it felt as though something happened *to me*, as though the poem did something with me. Today, however, I think that there was also an active moment at work. After all, I was the one who processed the transformation of the poem as it turned from a poetic paradigm into a poem about Holocaust memories. Moreover, the shock about this discovery released a considerable amount of energy, which irrevocably changed my attitude toward my chosen field of research so that I was no longer able to continue my studies the way I had set them up. For this reason I prefer to think about my experience not in terms of a return of the repressed that befell me but as a change of perspective in which I became involved. What guides me in this interpretation is not so much Freud's concept of the uncanny as Avery Gordon's thoughts on ghosts and haunting. Gordon writes:

> The ghost or the apparition is one form by which something lost, or barely visible, or seemingly not there to our supposedly well-trained eyes, makes itself known or apparent to us, in its own ways, of course. The way of the ghost is haunting, and haunting is a very particular way of knowing what has happened or is happening. Being haunted draws us affectively, sometimes against our will and always a bit magically, into the structure of feeling of a reality we come to experience, not as cold knowledge, but as a transformative recognition. (8)

When I say I was haunted by Kaschnitz I mean that her poem did not let go of me until I recognized that there was something important that I had missed in my study of parable hermeneutics. To be precise: the ghost for me was not simply Kaschnitz's "Zoon Politikon" but the piece of paper on which I had copied the poem and which I had taped to my desk. This piece of paper made me notice something that in Harnisch's book was "barely visible, or seemingly not there," or, in my own words, difficult to see and easy to overlook. What I noticed was not only Kaschnitz's jarring Holocaust imagery or what I alternately have called the poem's historical theme or its reference points. I also noticed the oddness of the poem's place in Harnisch's book and on my desk. The result, however, as Gordon says, was not "cold knowledge." It couldn't be, because the "haunting" of the poem affected me personally: the interpretation of the parables of Jesus through the lens of "living metaphor" had been important to me for several years. I had cared about Harnisch's hermeneutics.

I have analyzed my experience with Harnisch's work and its Kaschnitz quotation because the affect that was released through it, the "transformative recognition" I underwent, is the driving force for this book. The ghost of Kaschnitz's poem, I might say, directed me to questions of Holocaust remembrance but also redirected me in my own occupation and research. It involved me in a change of perspective that moved the poem to the center of my field of vision, which made me look anew at Harnisch's text and parable studies more generally and made me reread their discourse under a different sign.

When I now move from Harnisch's work to other instances of parable scholarship I am guided by a hunch that Harnisch's Kaschnitz quotation indicates a general, more widespread phenomenon in parable studies; that there is a relationship between the Holocaust and the way the parables of Jesus were interpreted in the postwar era. Let me formulate my hunch as a suggestion: Harnisch's Kaschnitz quotation might not be just a singular instance of what Huyssen calls "the excess of Holocaust imagery in our culture." Harnisch's book perhaps is not an accidental site of such excess. Perhaps there is a reason why Kaschnitz's poem appeared, of all places, in a book on parables. There might be something specific at work in some strands of parable hermeneutics, a desire or motivation or unconscious dynamic, that could explain its quotation of a text like "Zoon Politikon" or its production of passing references to "Auschwitz and Buchenwald." To deal with this suggestion, to figure out what this "something specific" might be, is the task I set for myself in the chapters that follow.

PART II

HISTORICAL CRITICISM AND THE LEGACY OF THE HOLOCAUST

4

Joachim Jeremias and the Historical-Critical Approach

> Jesus spoke to men of flesh and blood; he addressed himself to the situation of the moment. Each of his parables has a definite historical setting. Hence to recover this is the task before us.

My opening quotation is taken from Joachim Jeremias's book *The Parables of Jesus*, which came out in 1947, two years after the end of the war.[1] The time and place of the book's first publication are the reasons why I became concerned with Jeremias and why I have devoted three chapters to his work and to the kind of scholarship his work represents: historical criticism. In a 1984 essay, Elizabeth Schüssler Fiorenza and David Tracy argued that the historical-critical method, ironically, has been accompanied by "the loss of concrete history itself" (*Holocaust* 83).[2] Christian scholars, the authors write, have avoided rather than confronted history, "the real, concrete thing where events like the Holocaust have happened" (84). I would like to apply this argument to parable scholarship and suggest that Jeremias's work in its strict focus on the historical context of the parables is strangely isolated from its own context: Germany shortly after the Holocaust.

I have tried to break through this isolation. In my reading of his work, one could say I adopted the very strategies that historical critics apply to biblical texts. Jeremias, as my opening quotation indicates, wants to contextualize Jesus' parables in a "definite historical setting." In turn, I want to contextualize Jeremias's own work in a "definite historical setting." I want to historicize his text within the immediate postwar situation in Germany. Thereby I continue the task of my earlier chapters. While Kaschnitz's poem and Harnisch's quotation engaged me with questions of Holocaust remembrance during the 1960s and the 1980s/1990s, Jeremias's work made me think about the difficulties of responding to the "German catastrophe" as early as 1947.

This chapter has preliminary functions. I will introduce Jeremias's approach to the parables as an instance of historical-critical scholarship. I will do this in some detail, because I want to present not only Jeremias's treatment of the parables but also the general terms and categories of parable scholarship in the twentieth century. I also will spend some time discussing the critical work that has been done on Jeremias by historical critics during the last two decades. These presentations and discussions will set the stage for my own reading of Jeremias's work in chapter 5.

Jeremias and *The Parables of Jesus*

Joachim Jeremias's book *The Parables of Jesus* is well known in the field of New Testament and has been described and reinscribed as the classic of parable interpretation by many scholars over the decades. Even though research on the parables has taken several turns since the book's first publication in 1947, Jeremias's work is standard today, the kind of text that is indispensable for someone who wants to understand the rules and issues of the discipline. I have read Jeremias's book many times—more often than any other book during the course of my New Testament studies. It was a major source in Harnisch's 1990 seminar on parable interpretation and in every course I took on the topic after that. I was unwittingly familiar with Jeremias's work even earlier, because his approach to the parables was taught in religion classes in German high schools in the 1980s.[3]

Jeremias's interpretation of the parables stands for everything that I associate with traditional historical-critical exegesis: its research questions, its methodological apparatus, its procedures, and its passion. Jeremias's work is paradigmatic of a certain way of looking at the Bible that I learned during my first semesters at German universities and that, in the most general terms, can be called a consequence of the rise of historical consciousness: the Bible is not simply a timeless canon but also an accumulation of historical documents, each of which originated from a specific context. Theologically, the Bible might be understood as "the word of God"; historically, however, it emerged over time and out of various places. Historical critics are interested, among other things, in the process of transmission that the different parts of the Bible underwent before they became canonical. They assume that biblical texts did not fall from the sky, to put it crudely, but emerged out of historical, cultural, and geographical circumstances; that they turned from oral tradition into written texts, changed their function within communities (*Sitz im Leben*), and were translated, edited, collected, and framed.

Jeremias's Ancestor

Jeremias was not the first to read the parables of Jesus under these interpretive assumptions. The historical-critical approach to the parables was initiated half a century earlier by Adolf Jülicher's book *Die Gleichnisreden Jesu*, first published in 1886 (first volume) and 1899 (second volume). This almost one-thousand-page work defined the basic categories of modern New Testament parable interpretation and thus opened up the field of research in which, fifty years later, Jeremias would operate. At the center of Jülicher's concern is a hermeneutic error that, as he demonstrates, pervades the age-old tradition of parable interpretation. In numerous commentaries and sermons on the parables from the apostolic fathers to his own time, Jülicher detects the habit of treating the parables of Jesus as allegories—as coded texts whose elements have to be deciphered one by one. Jülicher claims that this interpretive practice distorts the nature and purpose of parables.

The notion that the parables contain hidden meanings that needed to be discovered through hard interpretive labor offended Jülicher because it radically contradicted his sense of the historical Jesus. Whoever constructs an allegorical story intends to conceal something, Jülicher emphasizes. An allegory prevents the reader or listener from having immediate access to what is said, makes the audience stumble over the narrative, and involves it in a process of speculation. Only those who possess the key to the allegory— who know, for instance, that a story about laborers who are hired at different hours by the owner of a vineyard is really about salvation history—will comprehend the actual meaning of what is narrated. For everybody else an allegory remains guesswork.

Jülicher points out that the alleged allegorical character of the parables implies a disturbing scenario. If it were the case that Jesus told allegories, it would mean that his preaching from the very outset was meant not to facilitate but to impede understanding; it would mean that Jesus unveiled his message only to a small group of chosen ones and refused to reveal himself to the common people.[4] According to Jülicher, this scenario is not only disturbing but also highly improbable. In line with the liberal theology of his time, Jülicher imagines the historical Jesus to be a caring teacher who passionately led his people to the proper knowledge of God and a powerful public speaker who won the hearts and minds of his audience.[5]

Jülicher's own theory about the literary nature of parables corresponds to his image of Jesus and his ministry. In contrast to the dark and obscure genre of allegory, "parables," properly speaking, are simple and clear illustrations of difficult and abstract matters. By presenting an incident within the familiar realm of everyday experience (*Bildhälfte*), parables make a point about a less familiar issue, usually from the religious, philosophical, or moral realm (*Sachhälfte*). What is plausible and convincing in the story then has to be applied by the audience to the more difficult and abstract sphere. What is true in the first case, the parabler suggests, is true also in the second case (*tertium comparationis*).[6] The parables of Jesus, particularly, are teaching devices at the service of Jesus' instructions about the kingdom of God. By telling parables, Jesus gently took his listeners by the hand and made sure that everybody was able to understand what he had to say. For example, the story of a landlord who pays full wage to laborers who have worked for only a little while illustrates something about God. The point of the story, according to Jülicher, is the landowner's right to be generous toward his laborers, and this point needs to be applied to God's relationship to repentant sinners (466–467).

If the meaning of a parable is not immediately clear to us today, Jülicher goes on to argue, the problem does not lie with the genre of parables, because in their first setting Jesus' parables were perfectly transparent to everyone. The problem is one of transmission: as the parables were collected and written down, the communicative situation and circumstances in which a parable originally was spoken were preserved only partially. The atmosphere, the questions, the events and experiences that occupied the minds of Jesus and his companions and that caused Jesus to tell a parable were forgotten. This means that the particular issue (Sachhälfte) which a parable was meant to clarify in many cases is lost to us.[7] What is worse, as Jülicher argues, the gospel writers themselves gave us misleading notions about the nature and purpose of Jesus' parables. Jülicher shows that the allegorical misunderstanding had already started in the gospels. Matthew, Mark, and Luke framed and edited the parables in a way that often made them look like allegories.[8]

The conclusions for the interpreter are serious: when it comes to the meaning of Jesus' parables, the gospels cannot be trusted. In many cases, the interpreter has to go beyond the traditional text and reconstruct the original version of the parable, its original communicative setting, and the subject matter about which the parable was to make a point. In order to understand the parables as they were intended by Jesus, the critic needs to take them out of the gospel context and place them within the life of Jesus.[9] With these conclusions Jülicher laid the groundwork for historical-critical research on the parables.

Searching for the Parables' "First Historical Setting"

Half a century later Joachim Jeremias adopted this groundwork for his own book on the parables.[10] Jeremias accepts Jülicher's generic distinction between "allegory" and "parable," his definition of the rhetorical function of parables, and their two-part structure (Bild and Sache), as well as the necessity of removing the parables from the gospel context in order to reconstruct their meaning in the context of Jesus' ministry. Like Jülicher, Jeremias believes that an adequate interpretation of the parables needs to focus on the communicative situation out of which a parable first emerged—that a parable's true meaning coincides with the meaning as it was intended by Jesus and understood by his audience. In Jeremias's own terminology this basic interpretive category is called the parables' "first historical setting."

What Jeremias criticizes about Jülicher is a certain naiveté with which he carried out the work of reconstruction. Jülicher wrongly assumed that he could just put himself in the position of Jesus and his companions in order to find out what kind of idea Jesus wanted to communicate when he told a parable. The result, Jeremias points out, has little to do with the historical Jesus and everything to do with Jülicher's own cultural background, the religious values of nineteenth-century liberal theology. Writing at a time when much of the so-called Leben Jesu Forschung had been exposed as a mere reflection of a scholar's own mindset, when the huge cultural and temporal gap between Jesus and European scholarship had been emphasized,[11] Jeremias, unlike Jülicher, knows that there is no easy access to the life of Jesus. The original meaning of the parables is not something that scholars can intuit. He writes, "The main task still remains to be done: the attempt must be made to recover the original meaning of the parables" (17).[12]

Jeremias's own critical energies are thus directed toward the problem of historical reconstruction. In a research situation in which the historical Jesus has withdrawn himself from the scholarly grip, Jeremias takes up the challenge to reconstruct the original words, the ipsissima vox, of Jesus.[13] This is not a dry scientific matter. Just as Jülicher was passionate about recovering the actual nature and purpose of Jesus' parables, Jeremias is passionate about his own work: "Our task is to return to the actual living voice of Jesus. How great the gain if we succeed in rediscovering here and there behind the veil the features of the Son of Man! To meet with him can alone give power to our preaching" (114).

Apart from this enthusiasm for the historical Jesus, Jeremias brings several skills to the task of reconstruction: a competence in historical-critical methodology, an expertise in the field of ancient Judaism, and knowledge about early rabbinical literature.[14] His work is divided into two steps. First, Jeremias tries to reconstruct the original version of the parables, the precise wording and form in which Jesus told them. Thereby he demonstrates the many ways in which the early Christian communities probably changed and reinterpreted the parables, for instance, by adding an interpretive last sentence to a parable or by placing a parable in a fictional context. In a second step, Jeremias attempts to recover the parables' "first historical setting": the audience for which Jesus told a parable and the issue or question that was at stake at the moment. By thus recontextualizing each parable in a specific situation in the life of Jesus, Jeremias imagines himself to have retrieved the original meaning of Jesus' parables, which he categorizes into ten basic ideas.

Generally speaking, according to Jeremias, the parables reflect something that Jülicher ignored and that only recent biblical scholarship has begun to take into account: Jesus' eschatology; in Jeremias's language, the recognition of an eschatology that is in process of realization' (die *Gewißheit der 'sich realisierenden Eschatologie*.[15] According to Jeremias, Jesus lived with the expectation that an era was about to come to an end, that a catastrophe was approaching that would destroy the forces of evil and bless the sick and the poor. Jesus and his companions thought themselves in a situation of crisis that demanded decisive change, penance, and conversion to God. Jesus' message, Jeremias argues, was an insistent warning against the coming disaster. He urged the people of Israel to wake up from their sleep and tried to shake them into action. However, as Jeremias emphasizes, Jesus' serious warning was met with increasing hostility by Israel's leaders, the Pharisees, scribes, and priests. Jesus consistently had to justify and defend his message against those who resisted him. The parables played a crucial role in this fight. Jeremias writes: "They were preponderantly concerned with a situation of conflict, they correct, reprove, attack. For the greater part, though not exclusively, the parables are weapons of warfare" (21). According to Jeremias's vision, Jesus was not the soft and gentle teacher Jülicher imagined him to be. Jesus was a fighter for the gospel. And Jesus' parables were not kindly constructed teaching devices but rhetorical weapons of Jesus' polemics against his opponents.

The Laborers in the Vineyard

In order to illustrate Jeremias's historical-critical approach, I would like to come back to the parable of the Laborers in the Vineyard in the gospel of Matthew, which I earlier quoted and addressed during my discussion of Wolfgang Harnisch's work.[16] This time I quote the parable in accordance with the gospel text:[17]

> 1 For the kingdom of heaven is like a landowner who went out early in the morning to hire laborers for his vineyard. 2 After agreeing with the laborers for the usual daily wage, he sent them into his vineyard. 3 When he went out about nine o'clock, he saw others standing idle in the marketplace; 4 and he said to them, "You also go into the vineyard, and I will pay you whatever is right." 5 So they went. When he went out again about noon and about three o'clock, he did the same. 6 And about five o'clock he went out and found others standing around; and he said to them, "Why are you standing here idle all day?" 7 They said to him, "Because no one has hired us." He said to them, "You also go into the vineyard." 8 When evening came, the owner of the vineyard said to his manager, "Call the laborers and give them their pay, beginning with the last and then going to the first." 9 When those hired about five o'clock came, each of them received the usual daily wage. 10 Now when the first came, they thought they would receive more; but each of them also received the usual daily wage. 11 And when they received it, they grumbled against the landowner, 12 saying "These last worked only one hour, and you have made them equal to us who have borne the burden of the day and the scorching heat." 13 But he replied to one of them, "Friend, I am doing you no wrong; did you not agree with me for the usual daily wage? 14 Take what belongs to you and go; I choose to give to this last the same as I give to you. 15 Am I not allowed to do what I choose with what belongs to me? Or are you envious because I am so generous?" 16 So the last will be first, and the first will be last.

Before developing his own interpretation, Jeremias recapitulates the various misreadings the parable has suffered over the centuries. One of these misreadings is manifest already in the gospel itself. The parable as we find it in Matthew does not end with the owner's question (verse 15) but with a generalizing sentence (verse 16): "So the last will be first, and the first will be last." With this sentence a particular meaning is given to the parable. The sentence suggests that the parable's emphasis lies on the order in which the different groups of workers receive their wages: "Call the laborers and give them their pay, beginning with the last and then going to the first" (verse 8b). However, as Jeremias is quick to point out, the order in which the wages are paid out is not at all central to the narrative. In fact, verse 16 misses the point of the story, which is not about the reversal but about the equalization of the different workers. Jeremias concludes that verse 16 was added to the parable by Matthew, who apparently understood Jesus' story as an illustration of the reversal of hierarchies at the Day of Judgment. The original parable, as it was spoken by Jesus, ends with the owner's question: "Or are you envious because I am so generous?"[18]

As soon as one disregards the misleading interpretation offered by verse 16 and looks at the story without any preconceptions, Jeremias says, the scandalous nature of the owner's behavior comes into view. To pay equal wage to people whose efforts and working hours greatly differ seems blatantly unjust, Jeremias suggests—like an arbitrary act of a capricious despot. As the laborers complain: "These last worked only one hour, and you have made them equal to us who have borne the burden of the day and the scorching heat" (verse 12). However, against this angry reaction, which might be shared by contemporary readers of the parable, Jeremias produces information about the living conditions in first-century Palestine that puts the owner's act in a different light. Jeremias points out that the wage each worker receives, one denarius according to the Greek text, is the amount of money necessary for survival; "the usual daily wage" is just enough to live at subsistence level (37). The landlord's decision to pay each worker one denarius is therefore not an excessive or whimsical act. Rather, as Jeremias argues, it is a indication of the landlord's pity for those who were without work most of the day. Even if it was the laborers' own fault that they were not employed during harvest time,[19] the landlord feels sorry for them and their families because he knows that without the daily wage, these people would face starvation.[20]

The point of the story, the Bildhälfte of the parable, to use Jülicher's terminology, is revealed in the final question. "Or are you envious because I am so generous?" the landowner asks and thus calls attention to his own generosity and kindness. Jeremias promptly applies this point to the Sachhälfte, the issue the parable wants to illustrate, which, according to Jeremias, has something to do with God and his Kingdom.[21] Jeremias writes: "This, says Jesus, is how God deals with men. This is what God is like, merciful. Even to tax-farmers and sinners he grants an unmerited place in his Kingdom, such is the measure of his goodness" (37). Just as the landlord in the story sympathizes with the poor day laborers who did not work enough to make a living, so does God have mercy with those who did not earn their place in the Kingdom.[22]

However, with this paraphrase, the parable's original meaning, according to Jeremias, is not yet adequately grasped. In order to properly understand the parable one needs to become clear about its first historical setting. On which specific occasion did Jesus tell the parable? Jesus did not simply want to proclaim God's benevolent attitude toward sinners. If the parable were just about that, Jeremias points out, the narrative might as well stop with the payment scene and leave out the dispute between the landlord and those who worked all day. But Jeremias shows that this dispute is crucial because it points to the first audience of the parable:

> The parable is clearly addressed to those who resembled the murmurers, those who criticized and opposed the good news, Pharisees for example. Jesus was minded to show them how unjustified, hateful, loveless and unmerciful was their criticism. Such, said he, is God's goodness, and since God is so good, so too am I. He vindicates the gospel against its critics. Here, clearly, we have recovered the original historical setting. We are suddenly transported into a concrete situation in the life of Jesus such as the Gospels frequently depict. Over and over again we hear the charge brought against Jesus that he is a companion of the despised and outcast, and are told of men to whom the gospel is an offence. Repeatedly is Jesus compelled to justify his conduct and to vindicate the good news. So too here he is saying, This is what God is like, so good, so full of compassion for the poor, how dare you revile him? (38)

With this interpretation Jeremias implies several things about Jesus' ministry: Jesus was known for the company he shared with people who were ostracized by society, the poor and the sinners, the prostitutes, the publicans. For this he was resented by members of the religious elite such as the Pharisees. Telling the parable of the Laborers in the Vineyard was a means for Jesus to justify his own behavior and to reproach his opponents for their resentfulness. The argument launched by the parable runs as follows: God is as generous and kind as the landowner in the story. I am God's representative. Through my own generous and kind behavior toward the outcast I make God's will known. You are wrong to oppose my doing.

Rabbinical Parallels

Jeremias underscores his interpretation by comparing Jesus' parable with a rabbinical one he found in the Jerusalem Talmud (138-139). From the Jerusalem Talmud he cites a story about Rabbi Bun bar Hijja, a learned man who died at the age of twenty-eight. The funeral oration was introduced by a parable that Jeremias renders in the following way:

> The situation was like that of a king who had hired a great number of labourers. Two hours after the work began, the king inspected the labourers. He saw that one of them surpassed the others in industry and skill. He took him by the hand and walked up and down with him till the evening. When the labourers came to receive their wages, each of them received the same amount as all the others. Then they murmured and said: "We have worked the whole day, and this man only two hours, yet you have paid him the full day's wages." The king replied: "I have not wronged you; this labourer has done more in two hours than you have done during the whole day." (138)

Jeremias continues: "So likewise, concluded the funeral oration, has Rabbi Bun bar Hijja accomplished more in his short life of twenty-eight years than many a gray-haired scholar in a hundred years" (138). Jeremias invokes this rabbinical story in order to make two comparative observations. The first concerns the question of historical precedence. Given the many parallels between Jesus' story and the rabbinical one, there obviously is a relationship between the two; one seems to be influenced by the other or they had a common antecedent. As to the question of which parable was first, Jeremias has no doubts. Not only did the protagonist of the Talmudic story, Rabbi Bun bar Hijja, live three hundred years after Jesus;[23] Jeremias also claims that the priority of the Jesus parable is evident also in the artificial nature of the rabbinical story. For ten hours the king is said "to take a walk" with the diligent worker; Jeremias implies that this is an unbelievably long time period, which makes the story dubious and unrealistic. In contrast, Jesus' parable distinguishes itself through its "clarity and simplicity." What Jeremias is claiming here is not only the historical precedence of Jesus' parable but also its superior literary quality.[24] While Matthew 20:1–15 tells a vivid and convincing story, the Talmudic parallel seems fabricated and unnatural.

According to Jeremias's second observation, the two parables drastically differ in their central messages. Jesus' story is about the generosity of a landlord who gives a full day's wage to workers who actually would have deserved only a small fraction of that wage. In the rabbinical version, by contrast, the worker who leaves his workplace after two hours and still receives the full wage has deserved what he receives, because he has accomplished in two hours more than the others in one day. The point of the rabbinical parable is not the king's generosity but the worker's diligence.[25] Jeremias concludes: "Thus in this apparently trivial detail lies the difference between two worlds: the world of merit, and the world of grace; the law contrasted with the gospel" (139).

This contrast between grace and law, between Jesus' message and that of the Rabbis, corresponds to the opposition Jeremias constructs between Jesus and the Pharisees: on the one hand is Jesus' sermon about God's mercy with sinners; on the other hand is a religious system that values strict observance of the laws and that often results, as Jeremias sees it, in a self-righteous, rigid, and loveless attitude. Jeremias's discussion of the rabbinical story, in some ways, is emblematic of his thoughts on Jesus in general. Throughout his work, Jeremias draws a great divide not only between Jesus and some of his contemporaries but, broadly speaking, between Jesus and the literary and religious traditions of Judaism during the first centuries.[26]

Jeremias's Critics

"Jesus Was a Jew"

While Jeremias continues to influence parable research up to this day, his work has also been criticized on many accounts by many scholars. In chapter 7 I discuss a reproach that was formulated within American scholarship in the 1970s, a reproach Perrin describes as Jeremias's failure to "sufficiently respect the integrity of the parables of Jesus as texts" (106). As I will show, this dissatisfaction with Jeremias's treatment of the parables initiated a broad shift from a strict historical to a literary approach to the parables of Jesus. In this chapter I am concerned with more recent criticism that emerged in the 1980s within strands of scholarship that represent a continuation of Jeremias's historical endeavor.

The first kind of criticism that needs to be addressed concerns Jeremias's construction of a stark contrast between Jesus and the Judaism of his time. In this particular scholarly practice Jeremias is not alone. Whole generations of (especially German) scholars based their reconstruction of Jesus' ministry on the assumption that Jesus sharply distinguished himself from his Jewish contemporaries—that his acts and teachings conflicted with what was practiced and taught by other religious leaders of his time.[27] Consequently, in their work with biblical or other first-century material, these scholars followed the rule of attributing to Jesus everything that, according to their judgment, stands out from a general Jewish background.[28]

This rule and its implicit assumptions have come under attack in the course of what nowadays is often called the "third quest" for the historical Jesus, a movement that has started to dominate the scholarly landscape and has produced a whole range of new versions of the life of Jesus, especially in the United States but also in Germany.[29] Like Jeremias, these scholars are eager to understand Jesus in the context of first-century Palestine. However, their research no longer proceeds on the assumption that there were deep conflicts between Jesus and Judaism. Instead, its starting point is an emphasis on the Jewishness of Jesus: "Jesus was a Jew; we should expect his teachings and actions to reflect Jewish ideas and customs" (Evans 20). Indeed, many of the new Jesus reconstructions are driven by an endeavor to integrate Jesus within a Jewish background and understand his ministry as part of a decidedly Jewish religious movement. Methodologically, the historical Jesus gains its contours no longer against a Jewish foil but in accordance with whatever seems plausible within the parameters of first-century Palestinian Judaism.[30]

E. P. Sanders's book *Jesus and Judaism*, published in 1985, is an early representative of "the third quest."[31] Not unlike Jeremias, Sanders is concerned with the relationship between Jesus and his contemporaries in Judaism. He is especially interested in trying to understand the conflict that led to Jesus' death. He investigates that "conflict" within a much more differentiated and richer historical framework than the one implied in Jeremias's binary of "Jesus" on the one hand and "Judaism" on the other. Sanders spends a great amount of time criticizing what he calls "an appreciable drive on the part of New Testament scholars to depict Jesus as transcending the bounds of Judaism" (18). Against this tendency Sanders believes that "we should be prepared to assume a broad ground of positive relationships between Jesus and his contemporaries in Judaism" (16).[32] Yes, there was an opposition between Jesus and certain groups within Judaism. But before that opposition can be grasped, one needs to thoroughly integrate Jesus within the historical reality of first-century Palestine.

At several places in his book, Sanders critically discusses Jeremias's work on the historical Jesus. Sanders takes on Jeremias's notion of the relationship between Jesus and the Pharisees, particularly the idea that Jesus' message of God's love and forgiveness for the poor and the sinners (which Jeremias detects, as I have shown, in Matthew 20:1–15) was offensive to the Pharisees and provoked their hatred against Jesus. This sweeping vision, in Sanders's opinion, has nothing to do with the reality of the time. Almost ridiculous for Sanders is the notion suggested by Jeremias that the Pharisees believed that "the poor" are excluded from salvation—that the Pharisees cut themselves off from the common people and despised them for their lack of education or their inability to observe special purity laws. The inhuman attitude that this view attributes to the Pharisees, according to Sanders, has no ground in any evidence. Keeping company with the poor and proclaiming God's love for them as Jesus did, Sanders emphasizes, was in no way extraordinary or provocative. Sanders writes: "Jeremias needs to make the Pharisees an extremely narrow and bigoted group in order to make an innocuous action—associating with common people—offensive" (196).

In regard to Jesus' relation to "the sinners," things are a bit more complicated.[33] On a general level Sanders points out that the alleged contrast between Jesus' good news about God's grace on the one hand and the Pharisees' insistence on merit and law on the other is a distortion of historical reality. The notion that offering forgiveness to sinners was a novelty and an affront to the Pharisees, a notion by no means held by Jeremias alone, "denies one of the things about Judaism which everyone should know: there was a universal view that forgiveness is *always* available to those who return to the way of the Lord" (202). Jeremias's argument that Jesus' message distinguished itself by putting grace *before* repentance is dismissed by Sanders. Which one comes first, repentance or forgiveness, might be an important distinction for modern theologians, but for Jesus and his contemporaries, Sanders argues, the issue of chronological order was irrelevant– (204–205). The only offensive aspect in Jesus' message was his claim that making restitution according to the law was unnecessary and that following Jesus and his movement would count as an act of repentance. The disagreement between Jesus and the Pharisees, Sanders concludes, far from being an abstract theological dispute over grace against law, was centered around a specific question: "Not whether or not God would be merciful and forgiving, but *to whom* and *on what condition*: to sinners on the condition of their accepting Jesus and his message? or to those who indicate their intention to remain within the covenant by doing what the law requires?" (280).[34]

In his critique of Jeremias and the scholarship Jeremias represents, Sanders repeatedly invokes evidence from first-century Judaism and reproaches his colleagues with a "loss of touch with historical reality" (40).[35] Sanders's readers consequently gain the impression that Jeremias's knowledge about Palestinian Judaism, though it has been acclaimed throughout the decades, is actually quite limited. What Jeremias appears to lack and what Sanders's work exemplifies is a commitment to research thoroughly the Jewish sources and to cooperate with Jewish scholars who are concerned with the same time period.[36]

There is another edge to Sanders's critique of Jeremias: Sanders suggests that the description of the Pharisees as self-righteous advocates of a rigid legalism or as merciless opponents of the masses has its source not in history but in Christian theological interests. Proponents of such a view, he writes, "have been carrying on theological polemic: we have love, mercy, repentance, forgiveness, and even simple decency on our side, and that is why our religion is superior to its parent" (199) (i.e., Judaism). Sanders suggests here that the contrast between grace and law, constructed by Jeremias and others, is in fact a means to demarcate twentieth-century Christian identity by setting it off from Judaism. A Jesus who attacks his Jewish antagonists' wrongheaded idea of God is a projection of Christian self-understanding onto the landscape of first-century Palestine.[37]

"Jesus and His Jewish Parables"

Sanders is not very interested in the parables of Jesus.[38] However, the critical concerns and arguments that are developed in his work and that I just addressed have informed parable research during the last decade as well. Behind book titles such as *Parable and Story in Judaism and Christianity* (by Clemens Thoma and Michael Wyschogrod) and *Jesus and His Jewish Parables* (Young), for example, are efforts to highlight the kinship between New Testament parables and rabbinical ones, to place Jesus' stories not against but within the context of Jewish literary traditions. The works of two German New Testament scholars, both published in 1990, can illustrate this trend. Eckhard Rau's *Reden in Vollmacht* and Catherine Hezser's *Lohnmetaphorik und Arbeitswelt in Mt 20:1–*

16 are attempts to make Jewish and particularly rabbinical parables fruitful for an understanding of the parables of Jesus. Let me briefly address both publications.

Rau's book builds an interaction between Luke 15:11–32, the parable of the Prodigal Son, and several Jewish parallels. At the beginning of this endeavor Rau problematizes Jeremias's claim of the uniqueness and superiority (*Unvergleichlichkeit*) of the parables of Jesus. It might well be the case that Jesus' parables "reveal a definite personal character, a unique clarity and simplicity, a matchless mastery of construction," as Jeremias says.[39] However, this does not mean that nothing in the ancient world compares to the parables. Rau emphatically challenges the apologetic tendency to elevate Jesus' parables, to play them off against the Rabbis (228–231); he deplores the failure of Jeremias and others to acknowledge that Jesus' mastery grew on the grounds of Judaism (231). Rau specifically calls into question Jeremias's claim of the priority of the Jesus parables, his notion that Jesus was the first in his cultural environment to tell parables and that the Rabbis, in their own use of the genre, were informed by Jesus. Against this claim, Rau offers a simple historical consideration: Jesus, in all probability, did not invent but acquired the ability to talk in parables (217). It is very likely, Rau surmises, that Jesus learned the skill so as to employ the genre of parables within educational establishments of his time. While the particular school or place cannot be determined with certainty,[40] there is no reason, Rau says, to think that Jesus' parables are without precedents, as Jeremias wants us to believe. Quite the opposite: Jesus' parabolic discourse—its technique and the everyday topics and theological traditions it takes up—is rooted within Jewish practices and Jewish institutions (226–227).

Even though rabbinical parables were written down much later than the New Testament parables, Rau argues, early versions must have circulated already during the time of Jesus. Rau furthermore suggests that rabbinical parables, although we find them today in the context of exegesis, once had a function (Sitz im Leben) like the parables of Jesus, namely to make a point about a specific issue in a specific communicative setting (227). It might even be possible that the Pharisees, addressed by Jesus in parables, talked back in parables, and that Jesus refined his mastery of the genre in conversation with his interlocutors (238). Be that as it may, Rau's emphasis is that the parables' alleged uniqueness is a misleading postulate for New Testament parable interpretation and that, instead, the affinities and similarities between Jesus and the early rabbinical material should be considered by the interpreter.

Hezser's work on Matthew 20:1–16, the Laborers in the Vineyard, is a powerful example of such an approach. Like Rau, Hezser problematizes the degradation of rabbinical literature that in her opinion is a result of the anti-Jewish attitude prevalent among Christian New Testament scholars (164).[41] And, like Sanders, she rejects the idea of a sharp contrast between Jesus' good news and the Pharisees' narrow-minded insistence on law and merit. Instead, she focuses on Matthew 20 as a test case to integrate Jesus' message within the multiplicity of Jewish thoughts and teachings (19). Through a close study of the notions of wage and labor, Hezser demonstrates that the message of God's generosity vis-à-vis human imperfection does not stand in opposition to but is part of Jewish theology.

At the center of Hezser's work is a multileveled comparison between Matthew 20 and twelve rabbinical parables that all tell about two groups of workers who are paid by their employers according to different criteria. The rabbinical parable, jBer 2,8, that is invoked by Jeremias is part of the comparison. However, while Jeremias uses this text as a negative foil for his interpretation of Matthew 20, in Hezser's work both the rabbinical parable and Jesus' parable are examined within a whole range of slightly diverging narratives.[42] Taking recourse to sociohistorical studies, Hezser argues that, in the rabbinical story, the king's decision to give the full wage to the diligent laborer, even though he worked only for two hours, is an extraordinary act. The king pays the laborer according to his proficiency, not according to the work he accomplished, and this is something that goes beyond the contemporary industrial law, which does not provide that diligent laborers should receive a special reward. The payment therefore needs to be considered a generous act on the part of the king. More generous is the landlord in Matthew 20, who pays wages according to the workers' needs. The destitution of those who are hired late in the day, not their accomplishment, becomes the criteria for payment.[43] However, Hezser discusses four parables that tell about even greater acts of generosity. These rabbinical stories tell about workers who receive a full wage even though they are either lazy or dishonest. Despite the worker's shortcomings, the king or landlord still makes the payment according to the workers' needs.

What Hezser suggests here is that Jesus did not have a monopoly on the topic of God's grace or love. Her comparative analysis shows that on the question of generosity Jesus' parable holds a middle position. Thereby Hezser relativizes the alleged uniqueness of Jesus' message and effectively invalidates Jeremias's interpretation of Matthew 20.[44] Hezser concludes that Jesus' teaching about godly rewards does not differ from contemporary teachings (296). His proclamation of God's grace belongs within the parameters of Jewish theology.[45]

Today, Jeremias's interpretations of the parables, which have influenced entire generations of scholars and students of the Bible, can no longer be read without serious reservations. How much the critique of Jeremias has started to inform the mainstream of scholarship can be witnessed in Gerd Theissen and Annette Merz's book *The Historical Jesus*, first published in Germany in 1996. This is a textbook written for students of theology. The many aspects of historical Jesus research are arranged into lessons to be studied. The authors frequently pose research questions and give exercises in which students are asked to process and apply the information that is offered in the various chapters. At the end of the chapter entitled "Jesus as Poet: The Parables of Jesus," the authors cite two long paragraphs by an unnamed New Testament scholar. The text is introduced as an example of the ways in which Christian exegetes have downgraded rabbinical parables. The first paragraph starts with the following sentence: "The clearness and simplicity with which our parable presents the Good News is thrown into sharp relief by comparison with a rabbinical parallel," and so on. The text is by Jeremias—the comparison between Matthew 20 and jBer 2,8 (5c). After the quotation, the students are asked to criticize what they just read: "What objections do you have to this interpretation in terms of method and content?" (346) Students who work on this study question learn to problematize the degrading treatment of rabbinical stories that characterizes Jeremias's work. In fact, Theissen's and Merz's textbook teaches students at almost every turn to be critical of anti-Jewish rhetoric in New Testament scholarship. Given Theissen's prominence within the current German theological landscape, I surmise that the book will significantly increase sensitivity toward the problem of anti-Judaism among the new generation of biblical scholars and theologians in Germany.

5

"In View of Catastrophe"

When I came to the United States in 1992, I was already familiar with the critique of Jeremias expressed in Theissen and Merz's exercise. In 1991 I had a seminar with Eckard Rau at the University of Hamburg on the topic of "Jewish parables." I remember how Rau, with a sarcastically exaggerated tone, read to us that flagrant sentence: "So scheiden sich . . . zwei Welten: dort Verdienst, hier Gnade; dort Gesetz, hier Evangelium" ("Thus . . . the difference between two worlds: the world of merit, and the world of grace; the law contrasted with the gospel"), and shook his head over what he emphasized was a crude kind of anti-Jewish stereotyping. Another teacher, Tim Schramm, who also taught seminars on the parables, strongly recommended to us Catherine Hezser's dissertation on Matthew 20, which at the time, had just been published. During those years in Hamburg I was made aware of the problem of anti-Judaism, specifically, of the anti-Jewish tendencies in Jeremias's work, and I was taught to appreciate and not to degrade rabbinical literature in my studies of the parables of Jesus.

However, I have to admit that I did not pay any special attention to these critical concerns conveyed to me through my teachers in Hamburg. I took account of them and acknowledged them as important scholarly insights. But the Jewishness of Jesus' parables was not an issue that caught my interest. I was bored with historical criticism, the general discursive space in which the work by Hezser and Rau is situated. I was fascinated instead with the literary approach to the parables as it was developed by Harnisch, for whom "first-century Palestine" and the question of "Jesus and Judaism" are irrelevant interpretive categories (chapter 3).

The shock about Jeremias that made my hair stand on end came in the spring of 1994. Not long after my uncanny encounter with Kaschnitz's poem on my desk, I started an independent study on the history of interpretation of two parables and for that purpose reread the classics of parable scholarship. After studying Jülicher and Dodd I engaged, once again, with Jeremias. I felt uncomfortable from the very start. I had already circled all the places in his book where rabbinical material was devaluated against the parables of Jesus. But beyond these specific and occasional paragraphs I felt that something was not right with the entire book. When I got to the chapter entitled "Im Angesicht der Katastrophe" ("In View of Catastrophe"),[1] I had to interrupt my study because I could not bear to read one more page.

Today this early reaction to Jeremias seems significant to me and I will spend some time investigating what precisely it was that upset me. I will also trace the process of how my reading of Jeremias after this experience changed; how I tried to articulate my concerns and how I nuanced my assessments. By laying out my different responses to Jeremias I intend to gradually historicize his book in the immediate postwar situation in Germany.

"A Nation Rushing upon Its Own Destruction"

Let me begin by looking at the sentences that disturbed me so much:

> Jesu Botschaft ist nicht nur Heilsverkündigung, sondern auch Unheilsankündigung, Warnung und Bußruf angesichts des furchtbaren Ernstes der Stunde. Die Zahl der hierher gehörenden Gleichnisse ist groß, erschreckend groß. Immer wieder hat Jesus warnend seine Stimme erhoben, um einem verblendeten Volk die Augen zu öffnen. (90)

> Ihr verblendeten Menschen! Die Wetteranzeichen vermögt Ihr zu deuten und die Zeichen der Zeit nicht? Ihr seid blind! Ihr feiert und tanzt—und der Vulkan kann jeden Augenblick losbrechen! (91)

> In einmaliger konkreter Situation sind die Gleichnisse, die von der drohended Krise handeln, gesprochen, das ist grundlegend für ihr Verständnis. Sie wollen nicht ethische Maximen einprägen, sondern sie wollen ein verblendetes, in sein Verderben rennendes Volk wachrütteln, vorab seine Führer, die Theologen und die Priester. (94)

> The message of Jesus is not only the proclamation of salvation, but also the announcement of judgment, a cry of warning, and a call to repentance in view of the terrible urgency of the crisis. The number of parables in this category is nothing less than awe-inspiring. Over and over again did Jesus raise his voice in warning, striving to open the eyes of a blinded people. (120)

> How blind you are! You can read the signs of the weather, but you cannot recognize the signs of the time. In your blindness you feast and dance, while the volcano may erupt at any moment! (122)

> The parables which deal with the impending crisis were each uttered in a particular concrete situation, a fact which is essential for their understanding. It is not their purpose to propound moral precepts, but to shock into realization of its danger a nation rushing upon its own destruction, and more especially its leaders, the theologians and priests. (126)[2]

What did I see in these sentences that they had such an effect on me? In my first attempts to articulate and explain my reaction, I referred to the anti-Jewish trope underlying Jeremias's language: the blinded people of Israel: "the Jews" who fail to recognize Jesus and his message. It is true that I had known about this aspect of Jeremias's work before. I had known that tropes like these frequently appear in Christian scholarship and those instances never had thrown me off balance. What distinguished my reading of Jeremias in 1994 above all was an acute awareness of the book's first date of publication. Throughout my reading there was a persistent thought in the back of my mind, namely, that Jeremias's book was published in 1947, two years after the end of the Second World War. What seemed to me absolutely scandalous about his work was, as I said, its perpetuation of anti-Jewish rhetoric *after Auschwitz*. How was it possible that anti-Jewish phrases and stereotypes could appear in a German publication only two years after the Holocaust?

However, this indignant question does not really capture my feeling of not being able to continue my work on Jeremias. Today I believe that what hit me in the sentences quoted here was not anti-Judaism but something less obvious and more difficult to pinpoint. Let me try to describe it: under the sign of "1947," the semantic field of Jeremias's sentences—"catastrophe," "cry of warning," "the terrible urgency of the crisis," "danger," "destruction"—became ambiguous and started to evoke for me the atmosphere of an impending catastrophe not in first-century Palestine but in Europe in the 1930s. Once the atmosphere of the Holocaust spread out in my mind I could not help taking Jeremias's phrases in a way other than they were intended. "A nation rushing upon its own destruction" conjured up images of deportation, of cattle cars, of Jews being marched out of their homes, Jews being dragged out of the ghettos. Jeremias's interpretive language had started to resonate with the events of genocide.

Jeremias unambiguously refers to the Jewish people of Jesus' time. There are no insinuations or allusions in the text that would justify seeking the reference points of Jeremias's sentences anywhere else than in first-century Palestine.[3] Yet, in light of the fact that these very sentences were published almost immediately after the end of the war, its terms and phrases became imbricated in my mind with events during and before the war. The distinction between the first century and the twentieth became blurred. Who are the "blinded people" who "cannot recognize the signs of the time," who "feast and dance, while the volcano may erupt at any moment," and "who are rushing upon [their] own destruction"?

As I started to read Jeremias's text as a post-Holocaust discourse, its language became overdetermined, but this overdetermination was almost impossible for me to deal with or to unpack because it was excruciating. Most clearly, this was the case with Jeremias's use of the trope of the "blinded people of Israel." This trope was never innocent. But during the 1940s it gained jarring meanings and resonances, and after the war "the blindness" of European Jewry, its supposed failure to anticipate the danger of German National Socialism, became a charged topos in writings about the Holocaust. The Italian Jewish survivor Primo Levi addressed this topos as one of the stereotypes that have frequently confronted survivors of the Holocaust: "Among the questions that are put to us, one is never absent; indeed, as the years go by, it is formulated with ever increasing persistence, and with an ever less hidden accent of accusation. . . . Why did you not escape? Why did you not rebel? Why did you not avoid capture 'beforehand'?" (Drowned 150–151) In his critical response Levi concedes:

> It isn't that the premonitory symptoms of the slaughter were lacking: from his very first books and speeches Hitler had spoken clearly. The Jews (not only the German Jews) were the parasites of humanity and must be eliminated as noxious insects are eliminated. But disquieting deductions have a difficult life: until the last moment, until the incursion of the Nazi (and Fascist) dervishes from house to house, one found a way to deny the signals, ignore the danger. (164)

These, I believe, are precisely the notions I read into Jeremias's trope of a "blinded people" "rushing upon its own destruction," unable to "recognize the signs of the time" and oblivious to the fact the "the volcano may erupt at any moment."[4] However, Levi also emphasizes how problematic and reductive these notions are. He admonishes his readers to "beware of hindsight and stereotypes" (165). Postwar judgments about the failure to read the warning signs and to escape in time bespeaks a lack of knowledge about the realities in Europe in the 1930s and 1940s. Emigration, Levi points out, was a much more complicated and dramatic process than it is today. It required financial resources as well as connections in the country of destination, and often it was made difficult or impossible by restricted immigration or closed borders (163). Moreover, says Levi, one should not forget that many Jewish families had been rooted in their home country for centuries and that many Jews were dedicated to their country's culture, language, law, and history. For many, emigration was a traumatic prospect (163–164).

A more vigorous critique of the readiness to reproach European Jewry for their blindness to the future has been developed by Michael Bernstein. Bernstein emphasizes that there was never a clear, predictable line that led from the anti-Semitic politics of the 1930s to the death camps. With hindsight "the road to Auschwitz" might seem like an inevitable course of events, but that was not at all obvious in the 1930s. On the contrary, the Nazi death machinery was something unimaginable at the time. Bernstein points out that even today one talks about "the unprecedented and singular nature of the Shoah" (Foregone 23). The notion, which Bernstein detects in much post-Holocaust writing, that the Jews of Europe were to blame for not saving themselves from the threat of Nazi Germany is based on a contradiction: "On the one hand, this contradictory perspective insists that the Shoah was an absolutely unprecedented event in human history, while on the other hand, it blames Europe's assimilated Jews for not having anticipated, and thus avoided, the plan for their total extermination" (34). Bernstein calls this *backshadowing*: "a kind of retroactive foreshadowing in which the shared knowledge of the outcome of a series of events by narrator and listener is used to judge the participants in those events *as though they too should have known what was to come*" (16).[5]

Bernstein adds an observation that is crucial to my concerns. The post-Holocaust practice of "backshadowing," of criticizing prewar Jewry for not recognizing the signs of an upcoming catastrophe, according to Bernstein, resembles an age-old Christian theological rhetoric:

> By now it ought to be apparent that there is a sense in which historical backshadowing unwittingly places the pre-war European Jews in a position disturbingly similar to the one assigned them by the early Church. Just as the first Christians condemned the Jews for having seen the Savior, witnessed his miracles, and still choosing to reject him, so the contempt of writers projecting backward from their knowledge of the Shoah convicts all those who failed to heed the initial signs of Nazism's reign. It is as though the Jews, initially cursed for not recognizing the Messiah, are now to be scorned again, two millennia later, for having failed to recognize the anti-Christ [i.e., Hitler]. To have been blind to "the truth" at Bethlehem and at Barnau [i.e., Hitler's birthplace], to have misrecognized first the eternal promise incarnated in the carpenter's son and then the mortal peril in the custom inspector's, are the terms to which Jewish history is reduced once its content is held accountable to the certainties visible from the standpoint of backshadowing. (34)

Before I channel this paragraph into my own argument it is important to acknowledge the specific rhetorical context of Bernstein's critical remarks. Bernstein is concerned with Holocaust literature, mostly by Jewish writers, some of them survivors. The paragraph I quote is part of an effort to raise an awareness of the problematic nature of backshadowing, of using current knowledge about the Holocaust to criticize the reactions of prewar Jewry to the rise of Nazism. It is historically questionable to talk about the Jews' blindness or self-deception since no one could foresee the genocidal outcome of Nazi anti-Semitism. This talk, Bernstein emphasizes here, has also highly suspect cultural undertones as it plays into the rhetoric of the supersessionist theology of the early church.

My own concerns are different. My point of departure was not Holocaust literature but a twentieth-century Christian discourse that arguably perpetuates the rhetoric of the early church. Jeremias does not exactly speak of Israel's rejection of the Messiah. But his notions of a blinded people and of an extreme antagonism between Jesus and the Jewish leaders is one facet of the larger Christian theology to which Bernstein refers. In what may seem like a backtracking of Bernstein's train of thought, the terms of Jeremias's discourse evoked for me the trope of a blinded people as it has emerged in narratives about the Holocaust.

Bernstein's remarks suggest—and this is why I find them helpful—that the resonances between Jeremias's discourse on Jesus and the Jews on the one hand and the events of the Holocaust on the other did not just vibrate within my personal imagination but are part of a deep cultural reservoir. Bernstein supports my idea that the distinction between the first century and the twentieth can become blurred on occasions as happened to me in 1994; that descriptions of "the Jews" in ancient times may become imbricated with descriptions of "the Jews" during the Holocaust. Bernstein also gives me a clue as to why my reading of Jeremias through the lens of the Holocaust was such a dramatic experience. For what I read in Jeremias's sentences was not only an excruciating thought— "the blind Jews of Europe who rushed upon their own destruction because they failed to read the warning signs"—but also a dubious thought, a taboo almost, something that raises, as Bernstein's work shows, one of the most painful debates in the study of the Holocaust. Even though I was not aware of it at the time, the charged nature of what I saw in Jeremias's text might have been the reason I put his book away from me so emphatically and did not want to touch it anymore.

But of course, I came back to Jeremias's book on the parables. In the summer of 1994 I started to write my way through the questions that Harnisch's quotation of Kaschnitz's poem had produced in my mind. At some point in the process, about a year later, I felt that I needed to look again at Jeremias, if only because his work plays such a dominant role in parable research. I needed to take account of these sentences from 1947 and figure out what they meant and what I would make of them.

My critical thoughts first were shaped in relation to Jeremias's phrase "Im Angesicht der Katastrophe"—the heading of the chapter that had made me leave off my reading. This phrase in fact became a focal point of my effort to deal with Jeremias.[6] In the context of Jeremias's reconstruction of the parables' first historical setting, "im Angesicht der Katastrophe" refers to eschatological events which are just about to happen. "Im Angesicht der Katastrophe" means, as the English translator puts it, "The Imminence of Catastrophe." Moreover, the German *im Angesicht* is equivalent to the English phrase "in view of." This figurative meaning may be included in Jeremias's heading as well. The parables subsumed under it are all told "with regard" to the fact that a catastrophe is approaching. "The message of Jesus is . . . a call to repentance in view of the terrible urgency of the crisis." However, there is a third way to understand the phrase "im Angesicht der

Katastrophe." Taken literally, the phrase would refer not to imminent events but to events that just took place and are looked upon—to a catastrophe whose outcome lies directly in front of one's eyes. This subliminal meaning, certainly not intended by Jeremias, became for me a sort of ironic emblem for the book's date of publication, 1947. "The catastrophe," in my reading, turned into the German catastrophe, the immediate postwar situation, the bombed cities, the millions of displaced persons, and most especially the atrocities of genocide that had been revealed by the Allies. The person who was face to face, im Angesicht with all this, according to my imagination, was Jeremias himself.[7]

My imagination was a timely one. It was 1995, the year of the fiftieth anniversaries of the end of the war and of the liberation of the death camps. On an almost daily basis the media covered the commemorations at the former sites of torture and death and shaped a broad public impression of the year 1945. The Holocaust museum in Washington, for example, had as an annual display the exhibit "1945: The Year of Liberation," which I referred to in chapter 2. What struck me most when I visited were the "images of confrontation" that showed Germans being forced to face the sight of liberated concentration camps. Unwittingly, I applied these images to Jeremias. What invigorated my critical thoughts, in any case, was the idea that Jeremias, when he published his book, was in the same position as the Germans on the Allied photographs. Even if he never confronted the "German atrocities" in the literal sense of standing im Angesicht of the sites of torture and death, he must have known about the facts, which now, in 1995, once again circulated in the international press. How could Jeremias talk about an imminent catastrophe threatening the Jews when he himself had just witnessed the catastrophic outcome of the Nazi assault? How could Jeremias write about "a nation rushing upon its own destruction" only two years after the literal destruction of the European Jewry had almost successfully come to an end and the full scope of Nazi atrocity had come to the surface? The recurrent trope of "the blinded people" in Jeremias's language gained a deeply ironic ring. For it seemed to me that the very use of this trope indicated Jeremias's own blindness toward contemporary catastrophe.

"Im Angesicht der Katastrophe" became the emblem, the stigma perhaps, of the entire book. Beyond the few charged sentences of this one particular chapter, the basic interpretive categories of Jeremias's work as a whole came, in my reading, under the sign of the immediate postwar situation. The construction of an antagonistic relationship between Jesus and the Jewish leaders, the notion of the parables as "weapons of warfare," the degradation of rabbinical material—all these problematic aspects of Jeremias's work, which I had known about without paying special attention to it, made me incredulous.[8] How could a German scholar develop such a discourse in view of the catastrophe of the Holocaust?

Germany, 1947

However, just as I eventually developed second thoughts on Harnisch's work, I also came to reconsider my astonishment and incredulity toward Jeremias's work. What I came to realize was that my reaction was in fact quite naive. Underlying my incredulity was the assumption that the Holocaust should have made an immediate and substantial impact on Jeremias's scholarly practice; that he should have seen the German atrocities and that he should have instantly drawn conclusions for his work; that upon learning about the terrible crimes done to the Jews in Europe, partly facilitated by Christian anti-Judaism, he should automatically have refrained from perpetuating any kind of anti-Jewish discourse; and that he should have been sensitive toward the way his interpretive language resonated with the fate of the Jews in the twentieth century. These assumptions are misconceptions of the realities of the immediate postwar years in Germany.

My first doubts came one day in the library when I passed by the volumes of the *Zeitschrift für Neutestamentliche Wissenschaft*, a preeminent journal that I knew from my theological studies in Germany. Spontaneously, I looked for the first issue that was published after the Second World War. It came out in 1949. When I opened the cover I saw a two-page dedication entitled by bold letters: "Den Toten," "To the Dead." I instantly thought that "the dead" referred to the dead Jews of Europe and that the dedication was intended to acknowledge the Holocaust as an interruption of New Testament scholarship. But I was completely mistaken. "The dead" in this piece refer to New Testament scholars who died during and after the war and above all to Gerhard Kittel whose name has become tainted because of Kittel's membership of the Nazi party.[9] The dedication configures the dead scholars and the New Testament profession in general as the tragic victims of historical and political circumstances. There is no mention whatsoever of the victims of "the final solution." I was dumbfounded. For the first time I suspected that my expectations of Jeremias were unrealistic, that they resulted from a position of hindsight; that they were informed by concerns and sensibilities proper to the 1990s but totally missed the state of affairs of the mid- and late 1940s, twenty years before the term "Holocaust" would even appear on the scene.

On a very general level and in the terms of psychoanalysis, Alexander and Margarete Mitscherlichs's work, *The Inability to Mourn*, offers explications of the difficulties that were involved in the task of recognizing the victims of the Holocaust. In order to acknowledge the enormity of the crimes committed in the name of Germany and to recognize the immense suffering caused by Nazism, Germans would first have to mourn for the loss of their collective ego-ideal represented by Hitler and to work through the traumatic shattering of their narcissistic identification. The Mitscherlichs are more concerned with the 1950s and 1960s than the first years after the war. But their description of the immediate postwar situation in Germany helped me to better understand the disturbing aspects of Jeremias's work. The Mitscherlichs would call unfounded the expectation that Jeremias should have felt empathy with the Jewish victims of his time. The period following Germany's collapse is theorized by the authors in terms of a psychological emergency that released a number of defense strategies, such as the derealization of the Nazi past. They write:

> The Germans . . . had received a blow to the very core of their self-esteem, and the most urgent task for their psychic apparatus was to ward off the experience of a melancholy impoverishment of the self. Thus the moral duty to share in mourning for the victims of their ideological aims—which for the rest of the world was self-evident—could at that time, be only of superficial psychic importance for most Germans. The mechanisms concerned here are emergency reactions, processes very close to, if not actual psychological correlates of, *biological* survival processes. Hence it is pointless to make of these immediate post-collapse reactions a subject of reproach. . . . It would be wholly unrealistic to expect a population in such a state of shock—with its insane goals and gruesome crimes newly laid bare—to be able to worry about anything but itself. (24)

Leaving aside the psychoanalytical concepts operative in the Mitscherlichs's think-ing, their work suggests, helpfully, I believe, that the primary challenge in 1947 for Germans was to cope with the collapse of an inflated national identity. This collapse was so drastic and the shift from images of Nazi grandeur to images of bombed cities and piles of corpses so extreme (Hüppauf, "Emptying" 3), that most Germans were busy dealing with their own struggles and disappointments, and that there was by and large very little capacity to recognize the suffering of others, particularly of the Jewish victims of the Holocaust.[10]

In a study of West Germany's postwar public memory, Robert Moeller makes a similar argument. In critical interaction with the Mitscherlichs' analysis of an "inability to mourn," Moeller points out that an intense work of mourning did take place during the second half of the 1940s and the 1950s.[11] It is not true that the Germans failed to mourn, Moeller argues, but the objects of mourning were not Germany's victims but the Ger-mans themselves. During the postwar years, Germans across the political spectrum were occupied by the fate of German POWs in Soviet captivity and of the countless Germans who were expelled from Eastern Europe. Postwar public memory in West Germany, Moeller's analysis shows, was centered around the Germans' own suffering.

Another argument to the same effect has been made by my grandmother, who was not expelled from her home but was nonetheless absorbed in her own distress. The postwar years, she said, were miserable times. All she could think of was how to feed her children. In fact, 1947 went down in history as the year of the most severe famine in postwar Germany. Karl Jaspers, in his immediate postwar considerations in *The Question of German Guilt*, testifies to this situation as well:

> The temptation to evade this question [i.e., of the German guilt] is obvious; we live in distress—large parts of our population are in so great, such acute distress that they seem to have become insensitive to such discussions. Their interest is in anything that would relieve distress, that would give them work and bread, shelter and warmth. The horizon has shrunk. People do not like to hear of guilt, of the past; world history is not their concern. They simply do not want to suffer any more; they want to get out of this misery, to live but not to think. There is a feeling as though after such fearful suffering one had to be rewarded, as it were, or at least comforted, but not burdened with guilt on top of it all. (27)[12]

Like the Mitscherlichs, Jaspers suggests that the conditions in postwar Germany—the time when Jeremias's book was published—were such that the Nazi past, the crimes and the question of guilt, for many people were just too much to deal with. These accounts do not excuse the problematic aspects of Jeremias's work. What they offer is a way to contextualize and to integrate Jeremias's book within the immediate postwar situation. Jeremias's work and its lack of sensitivity toward the fate of the Jews during the war is a document typical of the 1940s. What struck me about Jeremias, namely, that the events of the Holocaust apparently did not make an impact on his scholarship, is not surprising but symptomatic of the postwar years. As the Mitscherlichs would say, it is unrealistic to expect Jeremias to acknowledge and process the traumatic events of his time.

Eventually I also had to rethink my ironic emblem "Im Angesicht der Katastrophe." Especially in light of recent critiques of the photographs of atrocities, my idea of Jeremias standing face to face with torture and death calls for reinterpretation. While I still want to hold on to this idea, I need to call into question the assumption that the images of atrocities held clear, unambiguous meanings for the viewers in 1945. As Dagmar Barnouw has argued, the photographs were actually "too overpowering to speak for themselves" (xi). In some ways, my indignant question of how a text such as Jeremias's *Parables of Jesus* could have been published only two years after the Holocaust comes close to the rhetoric of the Allies in 1945 who, according to Barnouw, read and used the photographs from the camps as the clearest evidence that Germans should atone for their crimes. Just as the Allies expected the Germans "to see, accept and repent their complicity" (Barnouw xi), I expected Jeremias, upon looking at the horrors of the Holocaust, to at least show awareness of what had happened, which in the context of his profession would have meant to break with anti-Jewish interpretive traditions.

Barnouw argues that it was precisely the expectation imposed on the Germans to take responsibility for the millions of dead that blocked any response to the documentation of atrocities. Barnouw calls attention to "the audience's anxiety about expectations that Germans as a group should feel in some large general way responsible for these horrible facts, and therefore guilty. They could not articulate their profound shock at the evidence without fearing that answers would be demanded from them to explain 'how they could have let it happen'" (2–3). In Barnouw's opinion, "the real issue was not [the Germans'] refusal to look at and see the reality of the horror; it was, rather, their shrinking away from collectively accepting responsibility for that horror and showing remorse" (12).

But was it really the victors' expectations and impositions that made it so hard to look at and respond to these images? Was there not something in the photographs themselves that caused "a difficulty of seeing," that made it impossible for so many people to confront and react to them? Is the effect of newly revealed visual evidence of genocide not disconcerting enough to explain the silence and the lack of reaction? Have I not simply underestimated the traumatic and blinding impact of the images of catastrophe? Jeremias might very well have stood in front of the images—but how did he see and understand them? Did he let himself be affected or did he look with what Bernd Hüppauf calls an empty gaze, a gaze isolated from the cultural matrixes, the frame of an outside world (37), in which the act of viewing takes place? Have I not underestimated the immense work of reading and interpreting the images of catastrophe, of integrating them into one's moral and religious frame of reference in a way that then would result and reflect itself in a scholarly work on the parables, all this only two years after the end of the war?

6

Historical Criticism and the Return into History

I have narrated my different reactions to Jeremias because I wanted to recapitulate how his work gradually gained significance for me when situated within the immediate postwar situation in Germany. Giving space to my changing responses and thoughts, I described the process through which *The Parables of Jesus* turned for me from a classic text of parable research into a post-Holocaust phenomenon. In this chapter I want to point to some of the implications and consequences of my approach to Jeremias's work. Thereby I also want to explicate how this approach differs from that of the critical literature reviewed in chapter 4. What I would like to argue specifically is that the recent revisions of Jeremias's work, as long as they operate within a historical-critical framework, foreclose an understanding of Jeremias's publication in its own historical context. With their focus on the first century, these revisions mute important questions of remembrance that Jeremias's work as a post-Holocaust discourse poses.

Historical Critics and the Wicked Husbandmen

In order to concretize my arguments I want to narrow my focus, once again, to a particular parable. Here is the story of the Wicked Husbandmen, according to the gospel of Mark (12:1–11):

> 1b A man planted a vineyard, put a fence around it, dug a pit for the wine press, and built a watchtower; then he leased it to tenants and went to another country. 2 When the season came, he sent a slave to the tenants to collect from them his share of the produce of the vineyard. 3 But they seized him, and beat him, and sent him away empty-handed. 4 And again he sent another slave to them; this one they beat over the head and insulted. 5 Then he sent another, and that one they killed. And so it was with many others; some they beat, and others they killed. 6 He had still one other, a beloved son. Finally he sent him to them, saying, "They will respect my son." 7 But those tenants said to one another, "This is the heir; come let us kill him, and the inheritance will be ours." 8 So they seized him, killed him, and threw him out of the vineyard. 9 What then will the owner of the vineyard do? He will come and destroy the tenants and give the vineyard to others.

10 Have you not read this scripture: "The stone that the builders rejected has become the cornerstone; 11 this was the Lord's doing, and it is amazing in our eyes"?

This parable with its exaggerated and increasing violence—abuse, murder, destruction— is probably one of the most jarring texts in the gospels. For many contemporary listeners, the parable, moreover, has anti-Jewish undertones. In her book *Faith and Fratricide*, Rose-mary Radford Ruether cites the parable of the Wicked Husbandmen as an example of the anti-Jewish flip-side of early christology (92). According to this old tradition, Jesus, the Messiah, was murdered by the unrepentant and unbelieving people of Israel. Numerous interpreters over the centuries have read the parable against the background of this anti-Jewish myth: The murderous behavior of the tenants represents the murderous behavior of "the Jews" toward God's prophets and finally toward God's Son, Jesus Christ. The subsequent reprisal, the destruction of the tenants, represents God's abandonment of Israel, which is followed by his turn "to others," that is, to "the Gentile Church." Read in this vein, the parable expresses the central idea of Christian supersessionism.

I have chosen Mark 12 partly because of this legacy and partly because the parable appears in Jeremias's book under the rubric "Im Angesicht der Katastrophe" which has been central to my discussion. According to Jeremias, this parable, together with several other parables, was an "announcement of judgment, a cry of warning, and a call to repentance in view of the terrible urgency of the crisis" (120). It was one of those parables with which Jesus wanted "to shock into realization of its danger a nation rushing upon its own destruction, and more especially its leaders, the theologians and priests" (126). In the following, I will summarize Jeremias's treatment of the parable, then I will ad-dress an essay by Aaron Milavec that critically deals with Jeremias's scholarship and offers a reinterpretation of Mark 12:1-11. In the second half of this chapter I will draw some distinctions between Milavec's and my own approach.

Against Allegorical Interpretation

Jeremias discusses the parable of the Wicked Husbandmen as an example of allegorical interpretation (70–75).[1] As we read it today, each trait of the story seems to refer to some-thing else. "The vineyard is clearly Israel, the tenants are Israel's rulers and leaders, the owner of the vineyard is God, the messengers are the prophets, the son is Christ, the punishment of the husbandmen symbolizes the ruin of Israel, the 'other people' . . . are the Gentile Church. The whole parable is evidently pure allegory" (70). Previous scholars have therefore dismissed the parable as a creation of the early church.[2] In contrast, Jeremias argues for the parable's authenticity as *ipsissima vox* of Jesus by showing in detail how Mark, Luke, and Matthew, by slight changes, insertions or expansions, have added to the original story a deeper dimension and have turned it into an allegory.

As Jesus told it, the parable of the Wicked Husbandmen was a proper parable. Without primarily referring to God, Israel, and the prophets,[3] Jeremias argues, Jesus' story re-counts an incident that was familiar to its first listeners:

> The parable is, in fact, a realistic description of the Galilean peasants' attitude towards the foreign landlords, an attitude that had been aroused by the Zealot movement whose head-quarters were in Galilea. It is necessary to realize that not only the whole of the upper Jor-

dan valley, and probably the north and north-west shores of the Lake of Gennesaret as well, but also large part of the Galilean uplands, were parceled out as latifundia, and were in the hands of foreign landlords. (74–75)

For Jeremias, the rebellious and violent behavior of the tenants in Jesus' parable reflects the common attempts by Galilean peasants of the first century to get rid of their landlords' collectors and heirs in order to claim unoccupied property. There is thus no need to decode the meaning of the story or to seek the significance of the tenants' violent attacks on a "deep level."

The only trait that seems to contain allegorical significance is the sending and killing of the son. "It may, however, be asked whether the slaying of the son is not too crude a feature for a story taken from real life?" (76) Jeremias concedes that in the context of the gospels, "the son" indeed seems to refer to Jesus Christ.[4] However, within the parable's first historical setting this christological allusion was absent. When Jesus told the parable of the Wicked Husbandmen to his first listeners he did not intend to refer to his own upcoming death. Instead he told a captivating story that was geared toward a specific audience and that was meant to bring a point across.

Like so many other parables, this one was directed against Jesus' enemies, the Jewish authorities, most likely the priestly members of the Sanhedrin (166). How did they hear the parable? Jeremias supposes that they must have identified with the wicked husbandmen or, better, that Jesus compared their behavior with the behavior of the tenants. The point of comparison lies in the corruption of those peasants who rebelled against the wealthy landowner. The parable suggests that the leaders of the people acted toward God just as badly as the tenants acted toward the owner of the vineyard. And just as the tenants face the landowner's terrible vengeance, so do the Jewish authorities face divine punishment. This is how Jeremias renders the original meaning of the parable: "'You, it says, you tenants of the vineyard, you leaders of the people! you have opposed, have multiplied rebellion against God. Your cup is full!'" (76)

"The introduction of the figure of the only son," Jeremias argues, "is the result, not of theological considerations, but of the inherent logic of the story" (76). It serves to illustrate the utmost wickedness of the tenants: not only were they as unscrupulous as to abuse and to kill the owner's servants, they did not even hesitate to kill the owner's son. Originally, Jeremias concludes, the story of the Wicked Husbandmen was not an allegory but a proper parable, a vivid and realistic story, an authentic saying of Jesus.

Against Anti-Jewish Interpretations

Aaron Milavec's essay "A Fresh Analysis of the Parable of the Wicked Husbandmen in the Light of Jewish-Catholic Dialogue" is part of the 1989 volume *Parable and Story in Judaism and Christianity*, edited by Clemens Thoma and Michael Wyschogrod. This volume is the result of co-operative efforts by Jewish and Christian scholars to deal with the many relationships between their respective literary traditions and thus to engage in a kind of Jewish-Christian dialogue.[5]

Milavec's essay is concerned with the "long legacy of anti-Judaism" ("Fresh" 81) that is associated with the parable of the Wicked Husbandmen. An early expression of the anti-Jewish reading of the parable can be found, Milavec shows, in a fifth-century homily by John Chrysostom. For Chrysostom the parable expresses, among other things, the Jews' murderous disposition, their crime of killing the Son of God, and God's punishment and abandonment of the Jews. According to Milavec, Chrysostom's interpretation indicates "a pattern of exegesis surrounding the wicked husbandmen which became both the spontaneously given and the stubborn orthodoxy for future generations of Christians" (83). In fact, the anti-Jewish pattern of exegesis has been transported, Milavec argues, from the patristic period up to our own time.

"Our time," for Milavec, is the time period after 1945: he discusses modern scholarship on Mark 12 under the heading "The Interpretation of the Wicked Husbandmen during the Post-Holocaust Era." According to Milavec's assessment, anti-Judaism has been avoided, at least to a certain degree, after what he calls "the existential shock occasioned by the Holocaust" (84). However, "while overt anti-Judaism has been curtailed, the theological framework which engendered this devaluation of Judaism continues to operate under the untouchable rubric of being the objective content of what the wicked husbandmen originally meant for the inspired writers and their contemporaries" (84). At the heart of this theological framework, as Milavec understands it, is the identification of the owner's son with Jesus Christ and the implicit idea that the parable is about the Jewish killing of Jesus. "The allegorical identification of 'the son' with Jesus has been routinely accepted by almost every Christian scholar during the last forty years" (85).

For Milavec, Jeremias's influential work on the parables exemplifies this trend. It is true, Milavec concedes, that Jeremias denies any allegorical significance for the original Jesus parable. "Nonetheless," Milavec points out, "when Jeremias treated the Synoptic versions of the wicked husbandmen, he did not display the slightest hesitation in affirming that a program of progressive allegorization was in play which, at all points, served further to identify 'the son' with Jesus of Nazareth" (85). Jeremias's claim that the gospel writers applied the owner's son in the story to Jesus is precisely what Milavec tries to refute. The purpose of his essay is to argue, against Jeremias and others, that Mark 12:1-11 does not presume a son–Jesus identification and that this identification is the result of later anti-Jewish developments in the Christian community, as displayed for instance in Chrysostom's fifth-century homily.

Milavec's central strategy is to distinguish between the parable's anti-Jewish reception history and its original meaning as intended by the gospel writer Mark. His aim is to show that originally the parable of the Wicked Husbandmen was a "*true Jewish* story— the *true Jewish* account of how God does indeed act in history" (99). To make this case, Milavec recovers the Jewish horizon of understanding at the time of Mark. He argues that by rewriting the parable for his gospel, Mark evokes a theme familiar to a Jewish audience: persistently, God keeps sending his prophets, even though Israel again and again treats them badly. However, the punishment of the tenants does not represent the punishment of Israel as a whole. In contrast to the famous vineyard parable in Isaiah 5:1-7, which ends with the destruction of the vineyard, Mark has the tenants destroyed, not the vineyard. At stake is not the fate of Israel but that of its leaders, who keep misusing their authoritative power. Therefore, God will take this power away from them and entrust it to others. Milaves surmises that Mark deliberately does not give an exact clue as to who these "others" will be. What can be said, however, is that "the others" in Mark's understanding are definitely not the Christian church but a Jewish group; "not an alternative to Judaism but an alternative within Judaism" (106-107).[6]

Milavec concludes: "The legacy of anti-Judaism attached to the parable of the wicked husbandmen from the patristic period down to our present day cannot be judged as part of the original inspiration guiding Mark in the creation of his Gospel" (109). Instead, the parable's message, as Mark wanted it to be understood, was "decidedly favorable to Judaism": it holds on to the idea that the Jews are God's chosen people; it suggests that Israel will not be destroyed, and that "the others" who replace the wicked husbandmen will be a group within, not outside of, Judaism. This argument implies that the parable does not reinforce Christian supersessionism but, quite the opposite, asks its Christian audience to be self-critical. If the tenants can not be defined as "the Jews" as opposed to "the Christians," a Christian audience can no longer simply identify with "the others." Instead, contemporary leaders of the church may find in the wicked husbandmen a mirror image and are asked to remain cautious and self-critical vis-à-vis their own leadership. I quote from Milavec's final paragraph:

> In the end, consequently, critical inquiry carefully scrapes away the anti-Jewish image that had been carefully painted over the basic outline of the parable of the wicked husbandmen. Another image, older and fresher, appears. This image is not that of Christian superiority and Jewish guilt for the death of Jesus, which has for so long been displayed in the Church. Rather, this new image has the potential for unsettling the onlooker by tearing away those religious assurances which shield one from the terrible judgment of the living God. (110–111)

With this powerful proposal Milavec offers a way to read and make sense of the parable of the Wicked Husbandmen in post-Holocaust times. There are two things about this proposal that I would like to highlight and discuss. My first point pertains to Milavec's use of the category "post-Holocaust" and, related to this, his understanding of anti-Judaism. My second point concerns Milavec's understanding of the interpretive task that confronts post-Holocaust scholars of the New Testament parables.

What Is Post-Holocaust Biblical Scholarship?

"Post-Holocaust" and "Anti-Judaism"

What role does the category "post-Holocaust" play in Milcave's work? As I pointed out, Milavec contextualizes his essay vis-à-vis the events of the Holocaust. His rubric of "The Interpretation of the Wicked Husbandmen during the Post-Holocaust Era" suggests that the Holocaust represents a kind of break or caesura within the history of interpretation. Post-Holocaust scholarship on the parable, this rubric implies, has to be considered and assessed separately from previous scholarship. The main part of the essay, however, is focused on a different problem, namely, the "long legacy of anti-Judaism within the Christian tradition" (81). "Anti-Judaism," as Milavec understands the term, is as such independent of the Holocaust. One might take him to assume that Christian anti-Judaism facilitated "the final solution"—but this claim is not spelled out by Milavec. Anti-Judaism as a problem, in any case, did not result from the Holocaust. It has always existed and could be targeted without any reference to twentieth-century events. By anti-Judaism Milavec means an interpretive pattern that has been passed on from one generation to the next throughout the history of Christianity. Anti-Judaism, for Milavec, in its essence is the same whether we find it in Chrysostom's fifth-century homily or in Jeremias's twentieth-century scholarship: it automatically results from the Jesus-son identification and its implicit ideas: Israel gets destroyed; God's new favorite is Christianity.

What remains unclear is how exactly Milavec understands the relationship between the Holocaust and the anti-Jewish legacy of Mark 12. The Holocaust, Milavec seems to say, has put a damper on anti-Judaism. But how exactly this was the case remains unclear. Milavec talks about an "existential shock" that made scholars wary of subjectivism in their work, including the ideological bias of anti-Judaism. But Milavec does not explain how and for whom this shock led to the avoidance of anti-Judaism. His point, anyway, is that the anti-Jewish treatment of the parable did, in fact, live on after the Holocaust. Although less blatantly, Christian scholars, in their interpretive work on Mark 12, continued to operate within a theological framework whose effect is the devaluation of Judaism. Jeremias's work on the parable serves as one example of this problematic perpetuation. But how Jeremias might have been informed or affected by the events in Europe in the 1930s and 1940s remains unsaid. One gets the impression that the category "post-Holocaust," in Milavec's use, is not much more than a temporal marker.

Against Milavec I would argue that "interpretations of the Wicked Husbandmen during the post-Holocaust era," Jeremias's interpretation from 1947 especially, raise questions that cannot be reduced to the general Christian problem of anti-Judaism. As I emphasized earlier, Jeremias's work struck me not because of its anti-Jewish tendencies but because of something historically specific: not his use of anti-Jewish tropes as such but his use of the trope of "the blinded people" only two years after the end of the war. I also suggested that it was not really "anti-Judaism" that caught my attention but something more subtle: a tone, a particular choice of words, the atmosphere of urgency and catastrophe Jeremias conjures, the uncanny resonances between his language and the events of the Holocaust. Jeremias's interpretation of the parable of the Wicked Husbandmen, in my reading, would be an especially striking site of these resonances: Jeremias argues that Mark 12, perhaps more than any other parable, announces "the terrible urgency of the crisis," a "terrible threat" (124) to Jesus' enemies, the leaders of the people.

Milavec, in his discussion of Jeremias, focuses on the alleged son-Jesus identification in the gospel of Mark. Thereby, I would like to point out, he misses the heart of Jeremias's work. Jeremias's scholarly energies are not centered around the parable of the Wicked Husbandmen according to the gospel of Mark but around the original Jesus parable. What Jeremias passionately recovers and what he passes on to his audience in the academy and in the church is the parable in its first historical setting, where, as he emphasizes, the story did not possess any allegorical, that is christological, significance. Milavec focuses on a marginal aspect of Jeremias's work because Milavec's own interest does not lie with Jeremias but with an age-old anti-Jewish pattern of exegesis whose traces can be found, among many other places, in Jeremias's gospel criticism. I am not saying that such a concern is irrelevant or inadequate. I am saying that it fails to recognize an important dimension of Jeremias's classic work.

Besides being a reflection of an anti-Jewish pattern of exegesis, as Milavec rightfully argues, *The Parables of Jesus*, as I have argued, is also a historical document of the immediate postwar situation in Germany. Jeremias did not only perpetuate longstanding interpretive traditions; he also exemplifies an early and common response to the events of the Holocaust. The overdetermination of his phrases—"a blinded people," "the imminence of catastrophe," "the terrible urgency of the crisis," "a nation rushing upon its own destruction"—indicates a failure, typical for Germans in 1947, to process, work through, and integrate into their scholarly or everyday thoughts the contemporary trauma, the horrible fate of European Jews, and the German atrocities. Jeremias's overdetermined language testifies to a lack of sensitivity, a kind of blackout, an "empty gaze," which from hindsight might be hard to comprehend but which in the context of 1947 must be judged as a typical, perhaps understandable reaction to the Holocaust. This reaction is what I have in mind when I call Jeremias's work "a post-Holocaust discourse."

"Post-Holocaust," in my use of the category, is not just a temporal marker. I mean by it not simply the time period after an historical caesura, perhaps vaguely understood as a challenge to the Western world or an interruption of the course of world history. Quite specifically, the category "post-Holocaust," applied to Jeremias's work, entails for me the difficulties of dealing with the immediate past, the difficulties of mourning, to use the Mitscherlichs' term, that confronted the German public in 1945 and after.

Parables and Parable Scholarship

The second point I would like to raise vis-à-vis Milavec's essay pertains to the scholarly consequences Milavec draws from "the legacy of anti-Judaism." As the title of the essay already announces, Milavec's main task is "a fresh analysis" of Mark 12. The prevalent anti-Jewish reading of the parable provokes Milavec to show that this anti-Jewish reading has no ground in the gospel of Mark and that Mark's original intent was not anti-Jewish but "decidedly favorable to Judaism." Let me repeat a sentence from Milavec's conclusion: "critical inquiry carefully *scrapes away* the anti-Jewish image that had been carefully *painted over* the basic outline of the parable of the wicked husbandmen" (emphasis added). Earlier on in his essay Milavec places his "fresh analysis" of Mark 12 within the context of a general academic situation and a broad scholarly task: "Unhappily, the long-standing traditional religious interpretation of texts has not yet been *entirely emptied* of its anti-Jewish content, and this process will occupy the best efforts of scholars and teachers for many generations to come" (85, emphasis added).

I would like to highlight the metaphors in these sentences. Milavec suggests that the parable of the Wicked Husbandmen in the gospel of Mark, originally pro-Jewish, was transformed—"painted over"—with an anti-Jewish image. And it is Milavec's own critical inquiry that he thinks will "scrape" such image "away." Biblical interpretation in general, according to Milavec, has been filled with improper content, anti-Judaism, and therefore needs to be freed—"entirely emptied"—of this false substance. Milavec expects that a scholarly analysis such as his own, which puts the biblical text within its original, that is, Jewish, horizon of understanding, has the power to rectify misinterpretation, to undo Christian notions of superiority, and to get rid of anti-Jewish bias and stereotyping. Under all these layers, Milavec hopes to find an innocent text.

Some of Milavec's expectations may be justified. In the various contexts of Christian teaching, Milavec's work on Mark 12 could help Christian readers to unlearn deeply sedimented anti-Jewish interpretive patterns and to read the parable with new eyes, in a "fresh" way. Milavec's argument against the son-Jesus identification and his effort to read Mark 12 a as "*true Jewish* story" might engage many readers in an important process of rethinking Jewish-Christian relations.[7]

For several reasons, I will not join the effort proposed by Milavec. A historical-critical reconsideration of biblical texts, a recovery of their original meaning or the intent of their authors, may very well be an appropriate and important response vis-à-vis the Christian problem of anti-Judaism. Vis-à-vis the Holocaust a historical-critical turn to the Bible would bypass, I think, urgent questions of remembrance that still haunt us more than fifty years after the events. Jeremias's text needs to be explored not simply because it paints an anti-Jewish image over the parables but because it is emblematic for the difficulties of responding, confronting, or "seeing" the Holocaust. Jeremias's publication raises questions that concern not only the parables in their first historical setting but also, and more important, their interpretation after 1945.

Given that the most influential work in parable scholarship is symptomatic of the failure to deal with the events of the Holocaust, the most pressing question for me is this: how did scholars after 1947 take up the legacy of Jeremias—not a general Christian legacy of anti-Judaism but the post-Holocaust "legacy of an unmourned trauma" (Santner, *Stranded* 38)? Jeremias's 1947 publication can be explained, as I have attempted to do, by contextualizing it within what the Mitscherlichs have called an immediate psychological emergency. But what came after it? What happened within parable scholarship in the 1960s, 1970s and 1980s? The Mitscherlichs write: "The real problem is that, as a consequence of the de-realization of the Nazi period, even later on, when the immediate psychological emergency had passed, no adequate work of mourning was done by the German people for the masses of *fellow men* slain through their doing" (24). Can this assessment be applied to parable scholarship as well? Or did scholars after Jeremias belatedly engage in the work of mourning with regard to the Holocaust? If so, how? And how did the difficulty of seeing, to use my own language, transport itself through the postwar decades?

Historical Criticism and the Retreat from History

To sum up my considerations, I would like to generalize some of my points about Milavec's essay by connecting them back to the historical-critical work of E. P Sanders, E. Rau, and C. Hezser presented in chapter 4. What Milavec shares with these three authors is a commitment to historical criticism, a scholarly interest in and focus on the history and literature of first-century Palestine. While Milavec is interested in Mark's Jewish horizon of understanding, Sanders's work is concerned with the relationship between Jesus and his contemporaries in Judaism; Rau and Hezser are interested in rabbinical literature and in the sociohistorical realities as the Jewish framework of Jesus' discourse. Although their concerns and strategies differ—Sanders and Rau, for instance, are oriented toward the historical Jesus, while Milavec and Hezser are focused on the gospel text—they all move within the parameters of historical research. As such they represent a continuation of Jeremias's scholarship.

In fact, all four scholars understand their work as a continuation of Jeremias's historical research in stricter terms and on more objective grounds. Jeremias's vision of first-century Palestine, they suggest, was historically incorrect because it was clouded by apologetical interests (e.g., Sanders 199; Rau 230; Hezser 16) and anti-Jewish bias (e.g., Hezser 300; Milavec 84–85). Furthermore, Jeremias is criticized for his insufficient knowledge of Jesus' Jewish background. According to Sanders's assessment, the scholarly generation of Jeremias lacked some basic knowledge about Judaism at the time of Jesus (202), while Hezser mentions specifically that ignorance of the Hebrew language which prevented many Christian New Testament scholars from properly studying rabbinical sources (300). By enriching and expanding their understanding of first-century Palestine with facts and figures, by getting rid of anti-Judaism, and by being dedicated not to theology but to historical evidence, Sanders, Hezser, Rau, and Milavec carry on the project of historical criticism.

However, what motivates these scholars, it seems to me, is more than a commitment to objective historical scholarship. This at least is indicated in both Milavec's and Hezser's work.[8] Milavec is explicit about his motivation. The recovery of Mark's pro-Jewish mindset, Milavec hopes, will work against Christian feelings of superiority (111) and promote an awareness of the "common heritage which unites Christians and Jews" (117).

Hezser's work, in its main body, is a minutely researched and multileveled study that integrates Matthew 20 within a Jewish context. Only in her epilogue does the author point to the relevance of her analyses. I translate from Hezser's final paragraphs:

> For most Christian New Testament scholars, anti-Jewish bias and a lack of Hebrew language competence made it impossible to access the Jewish sources without prejudice. This did not change after the Second World War and after the destruction of great parts of the Jewish people. While Jewish New Testament scholars begin to bring Jesus "home" into Judaism, there are still Christian New Testament scholars who try to set Jesus off from Judaism. Only a few scholars have changed their views. . . . If we learn to see Jewish texts with different eyes, we will detect many commonalities between them and the teachings of Jesus. We will realize that the teachings of Jesus unites Jews and Christians. Perhaps Jesus can restructure our own perspective as well. Instead of degrading Jewish religious traditions, in order to valorize our own, we, too, should be glad about the religious truths and ethical doctrines that are contained in the rabbinical texts.[9]

Like Milavec, Hezser refers to the anti-Jewish bias of Christian New Testament scholars and specifically to their habit of degrading Jewish traditions. Moreover, Hezser describes the research situation in a way that very much resembles Milavec's assessment of biblical interpretation in the "post-Holocaust era" (his term). Even after "the destruction of a great part of the Jewish people," to Hezser's regret, Christian scholars continued their anti-Jewish practices. Finally, and again like Milavec, Hezser expresses hope that her effort to recontextualize Jesus' parable within Judaism will lead Christians and Jews to remember their common heritage.

Let me emphasize at this point that I consider the work of Hezser and Milavec valuable and important within the context of biblical scholarship. In some ways these scholars have taken up the task that, with my naive expectations, I thought should have been taken up already by Jeremias in 1947. After "the existential shock of the Holocaust," I assumed, Jeremias instantly should have "emptied" his parable interpretation "of its anti-Jewish content." That this task is carried out several decades later does not make it any less urgent or relevant.

However, I also want to say that historical-critical work has blind spots. It reduces the challenge of the Holocaust for biblical scholarship to the problem of anti-Judaism. Thereby it mutes or elides post-Holocaust questions of remembrance, which, as I have shown, emerge from the immediate postwar scholarship of Jeremias. The discourse of Hezser and Milavec has no place and no capacity to heed the "legacy of an unmourned trauma" that Jeremias's work represents. Historical criticism in general gives no room for the questions that arise from my struggle with Jeremias: what does it mean that the critique of Jeremias and of anti-Jewish interpretive patterns emerged as late as forty years after the Holocaust? Why did it take so long for scholars to concern themselves with this blatant aspect of their own scholarly tradition? And what has happened during the time in between?

Let me conclude this chapter by going back to Elisabeth Schüssler Fiorenza, David Tracy, and their essay "The Holocaust as Interruption and the Christian Return into History." This essay passionately advocates a confrontation with the Holocaust within Christian theology and biblical studies. Christian scholars, the authors demand, need "to face the interruption of the Holocaust." Schüssler Fiorenza and Tracy argue that the nineteenth-century rise of historical consciousness, in the context of Christian theology and biblical studies, paradoxically led to a retreat from the history of our own time, by which the authors mean especially the events of the Holocaust. With all its scientific vigor and critical potential, historical criticism did not return into history. "The gains of the historico-critical method . . . are plain for all to see. But the loss—the loss of concrete history itself under the paradoxical cover of 'historical consciousness'—was a loss whose full impact we are just beginning to realise" (83).

"The loss of concrete history," in some ways, is precisely what I detected in Jeremias's 1947 text. *The Parables of Jesus*, this classic of historical criticism, exemplifies the retreat from contemporary events at a crucial point in time. I wonder if the efforts by Hezser, Milavec, and others, forty and fifty years after the war, can be seen as steps toward a "return into history." By acknowledging the Holocaust and by letting one's work be motivated by it, these scholars break through the separation that historical critics have built between the Bible and our own time. The reconfiguration of the parables as *"true Jewish"* material, as attempted by Hezser and Milavec, might be what Schüssler Fiorenza and Tracy have in mind when they talk about the necessity of facing the interruption of the Holocaust.[10]

However, "facing the interruption of the Holocaust" for me, personally and academically, has meant to acknowledge and examine the fact that the Holocaust during the first three postwar decades by and large *did not* interrupt scholarly practices in my field of research—not in the way that Schüssler Fiorenza and Tracy demand. What I want to acknowledge as well is that these acts of omission have something to do with the enormous difficulties involved in "facing" this part of "concrete history," difficulties that exist beyond the realm of biblical research and up to this day. The "retreat from concrete history," as well as attempts to "return into history," are the themes of the following chapters. Looking at parable interpretation in the 1970s, I will examine how scholars after Jeremias continued to block out "concrete history" but also how they did engage in the events of the twentieth century.

PART III

JESUS AS POET OF OUR TIME

7

John Dominic Crossan and the Literary Turn in Biblical Studies

The teachings of Jesus . . . are best understood not only within their own contemporary situation by comparative historical criticism but also, and indeed especially, in confrontation with texts within our own world which are functionally, generically, and philosophically on the same literary trajectory, that is, through comparative literary criticism.

(John Dominic Crossan, *Raid on the Articulate*)

During the postwar decades Joachim Jeremias's work ruled the way the parables of Jesus were read in Germany and elsewhere. In the late 1960s, however, a group of American scholars began to take issue with Jeremias's interpretive assumptions, specifically with his rigorous focus on the parables' first historical setting and his insufficient awareness of their poetic powers. Incorporating various literary theories into the field of parable studies, biblical critics in the United States started to take seriously the form and language of the parables and turned them from historical artifacts into artful literature.

What interests me most about this shift from a historical-critical to a literary approach is a changed understanding of the "context" of the parables. While most American scholars did not entirely dismiss "the context of the parables" as Jeremias had defined it (their first historical setting), a new category entered the discussions: the category of genre.[1] Reconfigured as literary pieces, the parables became comparable to contemporary literature with similar generic qualities. This comparative focus on genre moved the parables out of the grip of their "first historical setting" in first-century Palestine and into the context of world literature.[2]

Crossan's 1976 book *Raid on the Articulate*, the source of my opening quotation, presents perhaps the most forceful and imaginative realization of this new understanding of context. The book is based on the premise that the teachings of Jesus "are best understood not only within their own contemporary situation . . . but also, and indeed especially, in confrontation with texts within our own world." For Crossan, "the texts within our own world" are primarily texts by the Argentinean writer Jorge Luis Borges. But in the course of his study, Crossan relates the parables of Jesus to a variety of twentieth-century writers, among them Kurt Vonnegut, Samuel Beckett, Franz Kafka, Albert Camus, and Elie Wiesel.

To confront Jesus with "texts within our own world" is an evocative idea. Crossan's choice of particular texts and authors is evocative as well. All the writers I just listed, in my mind, are associated in different ways with twentieth-century catastrophic events. My interest in John Dominic Crossan's comparative project is driven by a suspicion that something is at stake in the confrontation of Jesus' parables with "texts within our own world" that exceeds the notion of genre. My focus on *Raid* is invigorated by a hunch that the comparison between Jesus and twentieth-century writers has the potential to cross times and places on levels other than only the generic one and thus to break through the isolation that has kept Jeremias's scholarship from its own time. Crossan's hermeneutics, as I will show, in a complicated and not unproblematic manner, is a return into history that, according to Schüssler Fiorenza and Tracy, should lead biblical scholars to deal with the legacy of the Holocaust.

As I now turn from historical criticism to literary criticism, I will take up the questions raised in the previous chapter. I want to explore how Jeremias's "legacy of an unmourned trauma" has been taken up by the arguably most creative biblical critic of the scholarly generation that followed Jeremias: John Dominic Crossan. In my reading of his work I will ask if Crossan let his scholarship be affected by the Holocaust and if this history has or has not prompted him to change or at least to modify old anti-Jewish practices. My critical reading of *Raid* will also take up the historical narrative initiated and developed in the previous parts of this book. I have argued that Kaschnitz's "Zoon Politikon," Wolfgang Harnisch's use of Kaschnitz's poem, and Jeremias's historical-critical study were all symptomatic of different phases of Holocaust memory in (West) Germany. I now want to argue that *Raid on the Articulate*, in a similar vein, exemplifies problems typical of Holocaust memory culture in the United States in the mid-1970s.

This chapter will set the stage for these quests and arguments. In order to clarify the discourse in which Crossan participates, I will offer a brief account of the scholarly and institutional context of *Raid on the Articulate*, and, in a second step, I will place the book within Crossan's vast contribution to parable studies, highlighting its idiosyncracies and innovative nature. Finally, I will show how the book might be critiqued by biblical scholars today.

An American Endeavor

John Dominic Crossan's work on the parables belongs to a distinctively American scholarly endeavor that had its peak during the early and mid-1970s and that, today is known as the "literary turn" in biblical studies.[3] According to Norman Perrin's account, this turn was initiated when scholars in the United States perceived the hermeneutical discussions prevalent in German biblical scholarship to be insufficiently aware of the literary qualities of biblical texts.[4] Through interdisciplinary work in the realms of structuralism and the philosophy of language, American scholars, including Crossan, Robert Funk, Dan Otto Via, and Amos Wilder, brought a variety of literary theories into biblical studies and created a new framework for discussion.

These interdisciplinary efforts concentrated on the parables of Jesus as a kind of testing ground because, due to their narrative structure and identifiable form, the parables invited the kind of analysis that was practiced in the field of literary criticism of that time. As Perrin describes it, the general thrust of these new discussions was a commitment to take the parables of Jesus seriously as pieces of literature, to "respect [their] integrity . . . as texts" (106). Unlike historical criticism, which looks beyond the text into historical circumstances, the new American approach started to bring the parables' aesthetic qualities into focus and paid close attention to their language and configurations. Recent theories of metaphor supported the emergent appreciation of the parables as literary texts: Once it is claimed that the New Testament parables have the creative capacities of poetic metaphor, the interpreter is asked to concentrate on the parable as a place where new meaning is created and where new aspects of reality are discovered.

In one way or another, all the scholars involved in the early experimental project critically related themselves to Jeremias's work on the parables and, above all, to his claim that the parables' first historical settings in the life of Jesus must be considered the sole criterion of interpretation. Opinions were divided as to whether and how the two hermeneutical assumptions—the literary and the historical-critical understanding—could be combined. But whether the literary approach was considered a displacement or a complement, Jeremias was the common point of departure for the next generation of scholars in America.

The common indictment against Jeremias, as I mentioned earlier, was that he turned the parables into ancient artifacts with no literary value for today. Another point of concern was Jeremias's habit of treating the parables as dispensable devices for illustrating a message that could be separate from the stories of Jesus and could be categorized into clear-cut points. As Perrin holds against Jeremias: "The very nature of the parables of Jesus as texts forbids the reduction of their message . . . to a series of rubrics. Parables as parables do not have a 'message.' They tease the mind into ever new perceptions of reality; they startle the imagination; they function like symbols in that they 'give rise to thought'" (106).

Perrin argues that parables have the power to lead to "new perceptions of reality," which cannot be gained through any other kind of language. With this idea, the longstanding division of picture-part (Bild) and subject matter (Sache) broke down, which led to a broad shift in the binary oppositions governing the discourse. Jeremias based his work unquestioningly on the conceptual duality of "allegory" and "parable" that was introduced into parable scholarship by his own ancestor, Adolf Jülicher. Even though this duality was unwittingly retained by many American projects, a different binary gradually became more important: the distinction between descriptive and metaphorical languages—more precisely, between a didactic story that illustrates a point that is quite independent of the illustration, and a poetic story that discloses a referent unknown before and knowable only through the story itself. Just as historical scholarship valorized the simple and clear "parables" of Jesus over and against the obscure and incomprehensible "allegory," the literary scholars favored the disclosive power of metaphorical narratives over the didacticism of a dispensable example story and claimed that power for the parables of the New Testament.

Perrin points to two crucial institutional sites that provided the necessary space for these new emerging discussions: the Parables Seminar formed by the Society of Biblical Literature in 1972, which was supposed to meet for five years with John Dominic Crossan as chair; and the journal *Semeia*, whose first issues came out in 1974 and were designed to publish some of the results of that seminar's work. In his introduction to the first issue, Amos Wilder indicated the thrust of the journal: "the new concern as in so many fields today is with a better understanding of language in all its aspects" (3). While a certain interest in language and the forms of language governed previous generations of biblical scholars,[5] this interest now was guided by "new sophistications," as Wilder put it, which were gained in other disciplines and which concerned "matters such as the dynamics of human speech and communication, language modes and patterns, the apperception of hearer and reader, the social-cultural nexus of all language-phenomena, and the relation of language to referent and to reality" (4). Accordingly, one of the journal's main features was, and still is, its interdisciplinary impetus.

The essays published in the first issues of the journal focused on the parables and included discussions of structuralist methodology and questions of genre, metaphor, and the metaphorical quality of parables. A common focus was the parable of the Good Samaritan, which served as a test case for new investigations. With frequent reference to this parable, scholars such as Crossan offered various proposals, which were followed by critical responses from their colleagues. Taken together, these early essays convey much of the venturesome spirit of these days.[6] This venturesome spirit is a main feature also of Crossan's book *Raid on the Articulate*.

Crossan's Work on Parables

Raid on the Articulate, published in 1976, is the third of five books that, together with several articles, make up Crossan's prolific publication on the parables of Jesus between 1973 and 1980. Unlike many other publications by Crossan, *Raid on the Articulate* is not a well-known book and, to my knowledge, has been out of print for several years. In order to introduce this book I will offer a review of Crossan's work, dividing it into four broad themes that are central not only to *Raid* but to Crossan's thought on parables in general.

Parable as Paradox

Throughout his writings in the early 1970s, Crossan developed an understanding of the genre "parable" that is quite idiosyncratic and can be detected already in his first, most well-known, and also most conventional book, *In Parables: The Challenge of the Historical Jesus*, published in 1973. In this early publication, Crossan first appears to be following the mainstream of works of that time, which, as he sums up, "have insisted on the necessity of treating [the parables] as literature and placing special emphasis on their relationship to the world of poetic metaphor" (10). In line with other contemporary interpreters of the parables, Crossan goes on to establish poetic metaphor as a generic model for his own interpretive task. However, later on in the book one easily gets the impression that it is not so much metaphor that stands at the heart of Crossan's parable interpretation; much more important seems to be the formal concept of paradox: the subversion of previously held opposites.[7]

To claim paradoxicality as the formal quality of Jesus' parables, as Crossan does, is a distinctively different interpretive step from the one he announces in the introductory part of the book. Under the paradigm of poetic metaphor, as it was theorized by several American scholars, the "unexpected turn" in a parable comes to stand at the service of a disclosure of new meaning, a new view of reality. While a certain subversion of expectations is the necessary condition of the disclosure, this subversion is subordinated to and aimed at a "referent" that was previously unknown. As Crossan himself suggests in his theoretical introduction, the parable as metaphor leads to a participation in its referent. But obviously Crossan's recourse to paradox implies something quite different. For Crossan, really, Jesus' parables neither create nor discover meaning; they are not about new referents or new aspects of reality. Quite the opposite: they attack all those things; they subvert meaning, they challenge referentiality.

Let me illustrate the rather unusual implications of this shift from metaphor to paradox: Crossan's reading of the parable of the Wicked Husbandmen makes an excellent case study of what I mean by his idiosyncratic take on the genre parable. Crossan puts the parable under the rubric of what he calls "parables of action." These are stories about human behavior in the light of God's challenge. Crossan subdivides them into group A, normal stories about accepted ways of human action, and group B, parables that question and contradict precisely what was constructed as "normal" by the parables of group A. Of course it is group B, the cluster of subversive parables, that, according to Crossan, carries the actual thrust of Jesus' proclamation. At stake in the parables of action are, broadly speaking, ethics and moral guidelines that, although they are indispensable for human life, are, like any human construction, "undermined by the mystery of God." This broad interpretive scheme enables Crossan to make sense of a parable that has given numerous interpreters before and after him a particularly hard time. Crossan focuses on the parable's short version in the gospel of Thomas, which he considers the most authentic one:

> He said: A good man had a vineyard. He gave it to husbandmen so that they would work it and he would receive its fruits from them. He sent his servant so that the husbandmen would give him the fruit of the vineyard. They seized his servant, they beat him; a little longer and they would have killed him. The servant came, he told it to his master. His master said: "Perhaps he did not know them." . . . He sent another servant; the husbandmen beat him as well. Then the owner sent his son. He said: "Perhaps they will respect my son." Since those husbandmen knew that he was the heir of the vineyard, they seized him, they killed him. Whoever has ears let him hear. Jesus said: Show me the stone which the builders have rejected; it is the corner-stone. (*In Parables* 92)

Crossan offers the following interpretation of this story:

> Its meaning is quite clear as a parable of action. It is a deliberately shocking story of successful murder. The story . . . tells of some people who recognized their situation, saw their opportunity, and acted resolutely upon it. They glimpsed a way of getting full possession of the vineyard by murdering the only heir and, with murderous speed, they moved to accomplish their purpose. (96)

Remarkable about this interpretation is Crossan's perspective on the violence in the story. While most scholarship has interpreted the tenants' abuse of son and servants as a crime that is followed by the landlord's punishment, Crossan reads the tenants' behavior not as wicked but as smart action.[8] However, it is not self-evident what precisely the parable is achieving in Crossan's view. One might take Crossan to say that the parable makes a point about the necessity of recognizing one's chance when it arrives and of taking action.[9] But such a reading would bring Crossan's interpretation into the old didactic framework, where the parables are said to illustrate something for an audience. Strictly understood within Crossan's framework, the parable of the Wicked Husbandmen is not "making a point" but is effecting a subversion of moral expectations. Against the logic of an ethics according to which immoral behavior leads to a disaster of some kind, Jesus' parable forces upon the imagination a scenario in which a vicious but reso- lute action leads to success and to the achievement of one's goals. The emphasis lies on paradox: the parable refuses to give any positive insight as to how one should behave. Instead it is "upsetting and undermining" a specific ethical thought structure, in order to give a glimpse of the insecurity and incertitude that underlie the human effort of building moral systems.[10]

While the reader of *In Parables* could still hold some doubts as to Crossan's view of these matters, the paradoxical quality of the Jesus parables comes unambiguously into focus in Crossan's subsequent writing. By the time he publishes *Raid on the Articulate* three years later, Crossan self-assuredly unfolds his thought of Jesus' parables as shock- ing, radical, world-subverting stories, a thought that is detectable in the very title of the book. "Raid on the Articulate" is Crossan's own subversive rendering of lines from T. S. Eliot's "East Coker":

> And so each venture
> Is a new beginning, a raid on the inarticulate.

This little Crossanian play on in/articulate can be read as another piece of evidence that, for Crossan, the parables of Jesus are not poetic metaphors, ventures toward the "inarticulate," toward that which has not yet been put into words. On the contrary, they are small surprise attacks directed against what has been expressed already too many times, the known and familiar, the "articulate."

A Postmodern Vision

Between *In Parables* and *Raid* Crossan published *The Dark Interval: Towards a Theology of Story* (1975). I briefly want to refer to this little volume because it explicates the broader intellectual framework in which Crossan's thought on parables came to be embedded. The book shows how Crossan moves away from theories of metaphor and ventures into a direction that brings him close to a postmodern vision of lan- guage and reality.[11] The notion that metaphor discloses reality, Crossan would say, is still quite a moderate theoretical insight. *The Dark Interval* takes the far more radical position that reality as such is made up by human language. "Reality" itself is only a signifier, which human linguistic activity fills with meaning. Whatever we count as "real" depends on the stories we tell, and when the stories change, reality changes, too. In a sweep that today might be reminiscent of Jean Francois Lyotard's *Postmodern Condition*, Crossan dismantles three such stories: the great master claims of science, of progress, and of "the postulate that there is an external reality out there, extrinsic to our vision, our imagination, and our intellect and that we are gaining objective knowledge and disciplined control over this extramental reality" (6). For Crossan, these three master claims have lost credibility. He comments: "I admit that I can no longer believe in any of them" (6).

But Crossan also assures his readers that for him this loss of credibility is no reason for anxiety or nostalgia. No longer being able to hold on to any stable reality beyond language is not something to mourn but something to rejoice in.[12] Crossan finds it "exhilarating" to recognize that all we have is language. He finds it "fascinating" to feel the shifting grounds of story, because these shifting grounds, for him, are a gateway to transcendence. Postmodern indeterminacy in the course of Crossan's argument leads to what he calls a theology of limits. At "the edge of language and the limit of story," he says, "the excitement of transcendental experience is found" (29–30), the experience of the unknowable: God, the Wholly Other.

This kind of interaction between a postmodern sensitivity and a Christian theological concern with transcendence is carried through Crossan's work in the late 1970s and became most visible in the 1980 publication of *Cliffs of Fall*. It was, in fact, Crossan's attempt to appropriate postmodern themes for theology that caught the attention of several biblical critics. In his 1989 book *Literary Criticism and the Gospels*, Steven Moore, for example, devotes several pages to Crossan's work as a "forerunner of deconstructive theology." While traces of a deconstructive theology can be found in *Raid* as well, I would argue that here the concern with theology, the divine, and transcendence is subordinated to the postmodern concept of "comic eschatology," which, in 1976, is Crossan's central interpretive notion for discussing parables.

"Comic eschatology," broadly speaking, is, like its predecessor, "permanent eschatology," which Crossan developed in his earlier work, a challenge to and subversion of all human establishment.[13] It recalls the incertitude and indeterminacy that underlie all human stories and efforts at creating "reality." The shift from "permanent" to "comic" indicates the playful direction Crossan's work has taken. Both "play" and "comedy" are central tropes in *Raid*. While play, according to Crossan, is the foundation of human life—"to be human is to play" (27)—comedy is the kind of activity by which human beings remind each other of the ubiquity of play and thus of the relativity of all seemingly established notions about reality. Crossan writes: "The supreme act of play is world and when one player forgets or denies such playful creativity, it is necessary for another player to disintegrate world by comic eschatology and to renew thereby the springs of play and the relativity of world. Comic eschatology restores world *sub specie ludi*" (32).

It is Crossan's view that literature in general ought to do just that; and that parables, because of their paradoxical structure, belong to the kind of literature that does it particularly well. What Crossan's earlier work has called the "shattering" force of parables is now reconfigured as the restoration of primordial play. Thus the parables of Jesus are entering a postmodern scheme of things in which what counts is no longer the real versus the unreal but the excitement of shifting grounds over and against the boredom and dullness of reified norms and notions.

The Quest for the Historical Jesus

Notwithstanding Crossan's strong attraction to shifting grounds, there is one rather obvious stable point in his thoughts. As he made very clear in his first book and did not modify later on, Crossan's interest lies with the authentic Jesus parables. Crossan does not focus on the texts as they can be found in the gospels but on those texts that he thinks come closest to the original parables as they were uttered by Jesus, a distinction that, as I will explicate shortly, matters to Crossan quite a lot. This means that Crossan throughout his work is engaged in the labor of reconstructing original Jesus parables. It further means that Crossan operates with the whole array of traditional historical criticism. My brief discussion of his reading of the Wicked Husbandmen has already hinted at this aspect of his work. Crossan's decision to concentrate on the gospel of Thomas is based on a historical-critical retrieval of the most authentic version of the story. In many other cases Crossan cuts off layers of secondary interpretations until he arrives at what he considers the original text.

As several of Crossan's critics have been quick to point out, this reliance on historical-critical methodology and the investment in the historically authentic stands in tension with much of the postmodern theory Crossan engages in, a tension that is never resolved, not in *Raid* and not in any other publication.[14] In fact, it seems to me that it would have been quite impossible for Crossan to resolve this tension, because the distinction between authentic Jesus parables and the subsequent renderings of early Christianity is much too central to his thoughts. When it comes to the parables of Jesus, the postmodernism that shapes Crossan's view on what "parables" are is projected onto a particular historical situation and creates a chronological picture that can be found at every turn in Crossan's work.

At the time of Jesus, according to Crossan, the major strands of Israel's tradition had tended to become static, "trapped in . . . idolatry" (58), as Crossan describes it, an idolatry not of images but of words. The forms and genres of Judaism's legal, sapiental, and especially apocalyptic literature had become established a little too securely and had started to "hide the foundations of play on which and in which they operated" (61). Then Jesus appeared on the scene and recovered the buried tradition of iconoclasm (which Crossan today is still able to detect in parts of the Hebrew Bible), and by means of the comic eschatology embedded in his parabolic language he launched a comic attack on these overcultivated literary traditions to remind his contemporaries of their contingency on play. After his death, however, the early Christian groups that had inherited the records of Jesus' language were unable to hold on to the challenge of paradox. By means of moralizing and allegorizing reinterpretations they removed its sting and turned the parables of Jesus back into the old and normal forms and genres.

According to this version of the course of events, Jesus' parables are transient moments of subversion between two major reifications: Judaism's absolutized tradition (pre-Jesus), and Christianity's harmonizing reinterpretations (post-Jesus). This implies that the comic eschatology of Jesus' language, precious as it is, is also hidden beneath thick layers of misunderstanding that had its beginning in the first century and developed over the subsequent centuries up to the time of Crossan, who then, in the 1970s, saw himself faced with the task of breaking through the interpretive veil in order to get at the original Jesus (sub)version.

Let me point out that, methodologically, Crossan assumes that "original" is everything that stands in contrast to first-century Judaism and early Christianity, an assumption that historical biblical scholarship calls the criterion of dissimilarity, which, as I showed in chapter 4, has lately been called into question. As *Raid* reinscribes it:

> This criterion or principle proposes that the most likely authentic material coming from Jesus will appear where there is divergence from or dissimilarity with the emphases of the primitive community which both transmitted and transformed such materials. . . . Indeed, in many cases, one discovers that the material is being changed back into greater harmony with certain emphases in contemporary Judaism by the early church. (176)

Unlike other biblical scholars, Crossan applies this interpretive principle to the form rather than to the content of Jesus' message. Nevertheless it is precisely the interpretive tendency to theorize the sayings of Jesus in contrast to both a Jewish and an early Christian background that most clearly reveals Crossan to be an heir of Joachim Jeremias' scholarship. Despite his engagement with radical theory and despite all his idiosyncrasies, Crossan's vision of the parables of Jesus stands in continuity with Jeremias's historical criticism.

A Literary Tradition of Parable

However, in *Raid* the historical scenario just described is subordinated under the aegis of a larger theme: Crossan's construction of a literary tradition across the centuries. There are a few places in earlier publications where Crossan tries to bring into view a trajectory of the genre of parable that leads from the book of Jonah through Jesus to "some modern cases" (*Dark* 60) such as Kafka, Brecht, and Borges. However, it is only in *Raid* that this attempt is developed in full measure. In *Raid*, the comparison between Jesus and contemporary writers is not just one among many considerations for fleshing out a new understanding of the genre of Jesus' parables. Much more than that, the comparison is grounded in a hermeneutical assumption stated in the book's preface. The book claims, it says there, that the teachings of Jesus "are best understood not only within their own contemporary situation by comparative historical criticism but also, and indeed especially, in confrontation with texts within our own world which are functionally, generically, and philosophically on the same literary trajectory, that is, through comparative literary criticism" (xv).

What is explicated here is the complementary relationship of historical and literary criticism as the basis of Crossan's work. Subsequently, the quotation also points to two different but again complementary contexts in which Crossan intends to understand the teachings of Jesus: one is "their own contemporary situation," that is, the time and place of Jesus' life: first-century Palestine. The second context is the literary tradition that includes Jesus' sayings in the range of literature whose function is a comic attack on the world, whose genre is characterized by paradox, and whose philosophical significance lies in its capacity to restore primordial play. However, the literature that interests Crossan is not evenly spread over the centuries. Crossan says that the sayings of Jesus ought to be understood "in confrontation with texts within our own world," which in *Raid* are most notably texts written by Jorge Luis Borges, a contemporary Argentine poet. But in the course of *Raid*'s chapters the sayings of Jesus come in contact with a variety of literary texts whose places of origin lie on different parts of the globe but which all appeared in the twentieth century and are, in that sense, as Crossan puts it, "texts within our own world."

Accordingly, the reader of *Raid* is confronted with the following grand scheme. Imagine two poles in the air quite removed from each other. The first pole marks the first century where Jesus and his parables are located. The second pole marks the twentieth century and is occupied by a cluster of writers with Borges at the center. At both poles very similar things are going on: playful subversions of particular literary conventions and expectations, which Crossan likes to call raids on the articulate. Of course, the "articulate" at stake is different in each case. If Jesus attacks the legal, sapiental, and apocalyptic strands of Israel's tradition, Borges attacks the literary tradition of its own time: realism and its assumption that literature ought to mirror reality as it is. Borges's fictive reviews, pseudonotes, and summaries of nonexisting books, in Crossan's reading, are all part of a great "parody around the realistic novel" and its "mimetic fallacy." "Jesus has taught us the limits of word and the verbal form in the name of Israel's aniconic God. . . . Borges has taught us the limits of book and of literary genre in the name of humanity's playful laughter" (92).

Crossan investigates the activities at the two poles with equal scrutiny. However, what seems to be more interesting to him is the way these activities reflect each other. Crossan weaves threads through the air, from one pole to the other and back, and thereby creates a network that is basic to all subversions and comic attacks whether they are done by Jesus, Borges, or anybody else. This network is built throughout the five chapters of *Raid*. In the first chapter, "Comedy and Transcendence," Crossan introduces his notion of comic eschatology, which most fundamentally characterizes the verbal activities of both Jesus and Borges and which serves as the most central motif for their conjunction in the book. "Form and Genre," the second chapter, explicates how both Jesus and Borges attack the general literary establishment of their time. The third, "Parable and Paradox," looks at the genre of parable, "paradox turned into story," which is shared by Jesus and Borges as major weapons for the attack. The fourth chapter, "Time and Finitude," points to the particular theme of time that is discussed by both Jesus and Borges. "Person and Persona" finally attempts to understand Borges and Jesus beyond their authorial intentions and personalities as personae constructed in their respective language.

For all his investigations of Borges and Jesus within the context of their "contemporary situations," what ultimately matters to Crossan are less the historical specificities of their respective linguistic creativity. What matters more is the transhistorical foundation that combines Jesus and Borges: comic eschatology, iconoclasm, and paradox, all of which can be reduced to the one master theme in Crossan's thought: the ubiquity of the playful flux of language.

Raid on the Articulate: A Transgressive Reading of the Bible

I would like to close my introduction to *Raid on the Articulate* by locating the book within the current scene of biblical studies. From today's perspective, two major aspects of Crossan's 1976 book seem dated. First, Crossan's reading and appropriation of postmodern theory would be criticized by many scholars today. During the last decade the postmodern has been theorized by biblical scholars not in terms of play so much as in terms of scholarly ethics and responsibility, categories that do not exist in Crossan's thought in the 1970s.[15] Postmodernism since the late 1980s has been largely understood as an epistemic shift that challenges biblical scholars to critically examine their own entanglement with modernity and their situatedness in relations of power. What has been repeated time and again with respect to postmodern destabilizations is a call to historicize biblical scholarship, to take responsibility for the social and political consequences of biblical texts and their interpretations, and to respect and pay attention to differences and "the other."[16]

In light of this new postmodern sensitivity and its consequent emphasis on concrete history and heterogeneity, *Raid on the Articulate* and its apolitical argument, as well as its tendency toward reducing texts and writers across cultures and ages to the one theme of the flux of language, appears to be not only outdated but also a problematic misreading of postmodernism and its implications. However, this misreading itself has its time and place and needs to be historicized. It should be kept in mind that Crossan was one of the first biblical scholars to explore the challenges of postmodern theory for biblical studies. His venture took place at a time when the postmodern emphasis on indeterminacy prompted the playful reading practices of deconstruction in American literary studies, reading practices whose political or ethical implications, if such implications existed at all, were not spelled out. In the mid- and late 1990s, when the postmodern challenge had been picked up by a wider range of biblical scholars, leading to the 1995 publication of *The Postmodern Bible*, the ludic version of postmodernism had long been contested through a variety of debates outside of biblical studies.[17] Like the *Postmodern Bible*'s concern with power, politics, and ethics, Crossan's indulgence in play and comic subversion is at least partly reflective of the broader academic climate of a certain time.

The second aspect that dates *Raid* is Crossan's reliance on the criterion of dissimilarity. As I discussed in chapter 4, recent historical scholarship has pointed out the inadequacy of this principle because it precludes the possibility of understanding Jesus as part of and not opposed to his Jewish background. Furthermore, Crossan's vision of Jesus as attacking the "major strands of Israel's tradition" would make many readers today quite uncomfortable, not only for methodological reasons but because of the more or less explicit assumption that these traditions were in a state of decadence waiting to be recuperated by Jesus. Within the current context of biblical studies where attention has been paid to the problem of anti-Judaism in New Testament texts and scholarship, this assumption sounds like a problematic kind of twentieth-century anti-Jewish rhetoric.

I point to these recent and current developments in biblical studies, developments that critically lead beyond Crossan's 1976 book, because they shape the perspective from which I read *Raid on the Articulate*. My encounter with Crossan's text in the mid-1990s enables an engagement with the text that is marked by current concerns and sensitivities. The awareness of the problem of anti-Judaic interpretation and the desire to reclaim the history of this century and to give room for differences are reading assumptions that I have inherited from the work that has been done in American biblical studies during the two decades between Crossan's publication and my own reading.

However, I also want to emphasize that *Raid*, despite its dated aspects, is still of interest for postmodern biblical scholars today. This is suggested in A. K. M. Adam's 1995 book *What Is Postmodern Biblical Criticism?* Adam cites *Raid* as an example of what he calls "transgressive biblical interpretation," one of several postmodern reading practices that follow from the insight that discourses are not pure and homogenous but "socially constituted, the result of a 'bricolage'" (62). "These transgressive interpretive practices," Adam writes, "disregard the modern disciplinary rules and hermeneutical conventions to draw on resources that lie outside the boundaries of modern disciplined scholarship" (61). Transgressive interpreters, Adam continues,

> feel free to blur—and cross over ("transgress")—the borderlines that separate biblical interpretation from the literary criticism of fiction, from art history, from psychoanalytic dis-

courses, and so on. When interpreters obey the injunctions of the disciplines whose borders they are crossing, we may describe this dimension of postmodern biblical criticism as "interdisciplinary"; when they mix discourses and genres without careful attention to the rules of the realms they invade, their interpretation is called not so much interdisciplinary as "undisciplined." (61–62)

Adam does not explain why *Raid* falls under his category of transgressive readings, but it is not hard to see why he would think so. Obviously, *Raid*'s comparative literary project in and of itself could be called transgressive as it goes beyond the rules of historical-critical scholarship and understands the parables of Jesus within the context of twentieth-century fiction. What distinguishes *Raid* more specifically is the daring and unapologetic development of literary comparisons into an intertextual system that blurs the distinction between "secular" and "biblical" and ignores any religious or theological surplus value on the basis of which the parables of Jesus would be privileged over those of "secular" writers.

Raid is further characterized by what Steven Moore has called Crossan's "mischievous disregard for the proprieties of scholarly discourse" (*Literary* 143). In *Raid*, this disregard is reflected in the way Crossan engages with theory across the fields in order to shape his intertextual idea. This engagement is something different from the general effort in the 1970s to integrate literary theory and methodology into biblical studies, and it also goes beyond what the editors of *Semeia* meant when they introduced the journal's publications as "experimental." The applicability of new structuralist methods to the parables is not what *Raid* is about. Rather Crossan presents a tapestry of quotations and discussions from manifold and disparate realms. As I will illustrate shortly, *Raid*'s interdisciplinary endeavor is a plunge into various terrains that at times seems out of control, that is to say, uncontrolled by any discursive rule that would be recognizable to biblical or literary scholars—undisciplined, as Adam would say.[18]

According to Adam, transgressive readings "produce disruptive interpretive effects" (61). This might be one of the reasons why in my own reading of *Raid* I was able to make connections that in their turn are not warranted by any institutionalized discourse. This reading will occupy me in the following chapter.

8

Comedy, Play, and "The Horrors of This Century"

A Post-Holocaust Reading of *Raid on the Articulate*

A Web of Allusions

When I read *Raid on the Articulate* for the first time I was immediately captivated. From its very start, the book aroused in me a horror that did not go away as I continued reading. I had nightmares that are still in my head today. The strange connection between Holocaust material and parable studies, which I had seen in Harnisch's Kaschnitz quotation and in Jeremias's interpretive language, reappeared in Crossan's book in an uncanny way. Reading *Raid on the Articulate*, I saw the Holocaust continuously lurking through the surface, and although it never explicitly came to the front, it was always visible to me and threw its shadows over Crossan's discourse.

This uncanny feeling never left me. One of its sources is already apparent in the beginning of Crossan's first variation, "Comedy and Transcendence." Crossan starts his variation with the following Nietzschean motto:

> At the start of *The Joyful Wisdom* Friedrich Nietzsche wrote that "there is perhaps still a future even for laughter." This section is based on that hope but in the somber awareness that today, about a hundred years later, there is perhaps still a future for very little else.
>
> And I also presume that, since there is tragedy too great for tears, there must also be comedy too deep for laughter.
>
> This double awareness is continuously present throughout the First Variation which intends to establish the theoretical background against which I plan to compare the two great parablers Jesus and Borges. (9)

A "hope" and a "somber awareness" set the tone for Crossan's project. The hope concerns the future for laughter; the somber awareness concerns the hundred years that have passed since Nietzsche. What is striking about this opening is its allusive and suggestive phrasing. When I first laid eyes on the paragraph I was immediately struck by the thought that Crossan was beginning his comparison between Jesus and Borges by talking about the Holocaust. In my mind, a "tragedy too great for tears" could not refer to anything but the Nazi genocide. Similarly, I was only able to read "about a hundred years later" as indicating the caesura dividing these events historically, as before and after the Holocaust. If there were something within the last hundred years that could cause "somber" feelings in me, it was the Holocaust. Especially in combination with the expression "a somber awareness," Crossan's opening paragraph seemed to raise the question of laughter after Auschwitz.

However, this initial reading was quickly replaced by a hazy feeling that grew stronger as I turned the pages of Crossan's book. Crossan does not spell out what he means by "tragedy too great for tears." Neither in the beginning nor anywhere else in the book does he explicate what happened since Nietzsche that might lead one to reconsider Nietzschean thoughts on laughter. At the same time, Crossan's text did not allow me to forget my initial impression because similarly allusive references to the Holocaust kept reminding me of it. Throughout the text of *Raid*, words such as "Auschwitz," "Buchenwald," "final solutions," "Nazism," "totalitarian tyranny," "Nazi war criminal," and "destitution threatening the Jews" pop up at different places. These references enter *Raid* mostly via Crossan's quotations of twentieth-century writers. But Crossan's own discourse evokes the Holocaust as well when, for example, he throws in a remark such as: "One wonders that an author writing in the mid thirties of this century had no suspicion that the world needed a few less heroes and a few more fools" (11);[1] or when he in passing gives biographical information about a philosopher who had been dismissed from his University chair twice by the Nazis;[2] or when he begins a sentence with the phrase "Looking back over the horrors of this century" (15).[3]

This frequent appearance of the "horrors of this century" in Crossan's book was the cause of my anxieties and bad dreams during my first reading. At the same time it was precisely Crossan's allusiveness that created a sense of urgency about the book. Something important seemed to me to be going on, something that was hard to determine and therefore all the more captivating. What captivated me was in part the tension between an air of something grave and terrible produced by references to horrific events and *Raid*'s explicit themes of comedy, laughter, parody, paradox, and play. Crossan appears to bring the two together in his opening paragraph on Nietzsche: "since there is tragedy too great for tears, there must also be comedy too deep for laughter." But in fact, the causal connection between the two is not explained, and it is not obvious, when you think about it. The tension between tragedy and comedy, between tears and laughter, and, consequently, between the horrors of this century and comic eschatology is left unaddressed and unresolved—a source of irritation.

Crossan's allusions create a further and related tension: between the significance of twentieth-century history on the one hand and the timeless notion of comic eschatology on the other. As I emphasized in the previous chapter, his comparisons between Jesus' stories and "the texts within our own world" are based mainly in the focus on genre, a crosscultural interpretive category. As I further suggested, the focus on a specific historical situation, be it that of Jesus or of Borges, is subordinated in Crossan's work to the focus on the timeless play of language, the meeting-ground for all "genuine parablers" throughout history. This general ahistorical character of Crossan's explicit argument is disrupted by recurrent hints about the significance of historical time, such as the suggestion that "today," about a hundred years after Nietzsche, "there is perhaps still a future for very little else" than laughter.

The tension between the historical and the ahistorical became visceral for me through another striking peculiarity of *Raid*. Almost consistently, Crossan quotes the various literary and theoretical pieces around which he develops his themes by introducing each piece together with its year of publication. For instance: he introduces two stories by Borges in the following manner: "Both were written in 1940 and contained in the first volume of his short stories issued in 1941" (51). Or: "the first English translation of [Borges'] stories was *Ficciones* in 1962 and this contained two Spanish collections from 1941 and 1944" (77). This kind of meticulous citation is applied also to texts that Crossan quotes in other books but without giving the year of publication. In *Raid* the respective year is inserted into the reference. This preoccupation with years and dates creates a sense of the historically specific that stands in sharp contrast to the broad comparative vision of "comic eschatology in Jesus and Borges."

Since many of the quoted pieces by Borges and others appeared in the 1930s and 1940s, the text of *Raid* is covered with a web of years that are reminiscent of events related to Nazi genocide. Because of Crossan's allusions to "horrors of this century," the significance of these decades became a constant subtext in my reading. When Crossan, in passing, emphasizes that certain texts by Borges were published in the early 1940s, I read this emphasis as an indication that Borges wrote at a time when the Nazi death machinery was beginning to operate in eastern Europe.

American Holocaust Memory

However, numerous reviewers were able to read *Raid* without thinking about the Holocaust. Wasn't the attention I paid to what I called Crossan's allusive references to the Holocaust a result of my own personal preoccupations? Reading the year 1941 as an invocation of the beginning of the "final solution"—wasn't this a symptom of a certain kind of oversensitivity, a reading that had less to do with *Raid* than with my own concern with the Holocaust as a German?

These were the questions posed to me by the American friends and colleagues with whom I shared my reading of Crossan's book. How much did my own Germanness play into my reading? Wasn't I overreacting to something very marginal? A friend emphasized that Crossan, after all, was neither German nor American but Irish and pointed out to me the Irish Catholic concerns and sensitivities she saw reflected in *Raid*.[4] A colleague kept reminding me of Borges's South American background and the events in Argentina in the 1970s. If one wanted to find a historical subtext of *Raid*, would it not be much more reasonable to consider twentieth-century Catholicism, Ireland, or South America? How could I posit a viable connection between the Holocaust and a book on Borges and Jesus published in the United States by an Irish Catholic scholar?

There is no doubt that the subtext "Holocaust" in *Raid* is marginal, not central, but it is precisely the marginal character of Crossan's Holocaust references that I find significant. It seems to me that the allusive and often indirect ways that "Auschwitz" and "Buchenwald" enter Crossan's text illustrate a particular shape of Holocaust memory and are worth exploring. The fact that these allusions are irrelevant to Crossan's main themes, the fact that one can easily think of themes that are more relevant, as my colleagues did, are part of the phenomenon that interests me. Notwithstanding the Irish background of its author and the many other histories that inform the book, I wish to demonstrate that *Raid*, among other things, is also an illuminating instance of specifically American post-Holocaust scholarship. Published in the United States in 1976 as part of a distinctively American interpretive discourse on Christian Scripture, *Raid* with its web of allusions to "the horrors of this century" may reveal something typical about American Holocaust consciousness of the mid-1970s.[5]

Recent studies of the changes in Holocaust memory in the United States offer helpful venues for historicizing *Raid on the Articulate* as an American post-Holocaust discourse. While the analyses of these changes differ, most studies agree that a crucial turning point in the way the general American public remembered the Holocaust occurred in the late 1970s. Through the 1978 broadcast of the television miniseries *Holocaust,* narrating the fate of a German Jewish family under the Nazi regime, millions of Americans were turned into empathic witnesses of Nazi violence against the Jews. According to the critics, this event installed the Holocaust firmly in the public mind and marked the beginning of the "memory boom" as we know it today not only in Germany but in the United States as well. *Raid on the Articulate* was published two years *before* this big media event. This may mean that the book was first being read when awareness of the Holocaust was notably less prominent than it became in the late 1970s—that the book came out at a time when the term "Holocaust" had not yet entered common vocabulary, when courses on the topic were still waiting to be integrated in school curricula, and when Holocaust survivors had not yet gained the public visibility that was given to them forty, fifty years after the end of the war.

According to Peter Novick's chronology, the publication of *Raid* falls into "the years of transition," in which the Holocaust, for several reasons, gradually turned into a meaningful topic for American Jews. Novick's book *The Holocaust in American Life* describes the 1970s as a kind of interim between the postwar period, when neither Jews nor Gentiles had much interest in the Holocaust, and the more current state of affairs, when the Holocaust stands at the center of American public discourse. The silence in America around the Holocaust that Novick describes in the late 1940s and 1950s resembles the situation in postwar Germany, as I sketched it in previous chapters. Interestingly, however, Novick considers this silence the result not of a repressed trauma or an "inability to mourn" but of more or less conscious decisions of American Jewish communities not to publicly talk about the Holocaust. An important reason for these decisions, according to Novick, was the Cold War, which allied the United States with West Germany and created a political climate in which emphasis on West Germany's atrocious past fell into procommunist rhetoric. Jewish hesitancy to publicly dwell on the Nazi crimes derived from the fear of fueling anti-Semitic stereotypes equating Jews with the political enemy of the time, which was no longer National Socialism but communism (92). Another factor was wariness of the victim image, which talk of the Holocaust necessarily brought with it. In a situation where many Jews sought integration into the many levels of American life, to focus on the supposedly vulnerable and weak Holocaust Jew was, as Novick quotes a spokesperson of the time, "not in the best interests of Jewry'" (123).

Changed political and cultural circumstances were the reason why Jewish organizations in the 1960s and 1970s began to publicly talk about the Holocaust. Most prominent among those reasons were, according to Novick, first, "a certain loosening of the cold war culture" (127) which turned Germany's crimes from a taboo subject into a possible topic to talk about; second, the Middle East conflicts, during which the Holocaust, in different and complicated ways, began to be invoked in American Jewry's support of Israel; and third, the rise of identity politics that prompted different groups in America to tend to their respective "history of victimization," a process that in the case of American Jews centered around the Holocaust (171).

Novick's overall analysis suggests that the growth of the Holocaust consciousness of (Christian) America after 1978 was anticipated by developments among American Jewry during the 1960s and 1970s. What the analysis leaves open is the place of the Holocaust in American *Christian* consciousness during the 1960s and 1970s time, and specifically in the years when Crossan wrote and published his work on the parables. How can sporadic references to "Auschwitz" and "Buchenwald" in a Christian discourse that appeared in 1976 be understood in terms of the historical narrative developed by Novick? More concretely: how willing and able were Crossan and his first readers, American Christians in the mid-1970s, to make sense of the web of allusions to "the horrors of this century," to "Auschwitz" and "Buchenwald"?

Holocaust Guest Appearances

How much a general Christian audience was already being familiarized with the topic of the Holocaust in the 1960s and 1970s is suggested by Jeffrey Shandler in his book *While America Watches: Televising the Holocaust.* Shandler's study is based on the premise that "beyond any other medium or forum, television has brought the Holocaust into the thoughts, feelings, words, and actions of millions of Americans" (xvi). This was true for major events such as NBC's *Holocaust* or Spielberg's *Schindler's List* in 1993. But Shandler is equally interested in the many less spectacular television broadcasts that appeared on the screens even in those times when, according to other critics, the Holocaust was still rather marginal in the public mind, as in the mid-1970s.

According to Shandler's periodization, 1976 falls between two major television events: the miniseries *Holocaust* in 1978 and the coverage of the Eichmann trial in Jerusalem in the early 1960s. This is how Shandler describes these years:

> while this period offered no major works to rival the landmark broadcasts at its boundaries, the years between 1961 and 1978 saw the Holocaust become an increasingly frequent, even routine, presence on American television. In programs ranging from news documentary to science fiction, the Holocaust emerged during these years as a regular, if occasional, subject within American television's repertoire. (133)

At the heart of the 1960s/1970s repertoire were episodic series, and it was primarily via this genre that Holocaust figures entered American television. In Shandler's words:

> The appearance of the Holocaust on occasional installments of episodic drama series best characterizes the subject's presence on American television during this period. By the early 1960s, episodic programs had become the mainstay of prime-time television entertainment. Most of these offered a series of what amounted to self-contained dramas of a particular genre (e.g., court or police cases, espionage, westerns), which were linked together by the presence of continuing roles and locations (e.g., doctors, reporters; classrooms, spaceships). While rooted in consistent characters, plots, and settings, these series afford opportunities for guest performers in occasional roles, and, similarly, the appearance of "guest" locales and topics. The Holocaust figures as such a "guest" on a number of these series. (134–135)

Holocaust "guest appearances," as Shandler calls them, occurred in series such as *All in the Family, The Defenders, Twilight Zone, Insight, Lou Grant,* and *Star Trek.* In *Star Trek's* 1968 episode "Patterns of Force," for instance, the *Enterprise's* crew makes its peace efforts on a planet where Nazi German society has been rebuilt. As the plot progresses Captain Kirk and Mr. Spock successfully fight the people in power, the Ekosians, who hate and attempt to annihilate another group of people of a different race: the Zeons. According to Shandler, the rationale behind this and other episodes is the producers' wish to bring social issues to the attention of Americans, including racial tolerance or the antiwar movement. What characterizes those attempts, moreover, is the neglect of the specific historical circumstances in which Nazism emerged (142). Indeed, only a decontextualized approach to the subject matter is able to imagine a Nazi society far away from planet Earth several centuries after Hitler's rise to power. A thorough understanding of the Nazi genocide is clearly not the aim of these shows. Rather the Holocaust is used, as Shandler writes, "as a point of entry into more general issues—the limits of justice, the consequences of intolerance, or the nature of evil" (133).

Shandler's study of Holocaust television in the 1960s and 1970s resonates with my own study of Crossan's 1976 interpretive discourse. It shows that the marginal but frequent invocation of the Holocaust that I noticed in *Raid* was not unusual and was a cultural practice familiar to Americans of the time. I would like to suggest that the citation of "Auschwitz" and "Buchenwald" at the periphery of New Testament studies during this period is a cultural phenomenon similar to the one that occasionally places Nazis and persecuted Jews within established TV plots and settings. Shandler's notion of Holocaust "guest appearances" in American television of the 1970s may thus be an apt metaphor for Crossan's web of allusions to the "horrors of this century."

However, metaphors are ambivalent; Crossan's book is like and is not like Holocaust television. While Shandler's study offers helpful historical cues for my concerns, it also raises questions that force me to refine my critical focus on *Raid.* Shandler argues, as I said, that Holocaust "guest appearances" were part of an effort to include social concerns in television programs. But what about the rationale behind Crossan's practice? If the meaning and function of Holocaust television in the 1970s was to make its audience aware of what producers believed to be a "moral issue with universal significance" (154)—what about the meaning and function of such appearances in a book on parables? How are Crossan's readers to make sense of Holocaust "guest appearances" in relation to the teachings of Jesus?

I will begin to explore these questions by looking closely at two of Crossan's "guest appearances," two places in the web of allusions to the Holocaust, illustrations of thoughts which stand at the margins of Crossan's project: Crossan's quotation from Kurt Vonnegut's novel *Cat's Cradle* at the beginning of *Raid* and from Elie Wiesel's *Gates of the Forest* toward the end.

Piles of Corpses in Auschwitz and Buchenwald

Dark Comedy

Kurt Vonnegut's *Cat's Cradle* appears in Crossan's first chapter, which, broadly speaking, develops the concept of comic eschatology. More specifically, Crossan cites Vonnegut during a preliminary discussion of tragedy and comedy as competing "reactions to life."[6] "Tragic sense" or "comic vision"—which one, Crossan asks, is the "more important and adequate vision of our human condition?" (12) Crossan's answer, obviously, will be in favor of comedy.[7] The argument that leads to this answer is directed against the sedimented Greek prejudice against comedy as trivial and nonserious and is informed by various philosophers, theoreticians, writers, and poets. Starting out with the quote from Nietzsche and the affirmation of laughter, Crossan goes on to consider, among other things, the question of absurdity, the difference between contemptuous and compassionate laughter, the case of dark comedy, and a comic Greek epic until he finally arrives at the conclusion that comedy is a more pervasive and complete vision of life than tragedy: whatever instance of the tragic you look at, no matter how devastating or serious it may appear, it will eventually lead to a recognition of the relativity of it all, to laughter at our human limitations and therefore to the victory of the comic.

Shortly before he arrives at this conclusion, Crossan states that "it is necessary to look at a most contemporary facet of our comic sensitivity, black humor or dark comedy" (19). At stake is the question whether "real suffering or actual pain" preclude the comic—whether death and atrocity repudiate the victory of comedy. Crossan deals with this question in connection with the chapter "Black Death" in Kurt Vonnegut's novel *Cat's Cradle*. He writes:

> In *Cat's Cradle* Kurt Vonnegut has the son of a jungle doctor tell what happened during an epidemic of bubonic plague. The "grisly tale" describes in specific detail how the "House of Hope and Mercy in the Jungle looked like Auschwitz or Buchenwald" with bulldozers stalling as the mounting death toll left too many corpses for them to shove towards a common grave. His father worked without sleep for many days but was unable to do very much to save the doomed patients. After one sleepless and fruitless night with every bed eventually holding a corpse the doctor suddenly started giggling. "He couldn't stop. He walked out into the night with his flashlight. He was still giggling. He was making the flashlight beam dance over all the dead people stacked outside. He put his hand on my head, and do you know what that marvelous man said to me? . . . 'Son,' my father said to me, 'someday this will all be yours.'" (20)

Do horrible events such as a bubonic plague preclude laughter and the comic? It is true, Crossan says, whoever laughs at a story about plague victims is "a human swine." But after all, Vonnegut's piece is a funny story, and it might be precisely the proscription against laughter that provokes laughter, a laughter that ultimately keeps us sane. "Certain events are horrible and so are stories about them. Laughter at either event or story would be even more horrible still. But laughter at our inability to laugh is a narrow victory for the comic when faced with indescribable horror" (20).

This argument is the site of a brief guest appearance, to use Shandler's term, of images from the Nazi death camps. Piles of corpses resembling those in Auschwitz and Buchenwald serve as "a point of entry into more general issues," that is, the issue of dark comedy and the appropriateness of laughter in the face of atrocity. These images were mediated several times before they entered Crossan's discussion, and I would like to unravel the layers of quotations beneath Crossan's text.

Vonnegut's 1963 novel *Cat's Cradle*, the source of the "grisly tale," is a comic treatment of twentieth-century catastrophe, whose starting point is not the Holocaust but the dropping of the first atomic bomb on Hiroshima. It is the story of an American journalist who intends to write a book about this particular day, August 6, 1945, a book entitled "The Day the World Ended." In the process of doing research for his writing, the journalist becomes acquainted with the three children of one of the chief creators of the bomb, the late physicist Felix Hoenikker. Each of the children is in possession of another product of Hoenikker's scientific discoveries: Ice-9, a chemical with unknown destructive potential. Through his relation with the Hoenikker children, the journalist eventually becomes entangled with political events that distract him from his literary project and finally lead to the large-scale destruction of human life on earth through a piece of Ice-9.

The episode "Black Death" presents only a subplot within this narrative; the grisly tale about the bubonic plague is told by a minor character, and the tale as such is un-essential to the protagonist or the sequence of events. But the jungle doctor's comic remark, "Son, someday this will all be yours," embedded in the larger narrative of *Cat's Cradle*, has a specific resonance. Like the episode "Black Death," the novel is about tainted inheritance: three children literally inherit from their father not the outcome but the seed of catastrophe, the piece of Ice-9, which belongs to the same capital of scientific knowledge that led to the catastrophe of Hiroshima and that, a generation later, in Vonnegut's tale, will cause piles of corpses beyond measurement.

The reference to Auschwitz and Buchenwald, in Vonnegut's novel, is clearly subor-dinated to another history. The atrocity at the center of *Cat's Cradle* is not the Nazi genocide but the atrocity that is implicit in the work of American scientists who take no responsibility for their research results. The two infamous Nazi camps with their piles of corpses in Vonnegut's novel are like snapshots inserted into a larger frame, into a different thematic context. "Auschwitz" and "Buchenwald" are like snapshots in Crossan's discourse as well. But unlike Vonnegut's novel, Crossan's discourse gives no hints as to which specific human catastrophe its author is thinking of when he discusses the question of laughter vis-à-vis atrocious pain. While I can understand Vonnegut's laugh-ter because he explicates its historical points of reference, I am left guessing what kind of history is on Crossan's mind when he insists that comedy, not tragedy, is the "more important and adequate vision of our human condition" (12). Does he think about the Holocaust? About Hiroshima? About some other military conflict? Vietnam perhaps? About a possible nuclear war in the future? About an epidemic in some faraway jungle?

Atrocity Snapshots

Crossan offers almost no historical texture for his appropriation of Vonnegut's novel. He did, however, choose to include in his brief quotation the snapshots from Auschwitz and Buchenwald. Let me quote him once more:

> In *Cat's Cradle* Kurt Vonnegut has the son of a jungle doctor tell what happened during an epidemic of bubonic plague. The "grisly tale" describes in specific detail how the "House of Hope and Mercy in the Jungle looked like Auschwitz and Buchenwald" with bulldoz-ers stalling as the mounting death toll left too many corpses for them to shove towards a common grave.

Auschwitz and Buchenwald appear here without leading to any further reflection on Nazi atrocity; nor do the snapshots lead to a dramatization of Nazi violence, as is the case in the Holocaust television episodes examined by Shandler. What then is their function and meaning in Crossan's discussion? How did Crossan understand the piles of corpses in his own text?

In chapter 2 I discussed Holocaust photographs in the context of West Germany in the mid-1960s. Images of Nazi atrocities, which first appeared in 1945, reappeared in the course of the Auschwitz trials in Frankfurt in 1964, almost two decades later. This journalistic material, I argued, is the source also of the terrible images that haunted Marie Luise Kaschnitz, who attended the proceedings. Her poem describes how the forgotten images of atrocity reemerge in the private space of a German home, breaking through walls and floors and producing a paralyzing sense of devastation. Were such images readily available also for Crossan or for his first American readers in the 1970s? And if so, what meanings were attached to these images?

Barbie Zelizer's book *Remembering to Forget*, a study of American Holocaust photography, suggests that in the 1970s atrocity photographs, on the few occasions they were actually published and looked at, had rather nebulous meanings. From their first appearance in American newspapers and magazines, atrocity photographs, according to Zelizer, were used not to offer details about the different camps in Europe or the different fates of Nazi victims but rather to symbolize Nazi brutality in general. Instead of offering referential facts of the Nazi crimes such as places, dates, names, events, or biographies, images (in contrast to words) illustrated those crimes' grand scope (139). This function of atrocity photographs remained the same throughout the decades after the shocking news from Europe had settled. Looking at the time period from the late 1940s to the late 1970s, Zelizer argues that atrocity photographs, though moving from the center of public attention to the background, retained their generalizing effect. She writes: "Images . . . continued to do in memory what they had done at the time of the camps' liberation—to move the atrocity story from the contingent and particular to the symbolic and abstract" (158).

Zelizer's study suggests that in the mid-1970s images from the camps were not entirely forgotten or inaccessible to a general public but that the meaning of these images, if they were seen at all, were rather vague. "Vehicles of memory—words, photographs, artifacts—did not disappear, but they continued to exist as the background of unactivated memory" (168). Crossan's invocation of Nazi atrocity images can serve as an example of Zelizer's historical account. Rather than raising questions about the specific events, the names of the two Nazi camps symbolize atrocity in general. "Auschwitz" and "Buchenwald" are placeholders. They signify atrocity very broadly speaking. Crossan says he wants to contemplate "real suffering and actual pain" (19). To do so he lets the Holocaust appear on his stage, via Vonnegut's novel, and thereby he cites what in the mid-1970s had already become a paradigm for "suffering" and "pain" but had as a paradigm been stripped of any historical specificity. For Kaschnitz, Holocaust imagery is specific enough to affect her well-being, and this is because Kaschnitz writes as a German, as a bystander, because she belongs to the side of the perpetrators. The Holocaust imagery in Crossan's American discourse has no such power. It is the background of unactivated memory, as Zelizer says. The piles of corpses in Auschwitz and Buchenwald do not affect Crossan; they activate neither memories nor feelings of guilt. They are symbols of atrocity. Bad things happened. It is questionable whether "Auschwitz" and "Buchenwald" mean much more to Crossan than that.

Crossan's Laughter

That these names cannot mean a whole lot more is suggested in the section immediately following Crossan's contemplation of dark comedy. Shortly after his thoughts on laughter and pain Crossan concludes his discussion of "tragic response" and "comic vision" and makes the victory of comedy definite by positing comedy as the "Whole Truth." The text on which this final decision is based is Homer's *Odyssey*:

> In Book 12 of the *Odyssey* Homer records the tragic fate of Odysseus's crew caught between the monster Scylla and the whirlpool Charybdis. When the survivors finally landed on the Sicilian shore they prepared supper and "when they had satisfied their thirst and hunger, they thought of their dear companions and wept, and in the midst of their tears sleep came gently upon them." Tragedy knows of Death and of Tears. But the Whole Truth knows of Death, Supper, Tears, and Sleep. . . . Tragedy can and does insist there is only Death and Tears. Comedy responds that there is Death and Supper, Tears and Sleep. Only loss of critical nerve can avoid the implications of these statements. If the same life or world or reality can be judged by some as tragic and by others as comic, then the latter has clearly won because it is already comic that the same events could be interpreted in such diametrical opposition. Tragedy is swallowed up eventually by comedy. The sting belongs to tragedy but the victory to comedy. (21)

These sentences explicate why Crossan thinks that comedy, not tragedy, is the "more adequate and important vision of our human condition." Comedy gives a full, not a partial, picture of things. In contrast to tragedy, it includes the mundane matters and immediate concerns of daily human life such as food and sleep. And in that respect, comedy represents the "Whole Truth."

Together, Crossan's citations of Vonnegut and Homer exemplify the two irritating tensions that, as I mentioned in the beginning of this chapter, characterize the entire book: the tension between evocations of horrific events and the broad themes of play and comedy, here to be found between Vonnegut's "grisly tale," the "piles of corpses," on the one hand and Crossan's insistence on laughter on the other. The second tension is that between the historical and the ahistorical and lies between Vonnegut's tale and Homer's epic: Crossan introduces Vonnegut as a "most contemporary facet of our comic sensitivity," and by including the comparison with Nazi concentration camps in his rendering of the story he reminds his own readers of twentieth-century events. A few seconds later, however, he turns to an ancient Greek text and thereby gives his discussion a timeless scope and relevance.

Of course, Crossan's concluding evocation of the Greeks is apt insofar as the Greek tradition is the very source not only of the comedy/tragedy duality as such but of comedy's bad reputation as well. To counter the ancient Greek prejudice against comedy with an ancient Greek comic epic would seem logical. At the same time, the jump from contemporary atrocity to an ancient Greek story about "Death, Supper, Sleep, and Tears" shows me that "Auschwitz" and "Buchenwald" cannot be much more for Crossan than tokens that carry little historical meaning.

Capitalized as they are in Crossan's text, death, supper, sleep, and tears seem to be the universal and timeless aspects of human life. To some degree, they surely are. But in the specific context of Auschwitz and Buchenwald, all four of these things—death, supper, sleep, and tears—had gained meanings that should have made Crossan hesitant to speak so confidently about comedy as the "Whole Truth." It does not take much effort to realize the glaring difference between Homer's survival story and the situation of survivors in Germany and Poland after the war. The fact that Crossan easily moves from one to the other is a sign that the phrase "Auschwitz and Buchenwald" failed to evoke in Crossan's mind basic historical considerations. It obviously did not occur to Crossan, to give just one example, that the victims of Nazi atrocity, in contrast to Odysseus and his companions, had no resource to satisfy their thirst and hunger on request. Otherwise, it seems to me, Crossan would at least have nuanced his argument about comedy's victory.[8]

Crossan's failure to do so is not simply a sign of ignorance. It is a consequence of the vague nature of Christian American Holocaust consciousness of the mid-1970s.[9] What interests me is the historical phenomenon that a Christian scholar in America was able to quote the names of Nazi concentration camps, displaying familiarity with these names and perhaps even with Holocaust photographs, without however associating anything specific with those names and images.

My second example of the Holocaust "guest appearances" in Crossan's book will suggest that the Holocaust is not entirely without significance for Crossan and that there is at least one "guest" who does carry some more specific meaning.

Reverence for a Holocaust Survivor

A Hidden Treasure

Elie Wiesel's book *The Gates of the Forest* appears in Crossan's fourth chapter, which is generally concerned with what Crossan believes to be a central theme in the stories of Jesus and Borges: the problem of time. Time, according to Crossan, is not an objective reality but a human construct that becomes meaningful through storytelling. Its continuity is created by the respective narratives and myths of a culture—be it in terms of a circle, as is the case with the Greeks, or be it in linear terms, corresponding to the biblical understanding. Besides the great myths of the Greek or the Hebrew culture, however, there are small stories that playfully challenge normative notions of time. Both Jesus and Borges, Crossan claims, told such stories.[10]

Jesus' vision of time can best be explored through the story of the Hidden Treasure, a "short but devastating parable" (153), as Crossan calls it: "The kingdom of heaven is like a treasure hidden in a field, which a man found and covered up; then in his joy he goes and sells all that he has and buys the field" (Matthew 13:44, as translated by Crossan).

What distinguishes this little parable, in Crossan's view, is the peculiar course of events, which resists the usual development from past to present to future. Crossan comments: "For Jesus this linear time is broken so that the sequence is Future to Past to Present. Out of his unknown and unexpected Future comes the treasure's opportunity. For it he gladly abandons his entire Past by selling all his possessions. And thereby he obtains field, treasure, and a new Present" (156).

Jesus' parable, Crossan shows, is one of numerous treasure stories that can be found in various cultural settings. In order to illustrate the many different ways the plot of these stories can develop, Crossan goes on to offer "three modern examples . . . of stories of hidden treasure" (157). His third example is borrowed from Elie

Wiesel.[11] As Crossan introduces it: "Third . . . I would tell the story myself as I hear it at present. I do so as a variation on the epigraph Elie Wiesel used for *The Gates of the Forest* and I hope the adaptation will not be deemed irreverent" (157–158). Wiesel's version is as follows.

> When the great Rabbi Israel Baal Shem-Tov saw destitution threatening the Jews it was his custom to go into a certain part of the forest to meditate. There he would light a fire, say a special prayer, and the miracle would be accomplished, and destitution averted. Later, when his disciple, the celebrated Magid of Mezritch, had occasion, for the same reason, to intercede with heaven, he would go to the same place in the forest and say: "Master of the Universe, listen! I do not know how to light a fire, but I am still able to say the prayer." And again the miracle would be accomplished. Still later, Rabbi Moshe-Leib of Sasov, in order to save his people once more, would go into the forest and say: "I do not know how to light a fire, I do not know the prayer, but I know the place and this must be sufficient." It was sufficient and the miracle was accomplished. Then it fell to Rabbi Israel of Rizhin to overcome misfortune. Sitting in his armchair, his head in his hands, he spoke to God: "I am unable to light the fire and I do not know the prayer; I cannot even find the place in the forest. All I can do is to tell the story, and this must be sufficient." And it was sufficient.

What happens with Wiesel's epigraph in Crossan's hands? Crossan inserts into the plot the phrase "a hidden treasure would be revealed." This phrase replaces the words "the miracle was accomplished." First, the revelation of the treasure is placed parallel to God's averting the destitution. Midway it becomes unclear what is at stake in the story: is it the destitution or the hidden treasure? Here is Crossan's rendering:

> When the great Rabbi Israel Baal Shem-Tov saw destitution threatening the Jews it was his custom to go into a certain part of the forest to meditate. There he would light a fire, say a special prayer, *a hidden treasure would be revealed,* and destitution averted. Later, when his disciple, the celebrated Magid of Mezritch, had occasion, for the same reason, to intercede with heaven, he would go to the same place in the forest and say: "Master of the Universe, listen! I do not know how to light the fire, but I am still able to say the prayer." *And again the hidden treasure would be revealed.* Still later, Rabbi Moshe-Leib of Sasor, in order to save his people once more, would go into the forest and say: "I do not know how to light the fire, I do not know the prayer, but I know the place and this must be sufficient." It was sufficient and *the hidden treasure was revealed.* Then it fell to the Rabbi Israel of Rizhyn to overcome misfortune. Sitting in his armchair, his head in his hands, he spoke to God: "I am unable to light the fire and I do not know the prayer; I cannot even find the place in the forest. All I can do is to tell the story, and this must be sufficient." And it was sufficient. (Crossan 158, emphases added)

By the end of Crossan's adaptation of the story, the treasure seems to have replaced the destitution and Wiesel's epigraph has turned into a contemporary variation of Jesus' parable. How exactly he would draw comparative lines between the two remains unclear. Also unclear is, more generally, what this story means for Crossan, or what he means when he says that he tells the story "as I hear it at present." Wiesel's rewritten epigraph appears as a kind of afterthought. The only comment that follows the rabbinical story is this: "The hidden treasure in the story is the story of the hidden treasure" (158).

Again, let me unravel the layers of texts at stake. On the surface, Crossan cites and plays with a rabbinical story that, as an American Catholic friend of mine told me, had some currency among Christian communities in the 1970s as a word of wisdom.[12] However, Crossan cites (and modifies) the story not simply as a "rabbinical story" but as the epigraph to a novel by Elie Wiesel, a novel he provides no further information about. *The Gates of the Forest*, first published in France in 1964, is a tale about a young Jewish man in Hungary who survives the Holocaust by hiding, first in the forest, then in a village, and finally as a member of a partisan group. After the war the man (who calls himself Gregor but has lost his Jewish name) moves from Paris to the United States and continues to struggle with his religious tradition in light of his past. As an epigraph to this narrative, the rabbinical story has jarring connotations. The story tells about four rabbis who manage to avert a destitution threatening the Jews even though the means for effecting this "miracle" are forgotten over time. But what to make of this story when read in confrontation with Wiesel's Holocaust novel?

Crossan does not deal with that question in his appropriation of Wiesel's epigraph. Even though he cites the novel, Crossan ignores its meaning in Wiesel's book. Instead he modifies the story's theme from a destitution to a treasure and thereby makes the story readable in line with a story told by Jesus. As in his reading of Vonnegut's *Cat's Cradle*, Crossan lets instances of atrocity quickly appear on the scene and then focuses on something else. The twentieth-century meanings of "a destitution threatening the Jews" show up only to be replaced by Crossan's main intent, the search for hidden treasure stories.

A Raid on the Articulate

As with Crossan's Vonnegut quotation, I find it important to consider the immediate context of Crossan's use of Wiesel's epigraph. In his analysis of treasure stories Crossan considers not only "modern examples" but also ancient rabbinical material. A few pages before he arrives at *The Gates of the Forest*, Crossan compares Jesus' parable with "two other stories on the same theme taken from rabbinical literature to hear how his [i.e., Jesus'] version might have sounded to his contemporaries" (154). This comparison is based on Crossan's assumption that Jesus' storytelling stood in contrast to the Judaism of his time and that his parables were part of a comic attack on Jewish established literary traditions, "a raid on the articulate." In citing two Jewish stories circulating at the time of Jesus, Crossan therefore watches, as he says, "for hidden polemic in Jesus' story vis-à-vis the established authority of rabbinical versions" (155). For the sake of brevity I offer here only one of the two stories:[13]

> [A] man . . . inherited a piece of ground used as a dunghill. Being an indolent man, he went and sold it for a trifling sum. The purchaser began working and digging it up, and he found a treasure there, out of which he built himself a fine palace, and he began going about in public followed by a retinue of servants—all out of the treasure he found in it. When the seller saw it he was ready to choke, and he exclaimed, "Alas, what have I thrown away." (154, cited by Crossan from *Midrash Rabbah*)

According to Crossan, this story is part of the "traditional canon," from which Jesus' "artistic novelty" stands out. Crossan's interpretation goes as follows: "The . . . story represents a moral *example* which castigates laziness and extols hard work. It has a balanced negative and positive moral" (155). Crossan finds three differences between that story and Jesus' little parable:

First, [the rabbinical story] record[s] the activity of both the Seller and the Buyer so that the former's activity (sells . . . fumes) frames that of the latter. Second, and more important, the rabbinical Buyer traverses this sequence: *Buys, Acts (ploughs), Finds*; but Jesus' Buyer proceeds in exactly the opposite direction: *Finds, Acts (sells), Buys.* Put more simply: finding precedes buying for Jesus but buying precedes finding for the Rabbis. I would note in passing that Jesus' sequence makes the action of the Buyer if not illegal at least slightly immoral. It is not exactly what one would boast of having done except in carefully chosen company. Third, and most important, there is a very different sense of time behind that simple reversal of the main verbs, buying/finding. The time of the rabbinical stories leads logically and almost inevitably from Past to Present to Future. Its linear temporality shows the sweep from laziness and loss, through work-ethic and discovery, and projects into the future with the palace and the retinue in the forefront and the fuming seller in the background. (155)

Jesus' story, to paraphrase Crossan, distinguishes itself by turning upside down the normal sense of time, as well as by a certain recklessness and boldness in its protagonist. In contrast, the two actors in the rabbinical story, Buyer and Seller, represent the two types of the diligent and the lazy person, which correspond to what Crossan believes is the Rabbis' "work-ethic." In fact, the rabbinical story is not a "parable" in the proper—that is, in Crossan's—sense of the term but an "example." Its function is not a reversal of expectations but an illustration of right behavior based on a normative sense of time according to which success in the future follows upon hard work in the present.

These comparative practices stand in continuity with the problematic anti-Jewish aspects of Joachim Jeremias's scholarship, which I have discussed in chapter 4.[14] Like Jeremias, Crossan uses rabbinical literature as a foil for interpreting Jesus' parable. His terms and criteria, it is true, are different: Jeremias used that literature to contrast two different theologies and to point to the superior "clarity" and "simplicity" of Jesus' parables. Crossan opposes the moralizing, normalizing effects of the rabbis with the subversive thrust of Jesus.[15] In both cases, however, an arena of combat is conjured up in which Jesus in configured as a challenger of his Jewish contemporaries. For Crossan, as for Jeremias, the parables have a polemic function; they are "weapons of warfare" (Jeremias, 19) aimed at the Judaism of Jesus' time.[16]

Crossan's contrasting practices, his violent interpretive vision, his recourse to a "hidden polemic in Jesus' story," and the affinities with Jeremias's anti-Jewish tendencies throw a strange light on Crossan's subsequent reference to Elie Wiesel and *The Gates of the Forest.* A Holocaust novel written by a Holocaust survivor is cited and, at the same time, the scholarly valorization of Jesus over the Rabbis is perpetuated. What does this mean?

Anti-Judaism in the 1970s

The following short comment illustrates a third important dimension of Crossan's discussion of treasure stories. After contrasting Jesus with the Rabbis and before invoking Elie Wiesel, Crossan writes: "The comparison of Jesus' story with that of the Rabbis was not intended to exalt one over the other but to differentiate their functions as clearly as possible" (156). This kind of disclaimer frequently appears during Crossan's comparisons, not only in *Raid* but in other books as well.[17]

On the one hand, such apologetic remarks sound insincere to me. Crossan's distinction between two different functions—parable and moral example—is not neutral or value free. Indeed, Crossan's work in the 1970s constructs a huge binary, and on this binary "moral examples" are located on the lower side. This hierarchy is most clearly expressed at the end of *The Dark Interval*. Crossan distinguishes here "between mythical religion, a religion that gives one the final word about 'reality' and thereby excludes the authentic experience of mystery, and parabolic religion, a religion that continually and deliberately subverts final words about 'reality' and thereby introduces the possibility of transcendence" (105).

Crossan adds a final question: "Which do we prefer, comfort or courage? It may be necessary to make a choice" (105). There is no doubt about Crossan's own decision. He prefers courage over comfort, parabolic religion over mythical religion. And by way of implication he also exalts the subversive challenge of Jesus' parables over what he says are the moral examples of the Rabbis.[18]

On the other hand, Crossan's disclaimers are historically interesting, especially in light of Joachim Jeremias's postwar publication. In chapter 5 I argued that Jeremias's 1947 publication was characterized by a typical blindness toward the catastrophe of the war and to the Nazi genocide in particular. The degradation of Jewish material was carried out by Jeremias without any sign of awareness that what he was doing was odd vis-à-vis the contemporary destruction of European Jewry. I argued that the events of the Holocaust were too close and too recent for Jeremias to process them in a way that would make him avoid the problematic aspects of his own scholarship.

Crossan, who writes in the mid-1970s, three decades later, is more self-conscious. His assurance that he did not want to exalt Jesus over the Rabbis can be read as a sign that an awareness of the Holocaust has entered some corners of Christian scholarship. Crossan's apologies perhaps indicate the arrival of an awareness of the Holocaust not only as a paradigm of evil or a symbol of atrocity but as an event that critically concerns Christian biblical scholarship.[19] Crossan himself does not change his treatment of ancient Jewish texts. But reading them today, his apologies make me think of future changes. They foreshadow the efforts by New Testament scholars in the 1980s and 1990s to thoroughly recast their comparative strategies in light of the Holocaust.

Crossan's use of Wiesel's epigraph might be a similar sign of such newly emergent awareness. Let me quote once more the way Crossan introduces this third example of modern treasure stories: "Third," Crossan writes, "I would tell the story myself as I hear it at present. I do so as a variation on the epigraph Elie Wiesel used for *The Gates of the Forest* and I hope the adaptation will not be deemed irreverent." At stake here is more than a contemporary treasure story. As I said earlier, Crossan cites the rabbinical story not just as "rabbinical story" but as "an epigraph Elie Wiesel used for *The Gates of the Forest*." Wiesel's name is charged for Crossan, otherwise he would not be worried that his adaptation of the epigraph could be "deemed irreverent." Today the name Elie Wiesel, just like "Auschwitz" or "Buchenwald," has become a symbol of the Holocaust. Already in the 1970s Crossan knows that he invokes the name of a well-known Jewish writer and survivor of the Holocaust. Why would he be compelled to do so?

Perhaps Wiesel's name has a similar function to that of Crossan's earlier announcement of not wanting to exalt Jesus over the Rabbis. Perhaps Crossan wishes to ameliorate his treatment of rabbinical literature by first disclaiming any Christian superior intentions and then by making an indirect acknowledgment to the events of the Holocaust by referring to Wiesel and his epigraph. Whether this reference results from a conscious act or from an unconscious dynamic, I take it as a sign that the scholarly use of rabbinical material as a negative foil has already become tainted in light of the Holocaust and that the tolerance threshold for such misuse has decreased.

With the invocation of Wiesel's name, a concern with twentieth-century events flashes up, without, however, being explored by Crossan. It has no further effects on his discourse—and in that respect it resembles the snapshots from Vonnegut's *Cat's Cradle.* As I demonstrated earlier, Vonnegut's "grisly tale," in Crossan's text, is followed too quickly by the affirmation of a comic vision: "laughter at our inability to laugh is a narrow victory of the comic when faced with indescribable horror" (20). But Crossan never really looks at a particular instance of indescribable horror; he never identifies the victims of pain. Similarly, Crossan fails to really pay heed to Wiesel's epigraph. In transforming the rabbinical story into a "modern example" of hidden treasure stories and in perpetuating Jeremias's comparative practices, Crossan circumvents the historical legacy that, if my reading is correct, has provoked him to refer to Wiesel in the first place.

I have argued in this chapter that the Holocaust "guest appearances" in Crossan's book, his citations of Auschwitz, Buchenwald, the piles of corpses, Elie Wiesel, and the destitution threatening the Jews, are typical of Christian American Holocaust consciousness in the mid-1970s. These citations need to be historicized in a place and time when a process was still under way that would bring the Holocaust from the margins to the center of public discourse; a time when consumers of American television were used to the topic of Nazi persecution on episodic series not as an exploration of particular historical events but as "a point of entry in more general issues"; when images of the camps did not provide referential facts but symbolized the phenomenon of Nazi atrocities in its broadest sense. The Holocaust appears in Crossan's discourse, but it appears in a way that does not lead Crossan to reflect on the Nazi genocide as a specific historical event that concerns his work. The names of "Auschwitz" and "Buchenwald" carry no meanings, they are inconsequential for Crossan and they have no effects on his hermeneutic thoughts on the parables. How Jesus' parables can be read "after Auschwitz and Buchenwald," how they can be compared with Jewish literature after the Holocaust, how the significance of these ancient Christian stories might have changed in post-Holocaust times—all these questions are left unexplored in Crossan's book.

9

Parables for Our Time?

Crossan's comparison between Jesus' parables and twentieth-century literature is carried out within an uncanny subtext of twentieth-century catastrophes. This web of allusions to "the horrors of this century," to "Auschwitz" and "Buchenwald," distinguishes *Raid* from other publications by Crossan and from the work of his colleagues, and it has given me cues for situating the book within the history of Holocaust consciousness in the United States. I will now move from the margins of Crossan's discourse to the central theme of *Raid on the Articulate*, the affinity between the stories of Jesus and twentieth-century literature. In doing this, I also move from the idiosyncracies of Crossan's 1976 discourse to a more widespread effort among biblical scholars to compare the New Testament parables with modern and postmodern writings on the basis of structural or generic similarities. In this chapter I want to develop a post-Holocaust reading of such efforts, taking Crossan's project as a starting point. Is Crossan really driven by "structural" and "generic" interests alone when he cites Jesus' parables next to the work of Borges, Camus, Wiesel, and other twentieth-century writers? Isn't there something more at stake than "literary" questions when the writings of Franz Kafka are cited not only in *Raid* but, as I will show, in a whole range of studies on Jesus' parables? Isn't there a reason other than a concern with metaphors that prompted Wolfgang Harnisch to quote Marie-Luise Kaschnitz's jarring post-Holocaust poem?

I suggested earlier that there might be a reason why Kaschnitz's poem appeared, of all places, in a book on parables—that there might be a specific desire or motivation at work in some strands of parable hermeneutics that could explain its quotation of a text like "Zoon Politikon" or its production of passing references to "Auschwitz and Buchenwald." It is time to offer such explanation.

A Literary Tradition of Parables

Crossan's comparative project is based on a crosscultural notion of the "context" of Jesus' parables. This context is no longer solely the parables' first historical setting but is also, and more important for Crossan, literature that, across times and places, shares certain characteristics with Jesus' stories. The teachings of Jesus "are best understood . . . in confrontation with texts within our own world which are functionally, generically, and philosophically on the same literary tradition." (xv). In what follows I will show how this hermeneutic premise affects Crossan's actual treatment of particular literary pieces. In a chapter entitled "Parable and Paradox" Crossan combines into one trajectory Albert Camus's novel *The Plague*, Franz Kafka's novel *The Trial*, the biblical book of Jonah, and Jesus' parable of the Good Samaritan. This trajectory offers a good site for studying and evaluating the ambivalence of Crossan's comparative project—the tension between his rather rigid focus on the formal qualities of these texts and the historicizing gestures accompanying his discourse.

Contemporary Parable

Crossan's main tool in constructing a trajectory from Jonah to Camus is a generic definition of parable. Parables, as Crossan defines them, are constituted by the following core elements: "The first is paradox. The second is story. And the third is their correlation as paradoxical story. This is accomplished by effecting a structural reversal on a traditional or expected story at its deepest levels" (94). This brief definition, as I will show, both shapes and combines the literature that Crossan intends to include in his trajectory.

Crossan elaborates and refines his generic definition of parables as paradoxical stories by applying it to two twentieth-century novels: Camus's novel *The Plague*, the story of a deadly epidemic that breaks out in the city of Oran in the 1940s; and Kafka's novel *The Trial*, the story of Joseph K., a bank clerk who is sentenced to death on the morning of his thirtieth birthday without knowing why. Under the heading "Contemporary Parable" Crossan offers two commentaries on *The Plague* and *The Trial*. These commentaries are informed by the work of the German scholar Heinz Politzer and his essay "Franz Kafka and Albert Camus: Parables for Our Time."

> *The Plague.* "The only general insight Camus's plague coveys to the reader is the realization that there are no general insights to be gained." Politzer's summary finds its concentrated reflection in this comment of Jarrou [*sic*] to Rieux which Camus placed centrally in his novel. "A hundred years ago plague wiped out the entire population of a town in Persia, with one exception. And the sole survivor was precisely the man whose job it was to wash the dead bodies, and who carried on throughout the epidemic." Once again from Politzer: "For Camus . . . the incomprehensible remains incomprehensible, and a paradox takes the place of any rational maxim conveyed by the narration. It is a kind of meta-didactic prose: at the core of the secret a new mystery is hidden." . . .

> *The Trial.* We might expect a story structured in a nice, polite binary opposition as follows: The Law gives sentence of death to one convicted of serious crime but gives no death sentence to one innocent of such crime. Kafka furnishes us with a single reversal of this expectation: The Law sentences K. to death and he never knows of what he is accused. This paradox is concentrated once again in a central incident "Before the Law." (I admit to finding both central incidents in both novels much more devastating in their brevity than the full novels which now contain them.) A man seeks entrance to the Law but the doorkeeper continually denies him entrance. He waits and waits and just before his death he asks the doorkeeper why nobody else ever sought entrance to the Law. "No

one but you could gain admittance through this door, since this door was intended only for you. I am now going to shut it." One expects the Doorkeeper to admit those for whom the door was intended and to deny entrance to the unintended ones. But the parable has the Doorkeeper (the Law) deny entrance to the sole intended one. (94–95)

These two commentaries are typical of Crossan's whimsical style. For someone unfamiliar with *The Plague* or *The Trial*, the two paragraphs probably remain obscure. Crossan hardly addresses the general themes or plot developments of the books at stake. What matters to Crossan is the paradox that he, following Politzer, finds in the two novels. By means of this interpretive category, *The Plague* is rendered into "meta-didactic prose" that refuses to provide general insights other than the realization that the incomprehensible remains incomprehensible. *The Trial*, on the other hand, is rendered into a composition that effects a reversal of a binary opposition according to which criminals, not innocent people, are sentenced to death.

What is actually most conspicuous about Crossan's treatment of *The Plague* and *The Trial* is the way he narrows his focus down to the two short stories that stand emblematically at the core of the two novels: their "central incidents," as he calls them. In *The Plague* the central incident is the striking story of a man who is in constant close contact with the bodies of plague victims and, against all odds, is the only one who survives the plague. The central incident of *The Trial* is the story of a man who seeks entrance to the Law and waits at its door a lifetime in vain, only to learn at the end that the door was intended for no one but him. In fact, it seems that Crossan is little interested in the two novels themselves and that what interests him are the short stories. As he admits in brackets, he finds "both central incidents in both novels much more devastating in their brevity than the full novels that now contain them" (95).

"Devastating," in Crossan's scheme of things, is an attribute of appreciation. It captures the provocative and disturbing effects of paradoxical literature that are cherished by Crossan. While both *The Plague* and *The Trial* have such devastating effects in their denials of insights and reversals of binaries, "much more devastating" are the effects of the two brief paradoxical stories central to each novel. In only a few sentences Tarrou's story poignantly confounds the reader's expectation that physical contact with plague victims enforces the risk of infection, while "Before the Law," again within a short amount of space, effectively undermines the assumption that a door intended for one particular person naturally should be opened when that person comes along. In their short versions, the two novels have in fact become structurally the same: "paradoxical stories effecting a reversal of expectation."

Biblical Parable

Paradoxical stories can be found also in the Bible. Crossan makes this claim against what he considers a widespread misunderstanding of biblical parables. Literary critics such as Politzer (and biblical critics such as Jeremias, I may add) wrongly assumed that biblical parables are didactic stories with clear-cut messages. This is not so, Crossan argues, and points to a biblical incident that clearly and undeniably displays all traits of paradox turned into story. The incident can be found not in the gospels but in the Hebrew Bible: the book of Jonah, Crossan argues, is a classical case of how an established binary opposition gets reversed through paradox. The binary in question lies between good prophets and bad pagans. According to tradition, one expects prophets to obey the will of God and pagans to transgress it. In the story of Jonah, however, the prophet who is called by God turns his back and flees the mission, while the supposedly unredeemable Ninevites turn to God and perform an impressive spectacle of atonement. In Crossan's words: "the story presents us with a most disobedient prophet and with some unbelievably obedient Ninevites. I would emphasize the literary skill which effects a double paradox in this story as distinct from the single paradox of the contemporary parables seen earlier" (97). If there is a line to be drawn at all, Crossan suggests, it is not between contemporary paradox and biblical clear-cut messages but between superbly crafted double paradoxes and single paradoxes that are not so superbly crafted.

In order to demonstrate that Jesus' parables, too, are paradoxes, genuine parables, Crossan focuses on Luke's gospel and the well-known story of a Samaritan who helps his enemy, a Jew who lies beaten, robbed, and naked on the road from Jerusalem to Jericho. Crossan points out that "the Good Samaritan" has entered the general Christian cultural reservoir as a trope and model for helping those in distress. He writes: "The phrase ['Good Samaritan'] has become part of the language as a cipher for concerned assistance and we seldom realize that as first uttered it was, like square circle, an oxymoron" (101).

The square circle, the oxymoronic shape of the original parable, is what Crossan intends to recover. To do that Crossan has to free the parable of the moral grid imposed on it by time and tradition. He takes the parable out of its gospel context and rewrites it according to its most authentic version, that is, free from Luke's editorial interpretation. Crossan announces: "Here is the story, the whole story, and nothing but the story" (102).

> A man was going down from Jerusalem to Jericho, and he fell among robbers, who stripped him and beat him, and departed, leaving him half dead. Now by chance a priest was going down that road; and when he saw him he passed by on the other side. So likewise a Levite, when he came to the place and saw him, passed by on the other side. But a Samaritan, as he journeyed, came to where he was; and when he saw him, he had compassion, and went to him and bound his wounds, pouring on oil and wine; then he set him on his own beast and brought him to an inn, and took care of him. And the next day he took out two denarii and gave them to the innkeeper, saying, "Take care of him; and whatever more you spend, I will repay you when I come back."

After having thus isolated Jesus' story from its interpretive framework, Crossan closely scrutinizes the narrative. Calling attention to the implied narrator and the implied hearer of the story, he points out that the story is told by a Jew to a Jewish audience in Jerusalem. According to Crossan's next observation, the narrative shows a clear binary: the different protagonists of the story can be divided into the two groups of "us" and "them." On the one hand, there is the Levite, the priest, and the man who lies wounded on the street. All three of them are Jews and belong to the same group as the narrator and his audience. On the other hand, there is the Samaritan who, from the Jewish point of view, belongs to a group of outsiders and outcasts.

With this examination of Jesus' narrative, the category of moral example is already exposed as inadequate. Crossan's analysis shows that the story of the Good Samaritan does not work as an example for helping those in distress. If it wanted to make such a moralizing point, it would have to put one of the "insider" group, a Jew, in the position of the helping person, while the Samaritan, the outcast, would have to be the one lying on the side of the road. Only on the basis of such configuration could the story effectively launch an appeal to a Jewish audience to go and do the same. The story's actual point or emphasis, Crossan argues, lies in the surprising fact that it is not the good but the bad guy, the Samaritan, not the Jew, who offers help to the robbery victim. Crossan summarizes: "A Jewish narrator tells a Jerusalem audience a story in which Temple functionaries fail in human kindness and the outcast Samaritan succeeds superbly in helping the wounded Jew" (103). With this summary Crossan has put the parable into the mold of paradox. The Good Samaritan has become, like the short versions of *The Plague* and *The Trial*, a paradoxical story effecting a reversal of expectations. And like the book of Jonah, because of outstanding literary skills, it shows not only a single but a double reversal engraved in its pattern. Jesus' parable has turned into the type of material that fits Crossan's trajectory.

Following his treatment of *The Plague*, *The Trial*, and the book of Jonah, the Good Samaritan is the fourth concrete instance of parable understood as paradoxical story, the fourth instance of the same genre. Let me recapitulate: First we have a single reversal of an expectation according to which surviving a plague is least likely for someone who washes the bodies of its victims. Then we have a single reversal of the self-evident assumption that a person should be able to go through an entrance that is particularly assigned for him. The third case is a double reversal of the traditional theme of obedient prophets and disobedient pagans. Finally, there is the double reversal of a stereotype according to which Jews are good and Samaritans bad. Through Crossan's focus on paradox the four stories have thus become homogeneous. What makes them conform is, negatively, their "meta-didacticism," a refusal to give moral guidance, and positively, a provocation of an audience's cherished and unquestioned take on things.

Subordinated or even erased for the sake of conformity is everything that exceeds the generic definition. This erasure is especially striking to me in Crossan's reading of Camus's novel. Whatever can be said about *The Plague*, the novel is surely more complicated than Crossan's focus on its paradoxical aspects makes it appear.

The Plague: A Holocaust Novel

Published two years after the end of the war, *The Plague* has been associated by many readers with the experiences of the Second World War and the Holocaust. The plague-stricken town Oran and its residents' struggle to survive have been interpreted against the background of German-occupied France and the Nazi concentration camps. Terrence Des Pres's book *The Survivor*, which was published, like *Raid*, in 1976, illustrates this interpretation. Des Pres reads *The Plague* as a testimony of twentieth-century atrocity, a fictional account of survival in extremity. Camus's novel, he writes,

> respond[s] directly to the climate of atrocity which like a leveling wind has touched and unsettled every aspect of existence in our century. [Its] vision is informed by genocide and the concentration camps, and it becomes particular through individuals caught up in events which threaten to destroy not only populations but the human spirit itself. (10)

In the context of Des Pres's book, which is mainly a reading of Holocaust testimonies, *The Plague* foreshadows the unspectacular but intrinsically ethical behavior of survivors of the death camps. Especially the self-understanding of Dr. Rieux, Camus's protagonist, who works tirelessly against the epidemics and organizes a network of volunteers, highlights for Des Pres something crucial about life in extremity. Rieux calls his efforts "a matter of common decency" (150) and thereby suggests that survival in extreme situations depends not on heroism but on the simple desire to stay human.

The *Plague* has been studied by other Holocaust scholars as well. In his 1978 book *The Age of Atrocity*, Lawrence Langer reads Camus's work as a literary response to the trauma of the Second World War. Langer is particularly concerned with the question of how atrocity imposes itself on human consciousness. Death on a massive scale, as it occurred in recent history, Langer argues, is slow to make an impact on human comprehension. As Camus lets his narrator say in *The Plague*, "[a] hundred million of corpses broadcast through history are no more than a puff of smoke" (quoted by Langer 152). Camus, according to Langer, struggles with the issue of "how to press a vital nerve of the imagination so that a dead man can be given substance and one can avoid repeating indifference" (152). By choosing the metaphor of a plague epidemic, Langer argues, Camus tried to defy the unimaginable quality of the Holocaust. "The plague is Camus's way of dramatizing for his contemporaries atrocity's influence on the normal course of human fate" (151).

More recently, in a 1992 essay called "Camus' *The Plague*, or a Monument to Witnessing," Shoshana Felman adds another dimension to the novel. She is interested in Camus because his books show how the Second World War and the Holocaust have changed the relationship between history and narrative. Specifically, Felman argues that *The Plague* exemplifies how literature has become involved in history. She writes:

> To recognize in the dramatic allegory of the epidemic the recent history of the struggle against Nazism, readers did not need to know that Camus was himself during the war a member of the French Resistance, that he edited the French underground newspaper *Combat*, and that a long extract of *The Plague* had appeared clandestinely in Occupied France in a collection of Resistance texts. But in the context of the question of the dialogue between history and narrative, it is instructive to take notice of the fact that the novel was initially produced as an underground testimony, as a verbal action of resistance which, as such, is not a simple *statement* or description of the historical conflict it narrates, but an actual intervention in this conflict. Camus' narrative intends to be not merely a historic witness, but a participant in the events it describes. (98–99)

In different ways, Des Pres, Langer, and Felman are concerned with *The Plague* in relation to "an age of atrocity." Whether the novel is said to illuminate the meaning of survival during the Holocaust, to help the human imagination to grasp massive killing, or to exemplify the involvement of literature in twentieth-century history, for all three scholars Camus's novel is relevant in light of the catastrophes in Europe in the 1940s. I have given space to these three scholars because their readings of *The Plague* stand in such sharp contrast to Crossan's dehistoricizing treatment of literature, not only *The Plague* but also his other instances of "parables," ancient or contemporary. There are certainly many ways to read a novel; Crossan's way, however, distinguishes itself by a rigid reduction to form, which turns a historically charged text such as *The Plague* into timeless paradox, a reversal of expectation.

Crossan's ahistorical notion of paradox has its costs and its gains. What is gained is a new and interesting reading of Jesus' parables. What gets lost is an understanding of the historical significance of a novel such as *The Plague*, of how its paradoxical character is a response to historical events of its time.

A Hidden Hermeneutic Promise

Yet I have reasons to suspect that Crossan's comparative vision is motivated by more than structural considerations and that twentieth-century texts such as *The Trial* or *The Plague* mean more to Crossan than the sterile paradox to which he reduces these novels. Even though the historical significance of twentieth-century texts are erased in Crossan's actual comparisons, traces of twentieth-century catastrophes do appear in Crossan's work, not as clear historical backgrounds against which to understand certain literatures but as the web of allusions that are never explicated but give Crossan's work an uncanny subtext. In the previous chapter I argued that these allusions are typical of the way the Holocaust appeared within public discourses in the mid 1970s, vaguely symbolizing twentieth-century atrocity without, however, referring to the particulars of the Nazi genocide. Beyond this broad historical consideration I want to suggest an additional and more specific reason for the appearance of such allusions in a book on New Testament parables, a reason that is linked to the nature of Crossan's project.

What prompts a New Testament scholar to do research on twentieth-century literature, to study texts by "secular" and/or Jewish writers, and to suggest affinities between those texts and Jesus' stories? Because he is thrilled by their mind-challenging qualities? Because these texts point so powerfully to the shifting grounds beyond our norms and notions? Because he wishes Jesus' discourse to be mind-challenging and postmodern as well? All of this is certainly true for Crossan. But I believe that he is attracted to these texts also because they are "contemporary," because they are historically relevant, because they speak to "the horrors of this century." I suspect that Crossan is not entirely unfamiliar with the relationships between *The Plague* and the Second World War. I believe that the novel does carry historical resonances for Crossan, resonances that he cannot or is not willing to articulate or explore but lets come in through the back door, so to speak, in the form of brief "guest appearances"—indirect hints and allusions. The texts he cites are historically charged; I would be quite surprised if Crossan wasn't aware of it. Crossan is invested in books like *The Trial*, *The Plague*, or *Cat's Cradle*—at least partly—because of the air of urgency and contemporary relevance that comes with them. Why else would he insert constant reminders of twentieth-century horrors into his text?

My suspicions shed new light on Crossan's hermeneutic premise that the teachings of Jesus "are best understood in confrontation with texts within our own world." If what matters about those texts are not only forms and functions but also their meanings as twentieth-century testimonies, the confrontation announced by Crossan implies more than finding paradoxical structures and single or double reversals. If it matters to Crossan that these texts come form "our own world," our own time, and not from some faraway place, then his premise seems to open up the possibility of confronting the parables of Jesus also with the catastrophes of our own time, the possibility of reading Jesus' parables as a response to the "climate of atrocity" in which postwar generations find themselves. Hidden in Crossan's hermeneutic premise is a promise that Jesus' sayings, like the writings of Camus or Vonnegut, can be read and understood in confrontation with twentieth-century catastrophes.

On a surface level, Crossan at no time gives such a promise, and taking him up on it might seem unjustified. But I would insist that, on another level, Crossan effectively and continuously feeds a desire to understand his project in a way he does not address.

He does this, for example, by introducing his first chapter with that emblematic double awareness that today, a hundred years after Nietzsche, there is future for laughter despite a "tragedy too great for tears." He further does it by engaging in a discussion of dark comedy, the "most contemporary facet of our comic sensibility." He does it by choosing texts like Vonnegut's *Cat's Cradle* and Wiesel's *Gates of the Forest* to make his points. He continues to do it throughout his five chapters by infusing his text with dates, names, and terms that invoke the sites of Auschwitz or Hiroshima. Each of these little reminders of twentieth-century history belies Crossan's focus on genre and encourages readers to look for relationships between his comparative project and a postwar world.

Kafka's Limitless Horrors

I want to widen my thoughts on Crossan's project by addressing one twentieth-century writer whose texts are frequently cited in New Testament scholarship. Franz Kafka does not appear only in Crossan's comparative project. Comparing Jesus' stories with Kafka's stories has become a common practice, almost a cliche within the literary study of parables—a cliche worth examining. Especially the two Kafka parables "Give It Up!" and "On Parables" have become familiar devices in the hermeneutic repertoire of parable scholars both in Germany and in the United States. Wolfgang Harnisch's use of "Give It Up!" as an illustration of the metaphorical tension in parables, discussed in chapter 3, may serve as one example. Another example comes from the American scholar Robert Funk, who, like Crossan, was a prominent proponent of the literary turn in biblical studies. In an essay entitled "Jesus and Kafka," first published in 1972, Funk experiments with the thought that Jesus is the literary precursor of Kafka.

Even on the surface, it is not hard to see why an intertextual reading of Jesus and Kafka is an attractive endeavor for some New Testament scholars. Kafka's parables are clearly not about "clear-cut messages." They discourage interpreters to find in them easy, applicable lessons. What distinguishes Kafka's parables instead are what scholars alternately call their paradoxical structure or metaphorical tension that initiates a creative process on the part of the reader. Kafka's work is challenging—"devastating," as Crossan would say—and as such has engendered a number of interesting and provocative readings of the New Testament parables. Comparisons between Jesus and Kafka helped to establish the hermeneutic argument that Jesus' parables are not didactic stories with a message but narratives that, in the words of Norman Perrin, "tease the mind into ever new perceptions of reality" (106). But is this the only appeal Kafka has for New Testament scholars? I want to demonstrate that Kafka's name in some scholarly discourses plays an additional role.

A Dark Reading of Kafka

Funk's essay "Jesus and Kafka" explores the possibility that Jesus' stories stand within the same literary traditions as the parables of Kafka. If this were the case, Funk suggests, we would have to thoroughly revise our understanding of Jesus' parables: "Does Kafka modify the way we read Jesus? . . . is Kafka one of the authentic successors to whom Jesus gives rise?" (8) These questions seem to center around the genre "parable." But in the course of his considerations Funk suggests affinities between Jesus and Kafka that in fact have nothing to do with the form of parables. "Although Kafka has nothing to say about Jesus, the two men are nevertheless related. The curious will be struck by four remarkable affinities: both men were displaced Jews; both wrote or spoke in an alien tongue . . . both anticipated a holocaust; both were makers of parables" (6).

Both Jesus and Kafka "anticipated a holocaust," Funk notes, as though he was stating the obvious. Implicit in this remark, I take it, is the equation of the Nazi genocide with the destruction of Jerusalem by the Romans in the first century. In claiming affinities between Jesus and Kafka—which for Funk, as for Crossan, is mainly a matter of form and genre—Funk, as though he couldn't help it and only for a few seconds, lets his readers know that Kafka for him is more than a maker of parables.

Kafka's name is overdetermined for Wolfgang Harnisch, too. In chapter 3 I have pointed to the rich historical texture that accompanies Harnisch's otherwise ahistorical hermeneutic discourse. Twentieth-century history appears in his text not only by way of Marie Luise Kaschnitz's poem about the returning memory of Auschwitz but also in the following footnote, attached to Kaschnitz's text: "The poem repeats *ex eventu* the horrible vision about the fate of the Jews which Franz Kafka confided with cynical self-irony in one of his letters to Milena. This connection is indicated by the motif of the drawer in Kaschnitz's poem."

Harnisch refers here to the highly disturbing paragraph that I would like to offer once more. Kafka writes to Milena Jesenska:

> I could rather reproach you for having much too good an opinion of the Jews whom you know (including myself)—there are others!—sometimes I'd like to cram them all as Jews (including myself) into the drawer of the laundry chest, then wait, then open the drawer a little, to see whether all have already suffocated, if not, to close the drawer again and go on like this to the end. (*Letters* 59)

These sentences were written in 1920. In Harnisch's reading of the letter, Kafka's image of the drawer anticipates "the fate of the Jews" during the 1930s and 1940s. Harnisch further suggests that Kaschnitz, writing in the 1960s, takes recourse to the same image when she writes about the "drawer full of emaciated Jewish heads" breaking into her German home. Like Funk, only in a more complicated and subtle way, Harnisch's footnote suggests that Kafka anticipated the Holocaust.

Let me point to the similarities between Funk's and Harnisch's comments and Crossan's web of allusions to "the horrors of this century," which I examined above. In all three cases, the historical events of the Holocaust break into an interpretive discourse by way of brief remarks that are not further explored or explained. All three authors thereby put symbols of atrocity—the piles of corpses in Auschwitz and Buchenwald, the "drawer full of emaciated Jewish heads"—in the back of their readers' minds without ever making the connection to the actual subject matter: New Testament parable interpretation. As a reader of these discourses I get a vague impression about something dark, even horrific, but I wait in vain for this impression to be taken up and brought in explicit relation to Jesus' parables. In my study of Crossan's allusions to "the horrors of this century," I have argued that Crossan's investment in the "texts within our own world" is motivated by certain hermeneutic desires that go way beyond the generic characteristics of these texts. The same can be said about some New Testament scholars' investment in Kafka.

A good starting point for explaining my claim is an essay by the German Kafka scholar Heinz Politzer entitled "Franz Kafka and Albert Camus: Parables for Our Time." Politzer's work has been an important source for biblical critics' appropriation of Kafka. Especially his study of the paradoxical quality of Kafka's work has left its traces in the studies of New Testament scholars such as Funk, Crossan, and Harnisch. What interests me in this essay is an argument implicit in its title; Kafka's writings, Politzer suggests, are "parables for our time." Focusing on two novels, one by Kafka, the other by Camus, Politzer writes:

> The fascination both *The Trial* and *The Stranger* held for the same European generation—those who were young after the Second World War—arose from the questions posed by these books rather than from any specific answers they were able to give. A multitude of conflicting answers can be found in them, for neither novel is satisfied with copying reality in simple terms. What they contain is the evidence collected by modern man in that parabolic trial which he has instituted against a world deprived of any meaning. It goes without saying that, in this trial, he cannot hope for any other verdict than the pronouncement of the paradox on which his existence is based. (57)

Politzer contextualizes the writings of Kafka (and Camus) vis-à-vis a particular time and audience. He argues that paradox, the preference of questions rather than of answers, and the rejection of a mimetic mode of writing appealed to those who were born in Europe in the 1920s and 1930s and who encountered Kafka and Camus after the war. The insistence that "the incomprehensible remains incomprehensible," Politzer further suggests, strongly resonated with the postwar situation, a situation of general disorientation where human reality had lost its old coherence—"a world deprived of any meaning," as Politzer says. Camus and Kafka were fascinating because they gave expression to this dislocation. Their novels were conceived as "parables for our time" because they seemed to offer the only appropriate way of confronting life after the war. In the trial staged against the contemporary world, as Politzer puts it, there was no "hope for any other verdict than the pronouncement of paradox."

What strikes me about this fascination is its vague nature. Politzer does not really explain the link between the events of the war and paradoxical literature. He does not specify the questions that made the writings of Kafka and Camus so compelling for those who were young after the Second World War. Neither does he specify the "evidence," contained in the works of Camus and Kafka, that has caused "modern man" to institute a parabolic trial against the world. What exactly are the crimes? Who is the plaintiff and who the accused? The following sentences are a little more concrete.

> Camus fought with the French underground against the tyranny of a totalitarian system which Kafka seems to have anticipated in his chauchemars. Camus, that is, braved in reality all those persecutions from which Kafka had suffered only in his fearful dreams, without ever being forced to experience them in their physical brutality. However devastating the German occupation of France may have been, it had its limits and it found its end. Thus the younger writer was spared the limitless horrors the older had imagined in his eschatological visions. (52)

As Politzer suggests, Kafka did not live through horrific events, as Camus did; he anticipated them. Furthermore, Politzer seems to distinguish between different events:

while Camus witnessed the *limited* horrors of life in France under Nazi occupation, Kafka's horrors were "limitless"—why exactly is not entirely clear; perhaps Politzer thinks that Kafka foresaw not only a totalitarian tyranny but genocide. In any case, Politzer's idea that Kafka was tormented by an anticipation of the "limitless horrors" about to break over Europe strongly resonates with Funk's remark and Harnisch's footnote, and I wonder whether both Funk and Harnisch inherited the notion of Kafka's Holocaust visions from Politzer.

In his book *Foregone Conclusions* Michael Bernstein critically addresses the connection between Kafka and the Holocaust. Kafka as a Holocaust prophet, Bernstein says, is a powerful notion, which however fails to meet basic requirements of historical scrutiny. In regard to the passage from Politzer just quoted, Bernstein would point out that it is entirely unrealistic to think that Kafka, who died in 1924, could have anticipated, in some kind of eschatological vision, the extent of the Nazi assault and its "limitless horrors." According to Bernstein,

> it is actually the critics themselves who, encountering Kafka in the aftermath of the Shoah, have become prophets-after-the-fact and have found themselves unable to read stories like "The Penal Colony" without thinking of the concentration camps. But because of a lingering suspicion that something is seriously awry about interpreting a fictional text in this way, they have retroactively made Kafka into a prophet foreseeing the bestiality that they, not he, know occurred. (21)

Such questionable interpretations arise, Bernstein suggests, because in the face of evil as enormous as the Holocaust "there is a general freezing up of normal intellectual discriminations" (19). At the same time, such narratives contain "disturbing 'pleasures'. . . . [They] derive their energy from—and hence transport their audience to—an emotional register whose intensity supposedly places it beyond moral discriminations" (19).[1] In a post-Holocaust time it is probably impossible to read Kafka's letter to Milena without thinking about the Nazi killing machinery. Harnisch's suggestion that the letter expresses a "horrible vision" that reappeared in a postwar poem about the Holocaust, is therefore very persuasive. And yet, against Harnisch, Bernstein would point out the importance of trying to understand Kafka's sentences in their own historical situation, a situation marked by anti-Semitism and the difficulties of assimilation but where no one possibly could have foreseen the murder of millions.

Funk's comment that both Jesus and Kafka "anticipated a Holocaust" is a variation of the rhetoric around Kafka that is criticized by Bernstein for its lack of historical foundation and for the "disturbing 'pleasures'" it arouses at the cost of intellectual clarity. At stake in such ideas, as Bernstein suggests, is a certain fascination with horror that arises when that horror is not really looked at but functions as a kind of background for reading practices. The Holocaust as a reference point for reading Kafka is potentially energizing as it gives that reading an air of urgency and makes it disturbing and fascinating at the same time. This fascination, however, depends on keeping the Holocaust in the background so that its enormity is felt rather than known; its details and actualities vaguely sensed but never explicated.[2]

It seems to me that such fascination with horror is operative in Crossan's *Raid on the Articulate*, where, as I wrote earlier, the Holocaust continuously lurked under the surface without ever coming to the front. Bernstein's work furthermore suggests that the allusive practices I found in the work of Crossan, Funk, and Harnisch are effective not despite the fact but precisely because of the fact that they are not explicated, because they are in the background, because they are at the margins and not at the center. Funk's and Harnisch's work on Jesus and Kafka, like *Raid on the Articulate*, is energized by the Holocaust. Funk's brief suggestion that both Jesus and Kafka "anticipated a holocaust" sticks, if not with the author, at least with this reader and gives Funk's central hermeneutic questions a hidden meaning. "Does Kafka modify the way we read Jesus?" Funk asks and seems to be interested in purely "literary" issues. But beyond this explicit question I hear another one, which may or may not be on the conscious level of Funk's discourse: Does Kafka—and the limitless horrors he anticipated—modify the way we read Jesus? Do Kafka's visions change our understanding of Jesus' parables?

Harnisch's hermeneutic discourse is animated by the Holocaust as well. In my earlier discussion I have called Kaschnitz's Holocaust poem a ghost in Harnisch's book, and I think I know what the haunting is about. In combination with "Kafka's horrible vision about the fate of the Jews," Harnisch's choice of Kaschnitz's poem reveals a desire to have the parables of Jesus speak to this horrible legacy. Beneath the surface of Harnisch's investigation I detect a hermeneutic endeavor to show how the New Testament parables can continue to be meaningful in a situation marked by the countless dead Jews in Kaschnitz's home and in Kafka's dreams, the wish that these pivotal texts of the Christian canon are still relevant after Auschwitz, the wish to have in Jesus' stories "parables for our time."

This desire is a legitimate and important one. The wish to relate one's own religious tradition to contemporary catastrophe is perhaps the hermeneutic impulse par excellence. The problem with Harnisch's work, and with those other participants in the literary turn in biblical studies, Crossan and Funk, is that this desire is neither acknowledged nor explored. As critical revisions of Joachim Jeremias's rigid historical-critical take on the parables, as attempts to break through the isolation between biblical text and contemporary context, these literary readings of the parables both failed and succeeded. They were successful in so far as they moved the parables from their first historical setting into "our own world," into the context of twentieth-century literature. But they were failures because the historical meanings of these literatures remained in the background only, as guests or ghosts, held in check through concentration on "literary" issues. The journey of literary critics of the parables was a return into history, and it opened up the possibility of confronting the legacy of the Holocaust, of thinking about how the parables of Jesus can be read in light of this legacy. But instead of seizing this opportunity, the journey got sidetracked on the way by a preoccupation with the timeless themes of metaphor and paradox.

PART IV

THE PROMISE OF
METAPHOR THEORY

10

Paul Ricoeur's "Biblical Hermeneutics"

> The [parables'] "form" secures the survival of the meaning after the disappearance of its *Sitz im Leben* and in that way starts the process of "decontextualization" which opens the message to fresh reinterpretation according to new contexts of discourse and of life.
>
> (Paul Ricoeur, "Biblical Hermeneutics")

The literary turn in biblical studies of the 1970s produced a variety of experimental readings of the parables of Jesus, all of which were understood in one way or another as alternatives to Joachim Jeremias's historical-critical paradigm. I have discussed one such experiment: John Dominic Crossan's intertextual readings of the parables and twentieth-century literature. These readings, I have shown, are based on a hermeneutic model that prevents an actual confrontation of Jesus' stories with twentieth-century history.

I now turn to another protagonist of the literary turn in biblical studies who offered a different hermeneutic model, the famous French philosopher Paul Ricoeur. Up to this day Ricoeur's wide-ranging work informs Christian theology and religious and biblical studies.[1] Perhaps Ricoeur's most profound impact on biblical studies took place in 1975 when his essay "Biblical Hermeneutics" was published. In sum, the essay develops a detailed theory of the act of parable interpretation and is centered on Ricoeur's understanding of the metaphorical process that characterizes Jesus' parables. After 1975 Ricoeur's hermeneutics was taken up, interpreted, and applied by many biblical critics in the United States and in Europe, among them Wolfgang Harnisch in Germany.

What interests me in Ricoeur's essay is a hermeneutic thought that stands in contrast not only to Jeremias's historical criticism but to Crossan's work as well. In my opening quotation for this chapter, Ricoeur argues that the form or genre of the parables moves them out of their first historical setting, their Sitz im Leben. The same was argued by Crossan. But instead of taking the form or genre of the parables to be a fixed entity that remains the same across the centuries, Ricoeur suggests that it initiates a dynamic process that moves the parables also back into a second-, a third-, a twentieth-century historical setting. A parable's context, for Ricoeur, is not the timeless realm of world literature. Ricoeur reckons with a process that "opens up the message to fresh reinterpretations according to new contexts of discourse and of life." With every new act of parable interpretation, Ricoeur suggests, the context changes according to the time and place of the interpreter.

If the interpretive process theorized by Ricoeur leads to "fresh reinterpretations according to new contexts of discourse and of life," would it not be possible to interpret parables also in relation to a context marked by Holocaust memories? Ricoeur's thought seems to open up the possibility of a post-Holocaust hermeneutics of Jesus' parables. In the remaining chapters I will examine this suggestion.

This chapter introduces Ricoeur's essay as a part of the literary turn in biblical studies. I want to clarify Ricoeur's eminent role in the American endeavor of the 1970s to reconfigure the parables of Jesus as pieces of poetry. I also want to lay out the major arguments and themes of Ricoeur's hermeneutics in order to set up my critical discussion of his work in chapter 11.

A Comprehensive Theory of Interpretation

Introducing Paul Ricoeur

In 1975, Paul Ricoeur's "Biblical Hermeneutics" appeared in the fourth issue of *Semeia*, an "experimental journal" that served as a major site for the new American studies of biblical texts, parables in particular (see chapter 7). One of the interesting aspects of this publication is Paul Ricoeur's status as a scholar. While most of the scholars engaged in the literary turn were trained in traditional New Testament studies, Ricoeur represented the voice of a scholar from outside the field. Ricoeur clarifies his position somewhat modestly in the beginning of the essay: "As I am neither an exegete nor a theologian, I shall try to make a contribution to the discussion appropriate to my relative competence in the field of the philosophy of language" (29). This "relative competence" was very much appreciated by the editors of *Semeia*. Not only did they devote an entire issue to Ricoeur, they also chose to publish "Biblical Hermeneutics" together with a nineteen-page overview of Ricoeur's work in general. This overview introduced the reader of *Semeia* to the development of Ricoeur's thought from the late 1940s to the early 1970s, a time period during which Ricoeur was engaged in areas such as the history of philosophy and the philosophy of interpretation (Dornisch 1–2).

In 1967 Ricoeur published *The Symbolism of Evil*, a book that would also inform New Testament scholars because it offered a detailed theory of symbols in relation to ancient literatures.[2] In the early 1970s Ricoeur moved from symbol to metaphor and wrote his elaborated book *The Rule of Metaphor*. At that time, metaphors had already started to attract the interest of biblical scholars. The *Semeia* publication of "Biblical Hermeneutics" can be seen as a result of this intersecting research. It presents Ricoeur's attempt to make his own insights into the nature of metaphor fruitful for an understanding of the parables of Jesus. But "Biblical Hermeneutics," as the title indicates, is more than that. What made this text special and valuable for contemporary scholars was its integrative force. In the words of Loretta Dornisch's introductory essay, Ricoeur's work promised to open "the possibility of a comprehensive theory of interpretation" (17). Dornisch goes on: "[Ricoeur's] contribution to modern scholarship and to biblical interpretation will be unique and overwhelming in its implications. It will then be possible to unite the diverse sub-disciplines or thrusts now present within biblical interpretation, for example, the differing insights on the parables of Funk, Perrin, Via, or Crossan" (17–18).

"Biblical Hermeneutics" is designed to meet Dornisch's hopes. With an authoritative tone and on a fairly theoretical level Ricoeur leads his readers from a complex discussion of structuralist approaches to a thorough definition of "metaphor." Subsequently, he moves from a definition of the parables' metaphorical function to a discussion of their specificity as religious discourse and of the hermeneutic task that faces this kind of discourse. Throughout the essay, Ricoeur engages in discussions of Jeremias's historical-critical work and the new American projects. By doing this, he corrects interpretive mistakes committed by American scholars whose literary explorations had been undertheorized; and he also discusses and emphasizes the limitations of historical criticism within the context of a comprehensive interpretative theory. "Biblical Hermeneutics," in sum, is an expert hermeneut's effort at theoretically grounding the American endeavor and elevating the notion of the parable as metaphor to a sophisticated level.

Strikingly, Ricoeur hardly engages with the parables themselves. Apart from scattered and brief references to the parables, he does not apply his theoretical approach to the stories of Jesus. What Ricoeur offers is a theory for parable interpretation; he does not interpret a single parable.

Expert Talking

"Biblical Hermeneutics" starts by discussing the role and validity of structuralist analysis for parable research. Ricoeur points to several naive assumptions among biblical scholars regarding a proper "literary" approach to the parables (64). He specifically addresses Dan O. Via's attempt to link a structuralist analysis of the parables, without further ado, to historical-critical and existential interpretations.[3] Things are more complicated, says Ricoeur. For one, structuralism is antihistorical in nature and precludes the diachronic approach of historical criticism. Second—and this is Ricoeur's actual concern—structuralism is not interested in the meaning or message of a text.[4] Instead, it treats texts as codes, as systems of signs, which can be analyzed formally but not interpreted. The connection between a structuralist analysis and an existential interpretation therefore "calls for a distinctive kind of justification and cannot be simply taken for granted" (30). The relation between form and meaning (or code and message) is problematic, and the move from one to the other needs to be theorized.

The structuralist approach, which treats parables as systems of signs, is valid, Ricoeur argues, as a temporary strategy. Investigating the rules that govern the story of a parable can be a helpful step in the process of interpretation, as long as one does not buy into structuralist ideology. As long as one does not turn the antihermeneutical stance into a hermeneutical thesis, the structuralist method can and should serve as a formal explanation. Such an explanation of the parables is valid, even necessary, to the extent that the parables are indeed codifications; they are produced, "encoded," into a specific mode of discourse, namely, the specific literary genre of parables. This literary genre, however, is only a means to produce a message, and it is the message that represents the true interest of hermeneutics. The investigation of the genre needs to serve the interpretive quest for meaning. The parables are not only systems of signs; they also are articulations of our experience in the world.[5] How exactly this articulation comes about is the question Ricoeur tries to answer in the remaining parts of his essay.

In order to move from structuralist explanation to existential interpretation, Ricoeur says, he needs to make a detour through what he calls the metaphoric process by which the inner sense of a parable is "transferred" to an outer reference. By this he means that something in the parables functions in the way of metaphors; and because of this metaphorical function, the parables are not closed upon themselves—mere stories—but open toward the world. That is, they say something about reality. How is this the case? As a first step to answer this question, Ricoeur recapitulates the basic arguments of his metaphor theory.

For Ricoeur, a metaphor concerns not a single word but a whole sentence. Rather than speaking about "metaphor," one should speak about "metaphorical sentences." A metaphorical statement is a predication that brings together two words that stand in tension with each other. This tension produces a "semantic innovation." With the idea of a semantic innovation Ricoeur draws on the structuralist understanding of the polysemic nature of language. Language is polysemic in so far as single words can take on different meanings. These are the meanings that can be found in a dictionary. Ricoeur emphasizes the fact that the polysemic aspects of a word can increase continuously; a word can always gain additional meanings. Ricoeur calls this fact the cumulative capacity of language. "Normal" discourse reduces the polysemy of words in order to produce clear, unambivalent meaning. The opposite is the case with metaphors. A metaphorical statement activates all the potential meanings of a word *plus one*. Metaphor exploits polysemy in a creative way by bringing two words together that, according to their lexicalized meaning, do not go together. This procedure disturbs the order of discourse and produces a "semantic impertinence."

This "semantic impertinence" can initiate a creative process. A person confronted with the tension between two words may make sense of the statement on a level other than the literal level of lexicalized meaning. He or she may make "the words undergo a sort of labor of meaning, a twist by which the metaphorical statement obtains its meaning" (78). When the reader perceives some other, a new pertinence that is outside the common language system, meaning is created; a "semantic innovation" takes place. Although this innovation happens through interaction on the level of the sentence, it also has an effect on the word: as a result of the new pertinence, the word accumulates a meaning it did not have before, a meaning that violates the order of the code.[6] When a particular metaphorical statement becomes trivial, this new meaning enters the established language code and, eventually, the dictionary. Ricoeur calls this kind of metaphor a "dead" metaphor. "Living" metaphors, in contrast, cannot be found in dictionaries.

An important factor in the creative process initiated by living metaphors is resemblance. In the old rhetorical tradition, resemblance was always conceived as the basis for constructing metaphors: because one thing looks like another, its name can serve as a metaphor for the other thing. According to Ricoeur, however, resemblance plays a much more complicated role in the metaphorical process. A reader confronted with the semantic impertinence presented by a metaphorical statement may discover a resemblance between things that he or she has not perceived before. By seeing this new resemblance, the reader reduces the gap between two incompatible ideas and discloses a hitherto unnoticed relation of meaning: "What is at stake in a metaphorical statement is making 'kinship' appear where ordinary vision perceives no mutual appropriateness at all" (78–79). In this sense, Ricoeur agrees with Aristotle's dictum that "'to make good metaphors is to perceive likenesses'" (79).

The role of resemblance is a crucial aspect in Ricouer's argument because it suggests that the new meaning created by metaphors does not exist in language only but affects reality. By making a new kinship appear, metaphors tell us something new about the world. At this point, Ricoeur argues against a common assumption among literary theorists that poetic language is self-referential and suspends the ordinary referential dimension of language. Ricoeur does not exactly deny this, but he suggests that the destruction of the first-degree reference is the condition of a second-degree reference peculiar to poetic discourse and, consequently, to metaphor. From the newly perceived resemblance, from the sudden proximity of things that were distant before, Ricoeur argues, "a new vision of reality springs up, one which is resisted by ordinary vision tied to the ordinary use of words" (84). Ricoeur takes recourse to Max Black's notion of the heuristic power of scientific models. Models, at least in their theoretical versions, are scientific fictions that redescribe reality in ways that go beyond the normal vision of things. "To describe a domain of reality in terms of an imaginary theoretical model is a certain manner of seeing things 'otherwise,' by changing our language on the subject of these things" (85). Similarly, metaphors reach reality through a detour. The collapse of the literal or ordinary reference gives way to a centripetal movement: metaphors redescribe reality, they reveal new dimensions of our world and our experience.[7]

Extravagance, Limits, and Disclosures

Like metaphors, Ricoeur goes on to argue, the parables of Jesus redesribe reality and reveal new dimensions of our world and our experience. As it turns out, this argument is a complicated one. Applying the themes of his theory of metaphor to the parables of Jesus is not an easy project because at stake are no longer statements but entire narratives. How does the metaphorical process function in a story?

First of all, Ricoeur points to several important differences between metaphors and parables. While metaphors are located on the level of the sentence, parables are located on the level of composition, of a work. Metaphors are transient events of discourse. They last only as long as the tension between the two terms is perceived. As soon as they are taken for granted they enter into the established language system. Then they cease to be metaphors in the proper sense and turn into dead metaphors. This instantaneous existence does not seem to be true for parables. Even though the stories of Jesus are old and well known, they do not seem to die through habitual usage. This suggests that parables are characterized by some other kind of tension than that of metaphors. In fact, Ricoeur emphasizes that the metaphorical tension in a parable does not lie between single words or sentences. Where does it lie then? The tension, Ricoeur claims, is carried by the narrative as a whole. It exists between everyday life and what the story narrates, between reality as described and as redescribed. "The 'tension' is entirely on the side of the vision of reality between the insight displayed by the fiction and our ordinary way of looking at things" (95–96).

Instead of pursuing or exemplifying this line of thought, Ricoeur changes perspectives and asks the following question: what are the clues that cause readers and listeners of the parables to search for a referent in human experience? Do we just assume that a parable must have a point, because without a point the story would be trivial? Perhaps. Perhaps the main cause for the transfer from narrative to reality cannot be found in isolated parables but only in the parables taken together. At one point Ricoeur suggests that the main clues for metaphorical interpretation are given in the tension between the parables and other texts within the gospel. But Ricoeur makes a further suggestion. The parables, he says, are often characterized by strange traits that disturb their apparent realism. The everyday life settings of the parables are frequently interrupted by exaggerations, surprising developments, and improbabilities. Ricoeur calls this trait the "extravagance" of the parables of Jesus. And it may be this "extravagance"—"the presence of the extraordinary within the ordinary" (99)—which irritates listeners in such a way that they search for a meaning outside of the parameters of the narrative.

Let me interfere here for a moment. At this point in his discussion, Ricoeur's argument about the metaphorical tension of parables becomes diffuse. Especially since he does not provide any concrete examples, his discussion reaches a level of abstraction that makes it hard to follow. Where does the metaphorical tension lie? Does the tension lie between two versions of reality grafted in the narrative itself—a realistic story and an improbable story suggested by the improbable traits in the parable? Or is the tension between the narrative's surprising take on things and our normal ways of looking? But then, whose view is the normal view; how is it situated in time and place? Or is it useless to ask these questions, because the real tension, as Ricoeur suggests as well, lies within the contextual background of the parables?[8] In any case, one question remains, namely, how exactly can we imagine the transfer from a concrete story—such as the parable of the Wicked Husbandmen—to a new vision of reality.

The notion of a new vision, or the "referent" of the parables, according to Ricoeur's technical term, is the theme of the last part of "Biblical Hermeneutics." If it is true that the parables are more than systems of signs, that they are not just self-referential but have the power to redescribe reality, what kind of "reality" is at stake? The referent of the parables, Ricoeur shows, has something to do with the religious quality of the parables' language. Parables are *poetic* discourse insofar as they have the power to redescribe reality. But they are also *religious* discourse insofar as they have the special power to disclose a special referent. The preliminary task thus is to define the parables of Jesus as a religious kind of poetic discourse.

Here, again, Ricoeur takes recourse to the notion of extravagance. Their surprising, outlandish, excessive, and eccentric traits, Ricoeur argues, constitute the religious moment of the parables. They are a religious kind of poetic discourse in so far as they transgress, by means of their extravagance, traditional forms of parabolic discourse. With Jesus' stories, the ordinary and established language of the Jewish tradition is taken to its limits, or, as Ricoeur also would say, "is carried to the extreme" (122).[9] At last, Ricoeur offers some examples:

> Consider the extravagance of the landlord in the "Parable of the Wicked Husbandmen," who after having sent his servants, sends his son. What Palestinian property owner living abroad would be foolish enough to act like this landlord? . . . What employer would pay the employees of the eleventh hour the same wages as those hired first? (115)

What Ricouer highlights here is something that Jülicher and Jeremias ignored. For the two German historical critics it was important to emphasize the realism of the parables. Jeremias, for instance, had to envision the rebellious behavior of the "wicked husbandmen" as a realistic incident in first-century Palestine; he had to explain the murder of the son as a necessary factor in the climax of the story, and he did not find anything surprising in the behavior of the landlord. A parable needs to be realistic and convincing in order to fulfill the function Jülicher had assigned to the parables and Jeremias by and large had adopted: to clarify or illustrate a certain subject matter to an audience.[10] For Ricoeur, the function of the parables is no longer "clarification" or "illustration" but to disclose a referent that cannot be articulated in any other way than through the parable.

In fact, Ricoeur proposes that parables, as Jülicher had defined them, in their two-part structure of Bild and Sache, represent precisely the traditional form of language that actually has been transgressed by the parables of Jesus. "Can we not say, with some plausibility, that . . . the parable[s] treated as an illustration of general ethical truths within an exemplary and moralizing use still function as "Picture models," and that it is only when these forms of discourse are carried to an extreme that they exercise the power of 'disclosure'?" (125)

This special power of disclosure, according to Ricoeur, characterizes not only the parables but other sayings of Jesus as well. Jesus' proclamatory, proverbial, and parabolic sayings all show a typical procedure, a kind of intensification or transgression, a bringing-to-the-limit of an already constituted language. The sayings of Jesus are what Ricoeur terms "limit-expressions" under whose pressure traditional forms of discourse are shattered.

Now that the religious moment of the parables is defined—what do these "limit-expressions" redescribe? What is their referent? As a first answer to this question Ricoeur considers the formula "the Kingdom of God." This expression, by which many parables are introduced, seems to be the common referent of the sayings of Jesus. However, Ricoeur emphasizes that "the Kingdom of God" is merely a symbol that qualifies the parables in a certain way but should not be identified with their ultimate referent. The ultimate referent does not lie in some transcendent sphere but concerns a dimension of our own experience.[11] The extremity of religious language indicates an extremity on the side of human reality. As limit-expressions, Ricoeur claims, the parables disclose a corresponding aspect of human experience: limit-experiences. The parables redescribe human reality in its extreme. With reference to the philosophy of Karl Jaspers, Ricoeur suggests that the ultimate referent of the parables are experiences of limit- or boundary-situations:

> The human condition as such includes experiences which baffle discourse and *praxis*. Jaspers names death, suffering, guilt, and hatred as examples. But it is not just experiences of distress that have this power of rupture; culminatory experiences—"peak experiences"—especially experiences of creation and joy . . . are no less extreme than are the experiences of catastrophe. (128)

The "deciphering" of these limit-experiences, Ricoeur concludes, is the hermeneutical task in its broadest, but also most accurate, sense.

A Post-Jeremian Discourse

Ricoeur's essay lays the groundwork for a powerful alternative to Joachim Jeremias's historical criticism. In contrast to John Dominic Crossan, who claims and enacts his hermeneutic disagreement with Jeremias but never theoretically reflects on it, Ricoeur offers a detailed hermeneutic argument.[12] Ricoeur's theory of discourse invalidates

Jeremias's interpretive premise that the meaning of a parable today equals the meaning it had when it was told by Jesus. Parables, as discourse, undergo a "distanciation" in regard to their author, their original communicative situations, and their first audience. They gain autonomy from their "first historical setting" by being written down and subsequently by being read and communicated—actualized, as Ricoeur says—in ever-new situations.[13]

A parable thus is not to be subjected to the rule of its original context: "To say with Jeremias that the parables were intended initially as a vindication of Jesus' behavior and a 'defense of the Good News' is a way of limiting their 'application' to the situation of Jesus" (134). Against this reduction Ricoeur wants to keep open "the horizon for reinterpretation appropriate to new times and new places" (135).[14] This insistence characterizes Ricoeur's proposal for parable research as genuinely hermeneutic in Hans-Georg Gadamer's sense. Whereas Jeremias's reconstructions of the original meaning of the parables is what Gadamer considers a methodological reduction of the task of interpretation, Ricoeur turns parable interpretation into hermeneutics, properly speaking, by integrating our own situation, our own Sitz im Leben, into the interpreter's scope.

However, despite such decisive steps beyond Jeremias, there is one striking continuity between Ricoeur's "Biblical Hermeneutics" and Jeremias's *The Parables of Jesus* that needs to be addressed as well. Inconspicuously, Ricoeur has adopted a typical anti-Judaic procedure of Christian New Testament scholarship. In chapter 4 I discussed Jeremias's strategy of contrasting Jesus' parables with rabbinical material. The result was a frequent degradation of the latter. Jeremias found the rabbinical parables to be inferior in their literary quality and called them less clear and simple than the parables of Jesus. Or he suggested that the Rabbis in their parables expressed an inferior theology, one that was based on the Law instead of God's grace. Ricoeur, too, addresses the Jewish tradition and suggests a contrast between that tradition and Jesus' parables. Jewish parables, to put it simply, illustrate general ethical truths, whereas the parables of Jesus, by transgressing the traditional Jewish form of parables, "exercise the power of 'disclosure.'" This argument is not a blatant degradation. There is nothing wrong with illustrations of ethical truths. But of course, in the context of Ricoeur's work, and in the context of the American endeavor of the 1970s in general, "illustrations of ethical truths" have come in the shadow of another kind of parabolic language, namely, the kind of language capable of disclosing a new vision of reality. There lies a hierarchy in the binary between "picture model" and "disclosure model."

What might be more blatant is the fact that, on the basis of such binary opposition, Ricoeur defines the religious quality of the parables of Jesus. The moment of transgression, according to Ricoeur, not only alters the function and form of the Jesus parables but also makes them "religious discourse." For readers who are sensitivized to the problem of Christian anti-Judaism, this argument has odd implications. Is Ricoeur suggesting that Jewish parables at the time of Jesus lacked religious quality? Is Ricoeur suggesting that with Jesus the religious potential, the disclosive power, of parables is actualized?

The anti-Judaic undertones of Ricoeur's essay characterize the "American endeavor" of the 1970s more generally. They have come to the front, for example, in John Dominic Crossan's work on the parables, and I have discussed and historicized this problematic continuity to the work of Jeremias in chapter 8. Like *Raid on the Articulate*, "Biblical Hermeneutics" was published at a time before the legacy of anti-Judaism became a concern strong enough for some biblical scholars to change their treatment of ancient Jewish texts. Writing in the mid-1970s, Ricoeur shares the failure of his American colleagues to detect and/or take seriously the blind spots in Joachim Jeremias's work.

In the following, however, I wish to focus on those aspects in Ricoeur's essay that distinguish it from Jeremias's discourse: the genuinely hermeneutic character of Ricoeur's work and its claim that the parables of Jesus articulate "limit-experiences of human life." This claim, I want to argue, makes "Biblical Hermeneutics" an important instance of post-Holocaust biblical scholarship.

11

Limit-Experiences of Human Life

What Are Limit-Experiences of Human Life?

Ever since I encountered "Biblical Hermeneutics" I have been both intrigued and puzzled by the idea of human limit-experiences as the ultimate referent of the parables of Jesus. What keeps attracting my attention is particularly Ricoeur's suggestion that the parables are somehow pertinent to experiences of "death, suffering, guilt, and hatred." This is a remarkable and unique notion within the history of parable interpretation. Nowhere else to my knowledge are Jesus' stories said to express experiences of "catastrophe" or "distress" that belong to the "human condition as such" (128). It is true that Joachim Jeremias placed many parables in a situation of crisis; parables such as that of The Wicked Husbandmen were spoken, he said, "in view of catastrophe." But Jeremias understood this crisis to be a first-century crisis. When Ricoeur speaks of experiences of catastrophe he is interested in something that belongs to human life not only at the time of Jesus. Ricoeur emphasizes: "To speak of a limit-experience is to speak of our experience" (127).[1]

But I also wonder what exactly Ricoeur has in mind when he speaks of "limit-experiences" in relation to the parables of Jesus. Where would Ricoeur find the extreme aspects of human life in our time? Given his argument that the parables' message is open to "fresh reinterpretation according to new contexts of discourse and of life" (71)—how would Ricoeur describe such "new contexts"? Since Ricoeur does not exemplify his interpretive theory on the basis of a concrete parable interpretation, the parables' disclosive power remains an evocative but vague notion in his essay.

"Facts of Evil"

"Experiences of distress and catastrophe" will evoke all kinds of memories, depending on a reader's "context of discourse and of life." While Ricoeur gives us no clues about the kinds of experiences he would associate with "death, suffering, guilt, and hatred," the author from whom he borrows the phrase is more explicit. For Karl Jaspers the idea of limit-situations has Holocaust resonances.

Jaspers first developed his notion of limit-situation in the second volume of his *Philosophy*. In contrast to "situations" that always change and are contingent and historically unique, Jaspers defines boundary-situations as

> situations like the following: that I am always in situations; that I cannot live without struggling and suffering; that I cannot avoid guilt; that I must die—these are what I call boundary situations. They *never change*, except in appearance. There is no way to survey them in existence, no way to see anything behind them. They are like a wall we run into, a wall on which we founder. (178)

Boundary-situations, according to Jaspers, characterize human existence whether we are aware of them or not. Death, suffering, guilt, and hatred belong fundamentally and inevitably to human existence. When Ricoeur speaks of human limit-experiences, I conclude, he is informed by a philosophical discourse more concerned with the foundations than with the historical contingencies of "our experiences." Limit-experiences belong to "the human condition as such," as Ricoeur writes.

Jaspers's *Philosophy* was first published in 1932. Three decades later the notion of limit-situation reappeared in his 1962 book *Philosophical Faith and Revelation*, a work that attempts to distinguish Jaspers's own existential way of thinking in critical interaction with twentieth-century dialectic theology. In a central part of this work, Jaspers discusses how religious language, what he calls "chiffre," is able to illuminate (*erhellen*) human existence, particularly the limit-situations of disaster and evil (*Das Unheil und das Böse*).

During this discussion, Jaspers offers concrete examples of such limit-situations. He starts his contemplations with a series of "facts" (*Tatbestände*) that illustrate disaster and evil in history. Human beings have always done violence to each other, Jaspers says and mentions human sacrifice, the Inquisition, the cruelties in wartime beyond political reason, and the murder of millions of people by totalitarian systems. And then he writes:

> Under the régime that ruled in Germany from 1933 to 1945 Jewish children were torn from their mothers' arms, exposed to the agonizing fear of death, and killed only after a time of hunger and torment. An occasional delight in cruelty and a more frequent obedience in looking the other way—"Orders are Orders"—showed how men could turn into imagination-free, thoughtlessly functioning "operators" of an extermination machinery that went from arrest to transport to the actual killing. There would be no end to a description of the horrors that fill human history and strike us as unprecedented only where we personally witnessed them or knew about them, and thus came to share the guilt. (205)

Holocaust experiences exemplify here the "facts of evil" that constitute human life in general. It is true that Jaspers integrates the German "extermination machinery" into a long history of human cruelty. But he also suggests that for those who witness an evil such as the crimes committed under the Nazi regime, this particular evil is experienced like an "unprecedented horror" (*nie dagewesenes Entsetzen*). Especially in light of Jaspers's postwar contemplations in *The Question of German Guilt*, I surmise that in writing about those who witnessed evil, who knew about it and therefore became guilty, Jaspers refers also to himself. Notwithstanding his global approach to "disaster and evil," for Jaspers, writing in the 1960s, the Holocaust is at the center of contemporary actualizations of limit-situations.[2]

A decade later Ricoeur borrows Jaspers's notion of limit-situations in his essay on parable hermeneutics:

> I would like here to relate the concept of limit-experience, as elaborated under the rubric of the referent of limit-language, to a similar concept issuing from the philosophy of Karl Jaspers, that of limit-situation or boundary-situation. The human condition as such includes experiences which baffle discourse and *praxis*. Jaspers names death, suffering, guilt, and hatred as examples. (128)

In Ricoeur's appropriation of Jaspers' discourse the notion of limit-situation seems to refer to a timeless aspect of the human condition. However, it is critical to recognize that at the time Ricoeur wrote his essay the idea of the limit-situation had already accumulated particular post-Holocaust meanings, at least for Jaspers himself. Regardless of how Ricoeur understands his own interpretive claims, his limit-language, as a continuation of Jaspers's existential discourse, is not entirely ahistorical. It carries with it twentieth-century resonances. And I do wonder: if Ricoeur were to give examples of limit-situations of "disaster of evil," as Jaspers did, what kinds of examples would he choose? Where does Ricoeur find limit-experiences in his own context, and how exactly would he theorize a hermeneutic link to the parables of Jesus?

Limit-Rhetoric

Jaspers's examples of "the facts of evil" can bring into view a particular trajectory of terms like "limit-situation" or "limit-experience" beyond the discourse of existentialism. After the war notions like the ones used by Ricoeur in relation to the parables appeared in numerous writings on the Holocaust as a way to qualify the events under discussion. Survivors of the camps have frequently taken recourse to words such as "limit" or "extreme" in order to talk about their experiences. Tadeusz Borowski called his Auschwitz stories "a voyage to the limit of a particular experience." Jean Améry talked about the reality of the camps that brought his mind to its limits. In the 1970s, limit-terminology appeared in literary studies of Holocaust testimonies as part of the vocabulary with which interpreters like Terrence Des Pres and Lawrence Langer tried to read and discuss the growing literature coming out of the Nazi camps. In more recent studies, the notion of the limit has become a crucial epistemological and moral category with which scholars point to the difficulties of representing the Holocaust. In the introduction to his book *The Limits of Representation*, Saul Friedlander writes: "What turns the 'Final Solution' into an event at the limits is the very fact that it is the most radical form of genocide encountered in history" (3).

Limit-terminology has different meanings and connotations in these different Holocaust writings, but in all of them it functions as a kind of highlighting technique. What these writings share is what I would like to call "limit-rhetoric," language that serves to qualify the thing at stake as extraordinary or exceptional, as something "much more severe or unusual than you would expect" (Pons Dictionary 502). What does it mean that a similar rhetoric appears in Ricoeur's hermeneutic discussion of New Testament parable interpretation? What does it mean to deploy limit-terminology, which has become such a central rhetorical device in Holocaust studies, in relation to the parables of Jesus?

In order to explore these questions I would like to take a closer look at limit-rhetoric as it has been used in relation not only to the parables but to Holocaust testimonies as well. Des Pres's book *The Survivor: An Anatomy of Life in the Death Camps* powerfully illustrates the meaning and function of limit-rhetoric in American Holocaust studies at a particular moment in time; the book was published in 1976, one year after Ricoeur's "Biblical Hermeneutics" came out. This temporal coincidence is linked to another one: if Ricoeur participated in the literary turn in biblical studies, Des Pres was a proponent of a similar turn in Holocaust studies that took place in the 1970s. Writing from the perspective of a scholar of English literature, Des Pres offered one of the first literary studies of Holocaust testimonies and thereby changed the discursive rules of the discipline—not unlike the way Ricoeur helped to change rules in biblical studies.

Despite their different academic contexts, Des Pres's book and Ricoeur's essay emerged within the same cultural climate and were written for audiences whose Holocaust consciousness was characteristic of America in the mid-1970s. Comparing the two texts will therefore enable me to analyze Ricoeur's limit-rhetoric not only in general but in relation to a particular post-Holocaust point in time.[3]

Limit-Rhetoric and Holocaust Experiences

Life in Extremity

"To date," Des Pres writes in *The Survivor*, "serious study of the concentration-camp experience has been done almost exclusively from the psychoanalytic point of view" (155). Des Pres uses limit-rhetoric to challenge this point of view. Throughout his book Des Pres fights against what he perceives to be a degrading image of survivors that was painted in a range of psychoanalytic studies that dominated the postwar research on the Nazi camps.[4] According to these studies, the psychic developments of concentration camp inmates were characterized by "infantilism" and "regression." Focused on their bodily needs and depending on the camp guards' willingness to fulfill them, camp prisoners allegedly reverted to a childlike state of mind: they became submissive and self-centered. Whoever survived the camps, according to psychoanalytic studies, survived them only by means of ruthless selfishness and at the expense of others.

Des Pres passionately refutes this theory. In order to understand the experiences of survivors, he emphasizes, one needs to carefully consider the *extreme* conditions that were set up and maintained by the Nazis. Des Pres takes pains to describe the terrible details of daily life to which camp inmates were subjected. He includes testimonies of the cold, of physical pain, of the lack of clothing, of malnutrition, of the systematic exposure to human excrement, of the guards' random violence that could cause one's death at any moment. As survivors have pointed out, the conditions in the camps were such that, without some help or resistance, no one could survive for more than one month (194).

In order to set the tone for discussing survivors' experiences, Des Pres quotes from Reska Weiss's testimony *Journey through Hell*. One day during her imprisonment Weiss entered a tent where a group of women, called *Stuthofer* by the Nazis, waited for their execution:

Entering the tent from the blinding snow-whiteness, I could hardly distinguish anything in the semi-darkness, least of all the women lying on the ground. The stench was over-powering despite the airy tent. After awhile my eyes became accustomed to the light, and I was completely overcome by what I saw.

I screamed in horror and shut my eyes to the sight. My knees trembled, my head began to swim, and I grasped the central tent-prop for support. It was hard to believe the women on the ground were still human beings. Their rigid bodies were skeletons, their eyes were glazed from long starvation. . . .

For two months the Stuthofers had lain on the ground, stark naked. The meagre bundles of straw on which they lay were putrid from their urine and excreta. Their frozen limbs were fetid and covered with wounds and bites to the point of bleeding, and countless lice nested in the pus. Their hair was very short indeed, but the armies of lice found a home in it. No stretch of the imagination, no power of the written word, can convey the horror of that tent. And yet . . . they were *alive* . . . they were hungry and they tore at their skel-etal bodies with their emaciated hands covered in pus and dirt. They were beyond help. The SS guards denied them the mercy of shooting them all at once. Only three or four were called out daily to be shot. . . .

For days I couldn't swallow even a crumb of bread. The horror I lived through watch-ing this agony will remain with me to the end of my days.[5]

Des Pres adds: "We will not understand the survivor's behavior apart from its context. That is the context" (45). Limit-rhetoric helps Des Pres to make this point.[6] In his argu-ments against the claims of psychoanalysis, Des Pres repeatedly draws a sharp contrast between civilization and extremity, between ordinary living conditions as we know them and the camp conditions set up by Nazi policies for the purpose of destruction. The con-trast between civilization and extremity is a contrast between a cultural sphere—where meanings are multiple, especially the meaning of human behavior—and a sphere of bio-logical necessity, where the process of symbolization is reversed and human behavior is always a response to absolute necessity and has only one unequivocal meaning: survival. Applied to the first sphere, the interpretive methods of psychoanalysis might be appropri-ate. But they are not for the second. In extremity, there is no "hidden" meaning behind human action and, therefore, there is nothing for psychoanalysts to interpret.

Des Pres argues that the extreme living conditions in the camps did not lead to com-plete chaos or the loss of dignity. Rather, behavior in the camps, reduced as it was to the essential effort to survive, was of a moral and social nature. This, in fact, is already indicated in the will to bear witness and the need to remember that underlies numer-ous testimonies. For many, the sole motivation to survive was the wish to speak for the dead and "to tell the world"—an intrinsically collective act, as Des Pres points out. In contrast to what the notion of "regression" would imply, many survivors recount their efforts to resist the "excremental assault," to stay clean, as impossible as this was made by Nazi camp regulations. But even if it meant merely to use the morning coffee to wash one's face, these efforts were crucial, less for purposes of physical cleanliness than as a kind of ritual that helped to preserve human dignity.[7] Against the claim that pris-oners in the camps were selfish, Des Pres points to the communal network that the prisoners built up against all odds. While in order to stay alive one indeed needed to primarily care for one's own needs, mutual help and concern for each other also moti-vated the camp community. Life in the camps was "existence at its boundary" (177), "existence at its limits" (181), but was still human existence.

Suspicion against Survivors

At several points in his book Des Pres raises questions about the possible motivations that give rise to the psychoanalytic studies of camps experiences—and these questions provide me with important clues to the wider rhetorical situation in which Des Pres finds himself. Given the fact that a careful reading of testimonies quickly refutes psychoanalytic interpretations, even reveals their absurdity, Des Pres wondered whether there are certain reasons why these kinds of interpretations had emerged and prevailed up until then:

> Why is it easy to believe, despite the contradiction, that survivors were infantile *and* that they were cunning manipulators using every kind of betrayal and base trick to stay alive? ... Here is how one psychoanalytic commentator summed up the opinions of his colleagues in a symposium on the camp experience: "To one degree or another, they all stifled their true feelings, they all denied the dictates of conscience and social feeling in hope of survival, and they were all warped and distorted as a result." That word "all"—its assurance, its contempt—must be accounted for. (155)

What Des Pres wants to bring into view here has less to do with psychoanalysis itself than with the subject matter of the Holocaust. He suggests that the degrading notion of Nazi victims as childlike and amoral is of service to those who hold on to it. The "assurance" and "contempt" with which this notion is generalized and reinforced seems overdetermined and gives reasons to believe that there is more at stake than the wrong methodology. With this suggestion Des Pres not only addresses the group of psychoanalysts but uses the first person plural: why do *we* insist . . . ?

Des Pres does not give an immediate answer. But at several places in his book he discusses the wider cultural conditions that inhibit an adequate understanding of survivors' experiences. The Western tradition, and Christianity in particular, has produced and cultivated an image of the hero as a sacrificial victim (5), prominent for instance in Jesus and in the figure of the Christian martyr. The traditional hero is someone who gives his or her life for a higher cause. Death, consequently, has gained a certain grandeur. In contrast, "[s]urvival in itself, not dedicated to something *else*, has never been held in high esteem and often has been viewed with contempt" (164).[8] The common disregard or neglect of "mere" physical existence leads to suspicion of survivors and a general difficulty in hearing, understanding, and dealing with their stories.[9]

Des Pres offers another important reason why we have difficulty confronting what survivors lived through:

> The terror of the camps is *with* us. Some hideous impression of Auschwitz is in every mind, far removed from conscious thought but *there*; and not only as repressed perception of historical events but as an image which stirs up the demonic content of our own worst fears and wishes. The image is with us; and anything connected with it, anything which starts it into consciousness, brings with it a horror too large and intensely personal to confront safely. (170)

The sheer horror of what survivors have to tell, Des Pres observes, endangers our own well-being so that we refuse to take careful account of it. Des Pres also suggests that the Holocaust as an image does not necessarily imply a real knowledge about the German death camps or an active confrontation with the historical realities from which this image derives. To have "some hideous impression of Auschwitz" in one's mind is not the same as really engaging with survivors' experiences.

In fact, Des Pres suggests that an immersion in camp imagery is not beneficial to historical knowledge, especially when it is conflated with our archetypal conceptions of hell. While the comparison between Auschwitz and hell are prevalent in survivors' discourses, Des Pres warns:

> For us it is misleading because the archetype informs our perception and we end up seeing the SS as satanic monsters and the prisoners as condemned souls. When we imagine what the survivor's experience must have been, we thus project our own fantasies, our own worst fears and wishes. From our remote vantage point only the horror is visible; the real behavior of survivors goes unobserved because it was covert, undramatic, not at all in accord with our expectations of heroism. (172)

Vague notions about the camps as scenes from hell have very little to do with survivors' experiences or with the real concrete conditions in Auschwitz, the daily life of victims and their strategies for coping and surviving.

What Des Pres addresses in these quotes is a state of Holocaust remembrance that I encountered during my discussion of John Dominic Crossan's work. Like Crossan, Des Pres writes at a time when the Holocaust was still in the process of becoming a central issue in American public discourses. *The Survivor* was published during "the years of transition" (Novick), before the telecasting of Hollywood's landmark miniseries *Holocaust* in 1978—which may well explain why there is no reference in Des Pres's book to "the Holocaust," a term that entered common vocabulary only after this big media event. Des Pres writes at a time when the names and images of Auschwitz and Buchenwald for the majority of Americans functioned as symbols of atrocity, sources of horror, without evoking any specific historical considerations; a time when "Nazis" appeared in episodic television series not as particular perpetrators of particular crimes but as archetypes of evil, as "satanic monsters," to use Des Pres's expression. Des Pres writes for an audience that might have in its mind "some hideous impressions of Auschwitz," images of hellish places, piles of corpses, brutal SS men, smoke and chimneys, but no knowledge of what Des Pres calls "the real behavior of survivors," the actual conditions, the details.

Most important, Des Pres writes at a time when Holocaust survivors had not yet attained the authority they have today, and this circumstance is crucial in order to understand the rhetorical aims of Des Pres's book. Des Pres is not concerned with Holocaust memory in general. He is not concerned, for example, with the difficulty of making sense of atrocity images. He is concerned with the difficulty of understanding the experiences of those who lived through the Nazi camps. One does not learn about these experiences by looking at photographs; one learns about them by reading or listening to survivors. Therefore Des Pres's attention is directed toward their texts. Des Pres, I would like to suggest, struggles not with a "difficulty of seeing" but with a difficulty of approaching and reading survivors' testimonies.

Holocaust testimonies present problems different from those of the photographs of atrocity. Photographs reprinted in newspapers stare you in the face, whether you want them to or not, which is why the Allies were able "to make the Germans see," as Dagmar Barnouw puts it. The confrontation with written texts is a different matter. The reading of Holocaust testimonies requires a deliberate turn, an interest and openness towards

these texts, while the circulation and availability of such testimonies depends on pub-
lishers and on the willingness of survivors to write about their experiences.[10] This willingness, again, depends on the availability of an audience that will read and deal with
the texts and their content. According to Geoffrey Hartman:

> There have been three periods when survivors of the Holocaust recovered their voice and
> an audience materialized for them. The first was immediately after the war, when the
> camps were disclosed. That period did not last: a devastated Europe had to be rebuilt,
> and the disbelief or guilt that cruel memories aroused isolated rather than integrated the
> survivor. What has been aptly called a "latency period" intervened. A second opening
> was created by the Eichmann trial in 1960, and a third came after the release of the TV
> series Holocaust in 1978. (*Longest* 143)

Hartman further recounts that the complaint among survivors about the inadequate
representations of the Hollywood series gave rise to Yale's oral testimony project, an
effort to preserve survivors' accounts on videotapes for future generations. Today, I may
add, hundreds of visitors listen to survivors' video testimonies at the end of the exhibit
at the museum in Washington, and Steven Spielberg's Holocaust video project is under
way as well.

Des Pres's book *The Survivor* was published before such projects came into being.
While the book is based on a "vast body of literature" (30) produced by survivors, there
are clear signs that Des Pres's text belongs to a time when Holocaust survivors had
neither much public attention nor respect. Des Pres reckons with an audience that is
deeply reluctant to listen to Holocaust testimonies. Survivors "are suspect in our eyes"
(170), he writes; they arouse feelings of contempt and aversion. The subject matter of
Auschwitz might still cause feelings of revulsion, but nowadays those feelings are no
longer directed against survivors themselves, whose public image has improved since
Des Pres wrote his book.

I would like to mention another symptom of Des Pres's rhetorical situation, a point
that has been criticized by Holocaust scholars in recent years but needs to be historicized
as well. Des Pres's book reveals a striking lack of interest in questions of representation,
a lack of concern with the role of language vis-à-vis the events of the Holocaust. As James
Young points out, Des Pres seems to reckon with an automatic, somehow natural link
between testimonies and experiences without taking into account the interpretive activity
of language in remembering and reconstructing the past. He "implie[s]," writes Young,

> that in their enormity these experiences somehow force themselves directly into language
> as unvitiated facts, without being mediated or shaped by structures of mind, culture, and
> narrative that ultimately lend this testimony its voice. Like many readers, Des Pres seems
> to suggest that the literal facts of the Holocaust are both the primary aim and achieve-
> ment of a survivor's testimony. (*Writing* 16)[11]

However, this disinterest in questions of language or memory—issues that today are
at the center of scholarly concern—has nothing to do with a lack of sophistication and
everything to do with the time and the rhetorical situation of Des Pres's work. Des Pres
does not speak out of a context where a respectful and dignified discussion of survivors'
experiences is assumed and where the importance and urgency of survivors' testimonies is unquestionable—as is the case in American Holocaust studies today. Instead,

Des Pres sees himself confronted with an academic context where a shameful notion of survivors has been produced, accepted, and authorized.

The Rhetoric of Extremity

These contextual circumstances illuminate the meaning and function of limit-rhetoric in Des Pres's work. Des Pres wants to introduce an unprepared audience to the literature of Holocaust testimonies. He confronts readers, who might have certain impressions but not necessarily substantial knowledge about the Nazi death camps, with the concrete aspects of daily life, thereby replacing vague and misleading notions about "the horror of Auschwitz" with the details of survivors' struggle and of the conditions installed by reasoned Nazi policy.

Limit-rhetoric serves Des Pres's effort to vindicate survivors, to establish them as dignified human beings whose stories are of utter importance and should be read carefully and respectfully. As I have shown, "extremity" comes most directly into play during Des Pres's debate with psychoanalytic studies. By calling life in the camps a life in "extremity," where the meaning-making processes of civilization are suspended and human behavior is ruled by immediate necessities, Des Pres invalidates the psychoanalytic approach with its search for deeper meanings.

But "extremity" has a more general effect as well: by opposing "extremity" to the state of civilization, to everything we know and are familiar with, Des Pres sets a new tone for talking about concentration camp experiences. He makes conceptual space for the voice of survivors by consistently keeping the impulse to apply common interpretive concepts in check. With the notion of extremity, Des Pres makes it hard for readers to reduce survivors' experiences to familiar notions and thereby to distance themselves from what they read. Limit-rhetoric operates in Des Pres's discourse like a red traffic light: it asks readers to stop, to arrest usual sense-making strategies, and to realize that unfamiliar, alien matters are at stake.

In the preface to his book, Des Pres talks about the difficulties in finding a language with which to talk about atrocity. Employing a neutral, objective voice would lead to cynicism or despair, he says, while an emotional tone would end in inappropriate self-indulgence. "There seemed one language left," Des Pres goes on, "a kind of archaic, quasi-religious vocabulary, which I have used not as a reflection of religious sentiment, but in the sense that only a language of ultimate concern can be adequate to facts such as these" (vi). Des Pres's limit-terminology, besides being a rhetorical device against psychoanalysis and besides being a means to emphasize the exceptional nature of the subject matter and to pay respect to survivors, is also the result of a Holocaust interpreter's difficult search for adequate language.

Des Pres himself calls his language "a kind of archaic, quasi-religious vocabulary," "a language of ultimate concern." The notion of ultimate concern, another variation of limit-rhetoric, goes back to the Christian theologian Paul Tillich. Ricoeur, in his own search for language with which to describe the referent of Jesus' parables, writes: "I would have no objection to Tillich's concept of 'ultimate concern'" (128) and thereby amplifies Karl Jaspers's idea of limit-situation. What exactly is the meaning and function of limit-rhetoric, of this "quasi- religious vocabulary" in Ricoeur's discourse?

Limit-Rhetoric and the Parables of Jesus

Hermeneutic Revivals

Ricoeur's limit-rhetoric is not a means to call attention to neglected texts. Unlike Holocaust survivors' testimonies, which in the 1970s were still waiting to attain public attention, the parables of Jesus, as central stories of the Christian canon, were securely established within the various contexts of Christian American culture. In the special context of the literary turn in biblical studies, the parables in fact stood at the center of interest. In the 1970s, numerous New Testament scholars were invested in these texts as the testing ground for a poetic approach to the Bible.

The challenge of Ricoeur's rhetorical situation was not to propagate New Testament parables but to clarify very open and sometimes confused hermeneutic discussions. The shift from a historical-critical to a literary paradigm was no smooth transition. It was an experiment and raised multiple interpretive questions. How to combine a structuralist analysis with historical research, how to think together the form and the message of parables, how to define their metaphorical quality—all these things were up for debate at the time when Ricoeur published his essay. At stake were not only methodological difficulties. Ricoeur's essay was written for a scholarly context in which the meaning of parables, in a broad sense, was under question. What the parables are about, their point or referent, their significance or relevance, was no longer self-evident for American scholars in the 1970s.

Joachim Jeremias had been content to find the significance of a parable in Jesus' first-century ministry. For the literary critics in America this was unsatisfactory. In their view, historical criticism closed off the parables' hermeneutic potential for today. But how this contemporary hermeneutic potential could be conceptualized or actualized, what a hermeneutic alternative to historical criticism should look like, was by no means clear and had to be investigated.

This quest was not always successful, as Ricoeur shows in his essay. In assessing the role of structuralism for biblical hermeneutics, Ricoeur asks: "is it a new beginning or a dead end, the surest way of killing texts?" (63) Taken solely on its own terms, he suggests, structuralism has fatal consequences for parable hermeneutics because it reduces the parables to meaningless systems of signs without content (63). Therefore, Ricoeur argues, a structuralist analysis of parables needs to be opened up toward another mode of interpretation, one that takes account of the metaphorical process inherent in parables, a process that leads from the world of the narrative to an outside referent. But even metaphor theory, taken solely on its own terms, can not guarantee the referential value of parables, as Ricoeur emphasizes. Parables are metaphorical narratives, not metaphors, and this difference is important:

> Metaphors . . . have an instantaneous existence. They last as long as the semantic clash is perceived between the words. Their semantic innovations have no status in established language. As soon as they become common and taken for granted, they also become trivial and die as metaphors. Therefore, they must remain *events* of discourse, transient events. It seems that according to the theory of tension, *traditional* figurative stories should be *dead* metaphors. Of course this may be the case. (93)

Metaphors are alive only as long as they present original deviations from the common usage of words. Every deviation, however, if it takes place too often, ceases to be original and becomes trivial, which is why metaphors do not live long. But what then about "*traditional* figurative stories" like the parables of Jesus? Is it possible that these age-old, well-known stories, which have been read and listened to over centuries by millions of Christians, are dead, just as metaphors die once they enter dictionaries?[12]

Ricoeur's rhetorical situation is marked not only by methodological confusions but by a hermeneutic crisis. From various perspectives the parables of Jesus appear to be lifeless texts. As Ricoeur sees it, historical critics turn the parables into ancient artifacts with no relevance for today; structuralists treat them as meaningless codes; and Ricoeur's own metaphor theory, taken on its own term, suggests that the parables may be platitudes that have lost their innovative spark. To this hermeneutic crisis Ricoeur offers a striking response. His essay is filled with claims that all in one way or another suggest that the parables are anything but dead. As metaphorical narrative, Ricoeur suggests, a parable "says something new about reality" (80); "a new vision springs up," "a re-interpretation of reality" (84) arises, "we perceive new connections in things" (85), and "another power of speaking the world is liberated" (87). Not only are the parables not dead, they are the site of new visions of reality that cannot be gained through any other discourse.

Ricoeur's limit-rhetoric is embedded in this argument. "Biblical Hermeneutics" culminates in the idea that the parables, as religious discourse, make us see not just anything about the world but the limit-experiences of human life. What better way of affirming the contemporary relevance of Jesus' stories than that? The parables turn in Ricoeur's hands from apparently lifeless texts into rich stories capable of illuminating human life in its most important, urgent, *extreme* dimensions. Ricoeur's limit-rhetoric stands at the service of a passionate endeavor to bring new life to Christian texts, to affirm the hermeneutic value of New Testament parables.

Indeed, Ricoeur's skills in reviving the Christian canon for our time was appreciated by his readers in the 1970s and later. In her introductory essay to "Biblical Hermeneutics," Loretta Dornisch writes the following about Ricoeur's contribution to biblical studies: Ricoeur's hermeneutics, she says, "may *reanimate* or make possible a *renewal* of the fullness of the act of interpretation" and "may also lead to a greater or fuller *recovery* of the text, a primary goal, after all, of biblical interpreting" (19, emphasis added). Ricoeur gives new life to both the biblical text and its interpretation, Dornisch suggests here. What does such recovery of the text entail? Ricoeur's work shows, Dornisch writes, that a person can experience biblical texts "in a way that gives meaning to his life as nothing else does . . . more meaning than can be articulated or comprehended" (16).

Similarly, in a recent anthology of Ricoeur's essays on theological, religious and biblical themes, Mark Wallace talks about "the recovery of narrative" (10) accomplished through Ricoeur's work. Ricoeur's approach to the Bible, Wallace writes, is

a hermeneutic inquiry into the imaginative potential of myth, symbol, and story to aid our efforts to exist with integrity. Religious traditions use ontologically potent language and imagery to illuminate all that ultimately concerns human beings—our questions about life's meaning, our confrontations with death, our struggles to be at home in the universe. (14-15)

Here we meet again with the notion of ultimate concern. As Wallace says, Ricoeur recovers the capacity of religious traditions to "illuminate" something that "ultimately concerns" a person. The function Wallace attributes to Ricoeur's work in general, I would argue, is the function of "Biblical Hermeneutics" as well. The essay recovers the hermeneutic potential not of religious traditions in general but of Jesus' stories in particular and suggests that these old Christian narratives are able to give answers to "our questions about life's meaning, our confrontations with death, our struggles to be at home in the universe"—to the limit-experiences of human life.

An Inflated Rhetoric?

Not every reader finds Ricoeur's efforts persuasive, however. The Jewish scholar David Stern, for example, is skeptical about the interpretive language used by Ricoeur and other parable scholars. His assessment of Ricoeurian rhetoric is critical.

> The parables of Jesus are endowed with the full presence of an originary voice, with the plenitude of a revelation that not only need not be interpreted, but instead itself "interprets" its audience and transfigures its hearers. This is, in short, the parable become the Logos—a timeless, hermeneutically inexhaustible and rhetorically irresistible entity. Not surprisingly, some scholars have associated this conception of Jesus' parables with the idea that the literary form of the parables is itself informed by a kind of open-ended polysemy, a capacity for sustaining an endless number of interpretations. (49–50)

Stern calls this an "inflated rhetoric"; unconvinced about the kind of potency that is ascribed to the parables, he suspects that this "inflated rhetoric . . . indicates its author's desire to find in the parable an expression of language as pure, unmediated epiphany" (49). Stern specifically addresses Ricoeur's metaphor theory as it has been most influential for the literary conception of parables. Ricoeur, Stern says, "hopes that by concentrating upon the 'literary' aspects of the text he will be able to isolate its more permanent and abiding elements,—in sum, the keys to the contemporary relevance of the Bible and its powers of transformation" (50).[13]

Ricoeur's notion of the "ultimate referent" of the parables represents another instance of the kind of rhetoric criticized by Stern. The idea that the parables of Jesus refer to the limit-experiences of human life, that they point to the extreme aspects of human reality, could be called a rhetorical device for producing an impression of the parables' "contemporary relevance." By calling this rhetoric "inflated," Stern suggests that this impression is not grounded in anything substantial and that Ricoeur's claim is an intriguing promise that would break down as soon as one took him up on it; that his skills in reviving Jesus' stories seem convincing from afar and as long as they are not put to work. As long as one doesn't ask how exactly one moves from the parable of the Wicked Husbandmen to limit-experiences of human life, Ricoeur's essay may effectively reconfigure the parables as relevant contemporary texts—in theory. What Stern points out, however, is the danger that the air of relevance will pour out of Ricoeur's phrases once one tries to make them concrete.

Indeed, it would be difficult to defend "Biblical Hermeneutics" against Stern's critique. Ricoeur neither offers concrete examples of limit-experiences nor shows how his theory could be applied to a New Testament story. As I said in the beginning of this chapter, Ricoeur's limit-rhetoric is intriguing and puzzling at the same time.

But is Ricoeur's limit-rhetoric really merely a conglomeration of blown-up, empty phrases? I would like to qualify Stern's notion of an inflated rhetoric especially in regard to Ricoeur's idea that the parables of Jesus refer to limit-experiences of "catastrophe" and "distress." These phrases are inflated, but they are not empty. It is true, Ricoeur never specifies these phrases, leaving them open to all kinds of associations. But I would argue that limit-experiences of death, suffering, guilt, and hatred do have particularly strong resonances with the Holocaust, at least for certain readers. One such reader, as I have shown, is the philosopher who developed this interpretive language in the first place, Karl Jaspers. While Jaspers elaborated his notion of limit-situations before the Nazis came to power, this same concept, as it reappeared two decades after the Holocaust, evoked for him the "agonizing fear of death," the "hunger," the "torment" of Jewish children under the Nazi regime. When Ricoeur borrows the concept of limit-situations in his essay on the parables of Jesus in 1975, he leaves Jaspers's historical reference points behind. But it seems to me that the Holocaust still lurks behind Ricoeur's use of Jaspers's concept, ready to jump to the surface. The Holocaust is only one associative step away, so to speak, the step that it would take to make his interpretive claims concrete. If he too were to exemplify the notion of limit-experiences of death and suffering within the history of the twentieth century, wouldn't he meet with the subject matter of the Holocaust?[14]

Whether or not this is the case for Ricoeur himself, the Holocaust is a constituent part of Ricoeur's publication, a sort of semantic potential that will be actualized by some audiences.[15] Ricoeur's essay was published at a time when the Nazi crimes, generally speaking, were already part of the American cultural reservoir. What comes to mind when you read the expression "limit-experiences of death, suffering, guilt, and hatred"? Ricoeur's first readers were probably able to think of all kinds of things; among them, however, and perhaps even prominent, was the Holocaust. By the mid-1970s the Holocaust had not yet moved to the center of public discourses, but figures of brutal Nazis and suffering Jews had appeared enough at public sites for some American readers to make the associative step from Ricoeur's limit-rhetoric to Nazi atrocity. For some audiences Ricoeur's limit-rhetoric would bring to mind vague impressions of the Holocaust.

As Michael Bernstein argues, vague impressions of the Holocaust can energize reading practices. Especially if the Holocaust just rumbles in the back of a reader's mind, if it is only a trace of a memory of Nazi atrocity, it can effectively fuel the air of relevance or urgency that Ricoeur's discourse produces around its subject matter. The attraction and persuasiveness of Ricoeur's argument derive not only from limit-rhetoric in general but from the fact that this rhetoric is particularly charged after the Holocaust. It seems to me that Ricoeur's limit-rhetoric has a meaning and function similar to those of the citations of Kafka or Kaschnitz in the works of John Dominic Crossan and Wolfgang Harnisch. Not unlike these twentieth-century literatures, Ricoeur's notion of limit-experiences brings the Holocaust on the stage—not to the center but into the background, where it potentially invigorates the hermeneutic discourse.

Ricoeur's limit-rhetoric might be motivated by the same hermeneutic desire that prompts Harnisch and Crossan to cite historically charged literature, namely, the desire to have a connection between one's religious tradition and twentieth-century catastrophe, the desire to have Christian stories speak to post-Holocaust times. Again I want to stress the legitimacy of such desire. Jewish Holocaust survivors themselves, in writing about their experiences, have turned to the Bible, to its tales and figures of catastrophe. And, vice versa, Holocaust experiences have changed the way they now look at those biblical tales. Writers such as Wiesel, as James Young recounts, re-view antiquity through eyes now informed by new experiences that are so strong as to overwhelm and displace other figures. Experiences, stories, and texts of the ancient past remain the same in themselves; but their meanings, their echoes, causes and effects, and their significance all changed with the addition of new experiences in the lives of these texts' interpreters. (109)

Biblical tales of disaster are nuanced or recast so that they make better sense in light of what happened, or they are accused and repudiated because they are unable to express the full extent of destruction during the Holocaust. Could it be that Ricoeur's discourse got entangled in a similar exchange between Holocaust experiences and the New Testament? If so, would such entanglement not be valuable, the first step in a journey back into history?

The problem is, of course, that the exchange between the "extreme" events of the Holocaust and the parables exists only as an unexplored hermeneutic impulse. Parables will be reinterpreted, Ricoeur argues, "according to new contexts of discourse and of life," and thereby he opens up the possibility of a post-Holocaust hermeneutics. But these "new contexts of discourse and of life" are not thoroughly enough defined for this possibility to be realized or even addressed in Ricoeur's essay. The Holocaust appears not as clear reference point but in the form of vague resonances accompanying Ricoeur's discourse.

Ricoeur wants to offer a comprehensive interpretive theory; why should he be more specific than he is? What is wrong with offering hermeneutic impulses? For two reasons I find Ricoeur's rhetorical practice problematic. The first has to do with the difficulties of Holocaust remembrance. Ricoeur's deployment of limit-rhetoric fosters the state of Holocaust memory that Des Pres is struggling against. By using this charged interpretive language without ever specifying it, Ricoeur counteracts Des Pres's diligent effort to call attention to the details of survivors' experiences. The unexplored Holocaust resonances of Ricoeur's rhetoric contribute to a cultural climate where "Auschwitz" and "Buchenwald" tend to operate as mere symbols of atrocity and there is little knowledge about the historical particularities of Jewish suffering and Nazi violence. It was such a climate that prompted Des Pres to replace his contemporaries' vague notions about Nazi evil with concrete accounts about life in the Nazi camps. "Some hideous impression of Auschwitz is in every mind," Des Pres says. Ricoeur's discourse plays with such impressions and makes it hard to move from phrases, symbols, or images to actual events, persons, and fates. For Des Pres, limit-rhetoric functions like a stop sign that signals the exceptional quality of survivors' experiences, preparing his readers to approach and think through their testimonies. Ricoeur uses the same rhetoric as a way to energize his hermeneutic discourse, to produce an air of relevance and urgency around the parables of Jesus. Ricoeur's rhetoric is inflated rhetoric not because its phrases are empty but because it devalues the currency of limit-terminology, because it wears out an audience's reflex mechanism toward such language, because it decreases its *specific* relevance and urgency with respect to the events of the Holocaust.

My second concern goes back to the state of New Testament scholarship. I find the unexplored post-Holocaust hermeneutic impulse in Ricoeur's text problematic because it forecloses a critical examination of Jesus' stories in light of this historical legacy. A Christian exchange between the Bible and the events of the Holocaust will be different from Jewish efforts to reread biblical stories; a Christian post-Holocaust interpreter will have to struggle with different issues from those that face a Jewish interpreter. Parable hermeneutics is no innocent field of research, and the parables are not innocent texts. A Christian post-Holocaust hermeneutics would have to deal with the complicity of both parables and parable scholarship in the history of anti-Jewish violence. Ricoeur, writing in the 1970s, is not aware of the need for such work. The New Testament parables are capable of illuminating limit-experiences of human life, and they have this hermeneutic power, Ricoeur suggests, because they shatter traditional Jewish forms of discourse. Anti-Jewish rhetoric is a constituent part of Ricoeur's argument. Before a Ricoeurian interpreter could actually engage in a post-Holocaust reading of a parable, he or she would have to work through this legacy.

12

Toward a Post-Holocaust Biblical Hermeneutics

Ich hätte ehe ich gehe
Noch einige Fragen

Before I leave, I'd still have
A few questions.

(Marie Luise Kaschnitz, "Zoon Politikon")

I recently returned to the text that initiated the writing of this book, Kaschnitz's poem "Zoon Politikon." Several years have passed since I copied the poem on a small piece of paper and put it in front of me as an illustration of Paul Ricoeur's metaphor theory. Looking at it now I remember the feelings I had when I wrote the poem down. Most strongly I remember a feeling of curiosity, of "pushing something." By putting Kaschnitz's poem about the returning memory of Auschwitz on my desk, I pushed into my field of vision something that I had failed to recognize: the odd place of a Holocaust poem at the margins of a discourse on New Testament parable interpretation.

Holocaust imagery has been so prevalent in the 1990s, both in Germany and in America, that for a long time it was easy for me to overlook, to not really see Kaschnitz's poem in Harnisch's book. But by copying Kaschnitz's lines and by putting them on my desk I amplified Harnisch's citation and eventually forced myself to recognize the disturbing fact that Harnisch and I had used "dead Jews" as examples of "living metaphors." This book has offered a genealogy of this uncanny tension. I have focused on the works of Joachim Jeremias, John Dominic Crossan, and Paul Ricoeur because together these works represent the history of research on which Harnisch's hermeneutics is built: the literary turn in biblical studies. Working through the shift from historical criticism (Jeremias) to a poetic approach to the parables (Crossan, Ricoeur), I have traced the scholarly discourse that made it possible for an interpreter to quote a text like "Zoon Politikon" in a discussion of New Testament parables.

Harnisch's use of Kaschnitz's poem, however, is not only the result of changes in the scholarly discourse on parables but also the symptom of an important ambivalence that characterizes the literary turn. To a large extent, the literary turn was a response to Jeremias's rigid focus on the first historical setting of parables, which, in the words of Tracy and Schüssler Fiorenza, is characterized by a retreat from twentieth-century history and specifically from the events of the Holocaust whose terrifying evidence confronted the Germans in 1945.[1] When literary critics in the 1960s and 1970s departed from Jeremias's hermeneutic assumptions, the result was an often ahistorical discourse that treated the parables as autonomous aesthetic objects. In some cases, however, this reconfiguration of the parables was accompanied by unexplored first steps back into history. Most of the literary projects were attempts to recover the innovative, poetic qualities of Jesus' stories. But in some of these projects there was an additional desire at work, namely, to find in Jesus' parables poetic powers strong and innovative enough to shed light on twentieth-century catastrophes. When Crossan compares Jesus' stories with charged twentieth-century texts, he is invested in something historically more specific than generic and functional similarities. When Ricoeur suggests that the parables are able to illuminate limit-experiences of death, suffering, guilt, and hatred, he deals with something historically more specific than "the human condition as such." When Harnisch and Funk are unable to cite Kafka without mentioning, however briefly, visions of the Holocaust, their interest in Kafka must be historically more specific than the interest in paradox and metaphor. In all of these hermeneutic discourses I detect a desire to have Jesus' parables speak to post-Holocaust times.

As I look at my own copy of Kaschnitz's poem, which is marked by my handwriting, coffee stains, and traces of the tape that glued the piece of paper to my desk for many months, I realize that this hermeneutic desire is my own. Among the many things that prompted me to tape Kaschnitz's "Zoon Politikon" on my desk was also the wish to make a connection between Jesus' parables and the legacy of the Holocaust that Kaschnitz so powerfully articulates. I have always been attracted to the literary turn in biblical studies, to the works of Ricoeur and Harnisch, because, unlike historical criticism, they reckoned with the relevance of biblical texts for our time. "My own time," however, is prominently marked by the Holocaust. As a German, my "questions about life's meaning," my "struggles to be at home in the universe," are centered around the terrible crimes committed in the name of my country.[2] And as a Christian, I want to know how to make sense of the New Testament in light of this legacy.

A Post-Holocaust Reading of the Wicked Husbandmen

Revisiting the Wicked Husbandmen

Is it possible to take up the hermeneutic desires I found in the works of Harnisch, Crossan, and Ricoeur and bring them to an actual New Testament story? Is it possible to read Jesus' parables while explicitly working with the memories of the Holocaust and thereby participating in what Schüssler Fiorenza and Tracy have called a "Christian return into history"? Let me make the first steps in such a journey with a biblical text that crossed my way several times in this book: the parable of the Wicked Husbandmen, the story about a man who rents his vineyard to a group of tenants. During harvest time the tenants refuse to conform to the lease and instead beat or kill every servant sent by the owner to collect his share. After the owner sends his own son, the tenants kill him as well and subsequently are killed themselves by the owner, who then gives his vineyard to others.

In the course of this book, I encountered this story according to four different interpretations. Joachim Jeremias argues that the story reflects the rebellious behavior of first-century Galilean peasants and was used by Jesus to warn a blinded people of the approaching catastrophe. In John Dominic Crossan's rendering, the story confronts us with the striking paradox that the tenants' mischievously bold behavior leads to their success, not their downfall. According to a longstanding anti-Jewish tradition, the parable is an allegory for the troublesome relations between God, the Jews, and the Christian church. The Catholic scholar Aaron Milavec, finally, challenges the story's anti-Jewish reception history and offers a "fresh analysis," according to which the parable of the Wicked Husbandmen was originally a pro-Jewish story about inner-Jewish conflicts without any reference to Christianity.

These four interpretations are based on different assumptions of how to make sense of Jesus' parables. Jeremias seeks to understand the parable within its first historical setting; Crossan interprets the story within the context of paradoxical literature; the allegorical interpretation of Mark 12 places the parable within a supersessionist version of God's salvation history; and for Milavec, finally, the parable ought to be placed within Mark's first-century Jewish horizon of understanding.

Of all these interpretations, Milavec's "fresh analysis" comes closest to my own concerns. As I show in chapter 6, his analysis intends to offer an appropriate reading of Mark's story for post-Holocaust times and to work against the anti-Jewish trends in parable scholarship. However, I also show that Milavec's effort remains under the paradigm of historical-critical research and moves entirely within the parameters of ancient times. Therefore Milavec is unable to attend to the difficulties of Holocaust remembrance, difficulties that exceed the problem of anti-Judaism and that would explode a historical-critical focus on the gospel writer's first-century context.

In my own reading of the parable I would like to begin by foregrounding an alternative interpretive context: In the early 1990s, I participated in a Protestant church service in the south of Germany and was asked to read the Gospel. The prescribed text for that Sunday was Mark 12:1–12, the parable of the Wicked Husbandmen. I was familiar with the story but utterly unprepared to hear myself reading it aloud. Midway through the story, as I began to narrate the landlord's attempts to collect his share, my own words began to ring in my ears. "Sie nahmen ihn aber und schlugen ihn . . . dem schlugen sie auf den Kopf und schmähten ihn . . . den töteten sie . . . die einen schlugen sie, die andern töteten sie . . . und sie nahmen ihn und töteten ihn. . . . "[3] I heard my voice read what seemed to me a never-ending series of violent deaths, caught up in a plot whose violence had gone out of control. After my final sentence, I sat down with a vague but intense feeling of discomfort.

With this narrative I would like to bring into view a particular post-Holocaust context of reading the parable of the Wicked Husbandmen. The church service I attended was a "post-Holocaust context" in so far as my audience and I shared memories of the German past. I read the parable to a public whose cultural identity was bound up with Nazi atrocities. What I find significant about this context, moreover, is the fact that my reading was institutionalized. The parable was read (and will continue to be read) because it is included in my church's lectionary.[4] I read the parable and, according to custom, sat down without comment. And since this reading was not framed by any explicit interpretive discourse the parable's meaning was highly ambiguous. I cannot tell how the story was heard by the people in the church nor am I exactly sure how I read it. But I still vividly remember my feeling of discomfort.

Reading one of the fiercest anti-Jewish stories in a German church is an awkward thing to do. No wonder I felt uncomfortable. However, I believe that my feelings were caused not only by the story's anti-Jewish resonances. If it had been the implicit tale of supersessionism only that caused my unease, I could have worked through the experience. I would have been able to pinpoint the problem and come to a conclusion, such as, next time I refuse to read this text, or next time I will add some critical comments. But things were much more complicated. Something else was at work that needs to be explored.

Historical criticism offers no tools to work through my experience. However diligently I explore the parable's first-century Jewish horizon of understanding, this research will offer no explanation for the story's meanings and connotations in a German church in 1992. What I need is an interpretive approach that reckons with the story's capacity to engage and haunt a contemporary audience, to evoke feelings, to upset and disturb. In order to explore my memory I need to tend to the *poetic powers* of the parable. I need a hermeneutic technique that will get at the transfer that obviously took place during that church service, a transfer from the world of the story to something that concerned me in my own context. I need an interpretive approach that does not subject the story to its original context, that does not look for its meaning in its first historical setting, but reckons with the fact that the story of the Wicked Husbandmen has gained autonomy from its author and its first audience, by being read and communicated in ever-new situations.

These are, of course, the hermeneutic premises of Paul Ricoeur. In the following, I would like to offer a reading of the parable of the Wicked Husbandmen that takes its cues from Ricoeur's essay and offers an alternative to Milavec's "fresh analysis." Just as Milavec revised and reinvisioned the historical-critical discourse in which he participates, I would like to revise and reinvision the discourse in which I have been participating all along: the literary approach to the parables, represented by Ricoeur's "Biblical Hermeneutics." Let me take Ricoeur up on his argument that the parables, thanks to their poetic powers, can be reinterpreted "according to new contexts of discourse and of life" (71).

The Extravagance of the Wicked Husbandmen

According to Ricoeur's overall hermeneutic claim, the parable of the Wicked Husbandmen can be understood as a metaphorical narrative. As such it is endowed with the power to lead its readers to a new vision of life beyond established ways of looking at the world. The main challenge in the act of interpretation is to find the metaphorical tension that prompts readers to see things that they have not seen before. In metaphors, the tension clearly lies between two terms that according to their lexical usage are incompatible (e.g., this book is a dungeon) but whose irritating combination provokes the reader to make sense of that tension. In parables, the tension is less obvious. What exactly is it that causes an audience to move from the story to something outside of it, that makes me aware of the fact that the parable is not just an autonomous world in itself? As I explained in chapter 10, Ricoeur himself is ambiguous about this question and suggests more than one possibility. To continue with my task I will orient myself to the following suggestion: "the trait which invites us to *transgress* the narrative structures . . . is, to my mind, the element of extravagance which makes the 'oddness' of the narrative, by mixing the 'extraordinary' with the 'ordinary.'"[5] Jesus' stories are about normal, quotidian situations, Ricoeur observes, but their plot developments are often surprising, sometimes even bizarre. These strange traits are the "signs of metaphoricity" (97) that refer an audience to something outside the narrative. To determine the kind of extravagance that characterizes the parable of the Wicked Husbandmen, Ricoeur would ask us to take a close look at the dramatic structure of the narrative, by which he means "the challenge which the *plot* displays for the main characters, and . . . the answers of these characters to the *crisis* situation" (97). The dramatic structure of the parable of the Wicked Husbandmen can be described as follows.

The parable's main characters are the owner of the vineyard, the tenants, and the collectors, including both the servants and the owner's son. As the plot develops, three interactions between these people occur: the contractual agreement between the owner and the tenants, the tenants' recurrent rejection of the collectors, and finally the owner's destruction of the tenants. The first interaction sets up the situation and opens up a variety of possibilities. Will the tenants conform to the agreement made with the landowner or will they break the contract?

The second interaction answers this question in a startling way. Not only do the tenants refuse to deliver the owner's share, not only do they break the contract, they also violate basic human relations by beating and even killing the collectors who are repeatedly sent to them. This second interaction is a process of increasing brutality that has its climax in the owner's decision to send his son and the subsequent deliberate murder of the son by the tenants. At this point the plot has led to a crisis situation, which, again, opens up various possibilities. Will the tenants' violence persist? Will it lead to their final victory over the owner, or will the owner repay the tenants for their outrageous crimes? The tension of this crisis situation is enforced and prolonged by the question: "What then will the owner of the vineyard do?"

The third interaction is narrated in the future tense: "He will come and destroy the tenants and give the vineyard to others." With this sentence, the crisis is already resolved: the tenants do not triumph but lose their lives. The handing-over of the vineyard to other tenants is an epilogue that has no further influence on the basic structure of the plot.[6] The dramatic structure of the parable leads from a peaceful business deal to an outburst of violence and finally to an equally violent revenge.

Again, this examination of the parable's plot is necessary because it "provides an appropriate basis for the *metaphorical* process" (97), as Ricoeur says. We should now be able to determine the element of extravagance that compels the reader to take "the narrative as referring to some similar structure of human experience outside the narrative" (98). Ricoeur himself detects this element in the behavior of the owner who puts his own son at the mercy of the murderous tenants. He writes: "Consider the extravagance of the landlord in the 'Parable of the Wicked Husbandmen,' who after having sent his servants, sends his son. What Palestinian property owner living abroad would be foolish enough to act like this landlord?" (115)

At this point, I would venture to disagree with Ricoeur. The realism of the story, according to my reading, breaks down and gives way to surprising developments long before the landlord decides to send his only son. My own analysis points to the strange discrepancy between the possibilities opened up by the first interaction—the leasing of the vineyard—and the actual way the plot develops. The tenants do not just refuse to comply with the collector, they grab him and beat him up! This is where the "extravagance" begins. When the landlord sends his second servant, the violence persists. According to the gospel of Mark: "This one they beat over the head and insulted. Then he sent another, and that one they killed. And so it was with many others; some they beat, and others they killed." This is out of all proportion to how one would imagine a quarrel over real estate.

The scene of destruction with which the story ends—the servants murdered, the son murdered, and finally the tenants dead as well—contrasts drastically with the everyday setting with which the parable begins, a landowner leasing his vineyard to a group of tenants. This tension between the familiar world of business and the eruption of multiple beatings and killings seems to me to be "the extraordinary within the ordinary" that Ricoeur makes responsible for the metaphorical process. It is here where I find the "element of extravagance" that, according to Ricoeur, lets the reader know that this story has an "outside referent."

This referent in human reality is not just of any kind, if I follow Ricoeur. In reading the parable of the Wicked Husbandmen, in being receptive to its strange traits, in letting oneself be moved and irritated by the clash between a familiar setting and the subsequent scenes of savagery, a Ricoeurian reader makes a transition from the world of the story to human limit-experiences. The accumulation of physical violence that I have claimed to be the element of extravagance within the parable refers readers to a boundary-situation of the human condition, to experiences of catastrophe and distress, death, suffering, guilt, and hatred, to use Ricoeur's language (128).

Ricoeur claims that an interpretation will always be related to "our particular situation" (134). When I read the parable in the German church in 1992 I heard the anti-Jewish echoes of the story, its allegorical links to the alleged Jewish killing of God's prophets and God's son. *At the same time,* I was a recipient of the parable's poetic powers, released by the story's excessive violence. I felt myself being powerfully referred to limit-experiences of "death, suffering, guilt, and hatred" in my own time, memories of excessive violence that shaped my own "particular situation." Images of Nazi atrocities flashed up before my eyes as the story took its catastrophic course. The tenants' brutality seemed so exaggerated to me, the multiple killings so out of proportion to common sense and in fact, the whole outcome of the story so horrific that I did exactly what Ricoeur's theory suggests: I made a transfer from the world of the story to my own "context of discourse and of life."

This transfer was as powerful as metaphors can be. Poetic language, according to Ricoeur, makes us "perceive new connections in things" (85). The parable of the Wicked Husbandmen reminded me of the Holocaust more forcefully than descriptive language does. I was "struck" by its images, yet I was unable to articulate or think about what I "saw." What the story evoked in my mind was a vague impression that shook me up but that I could not explicate. This impression was all the more difficult to identify because it was imbricated with another layer of meaning: the anti-Jewish Christian tale of supersessionism.

Ricoeur argues that metaphorical narratives cannot be reduced to a clear message but can be interpreted: "the connection between the narrative form and the metaphorical process paves the way for an open-ended series of interpretive attempts" (35). What kinds of interpretive attempts, then, should follow the metaphorical process I just described? What kind of hermeneutics could appropriately address the post-Holocaust meanings of the parable of the Wicked Husbandmen? I cannot offer here a comprehensive answer to these questions. But I can begin to outline what Ricoeur calls an open-ended series of interpretive attempts.

A Post-Holocaust Biblical Hermeneutics

Claiming a Post-Holocaust Context

The hermeneutics I propose should begin by claiming clearly and consistently a post-Holocaust context for engaging with New Testament parables. The question of context is the starting point of every interpretive endeavor and needs to be answered carefully. The *primary* context for the kind of hermeneutics I am envisioning here is neither the "first historical setting" of these texts nor the gospel writer's first-century horizon of understanding, nor a literary tradition of parable and paradox, nor limit-experiences of the human condition. The primary context I propose we consider are the post-Holocaust times in which we find ourselves. I use the term "post-Holocaust" not just as a temporal marker but in order to describe a particular kind of interpretive challenge that involves the difficulties of dealing with the legacy of the Nazi crimes and of integrating this legacy into one's religious and cultural identity.

I began to describe this context earlier in this chapter when I referred to the German church service in which I read the parable of the Wicked Husbandmen. By positing such a post-Holocaust context I was following Ricoeur's argument that a parable's message is open to "fresh reinterpretation according to new contexts of discourse and of life" (71). But in contrast to Ricoeur, who never specifies any contexts, a post-Holocaust reading of the parables cannot avoid the work of foregrounding its dependence on a specific social location.[7] The metaphorical process released by the parable can only be explored in concrete terms. Who is reading the parable? When, where, and how does this reading take place? These specifications necessarily highlight the contingent nature of the interpretation. What that means is that not every contemporary reader of the parable of the Wicked Husbandmen will be reminded of the Holocaust. When I teach the parable in an American classroom, for example, my students respond to the story's poetic powers with different memories and associations from mine. They, too, are receptive to the story's exaggerated violence. But for them, this violence evokes memories that are part of their own distinct cultural reservoir, a cultural reservoir that is shaped by nationality, religious background, and age. My American (and mostly Christian) students associate not Nazi atrocities with the parable of the Wicked Husbandmen but things that are much closer to home, such as the recent shootings in American high schools or the handling of illegal immigrants by U.S. officials.

The post-Holocaust setting in which I place my own work is not the only legitimate context in which the parables of Jesus can be read. There is nothing intrinsic in the biblical text that can ground or even demand a post-Holocaust hermeneutics. Similarly, there is nothing intrinsic in the events of the Holocaust that can ground or demand a post-Holocaust reading of New Testament parables. Nevertheless, my experience in the German church service must be recognized as more than a private one. By deploying this memory I am engaged in more than a self-reflective act of working through my

German biography. Throughout this book, my autobiographical interventions have pointed to the many ways my concerns with parable studies rely on specific social, cultural, and historical circumstances and therefore reflect a particular horizon of understanding that I share with others. When I read the parable in 1992 I was engaged in a public act that involved an institutionalized setting and an audience. In this setting, the parable of the Wicked Husbandmen, because of its power to evoke memories of Nazi violence and because of its anti-Jewish reception history, raises the question of how to read this text after the Holocaust.

The parable of the Wicked Husbandmen can raise post-Holocaust questions not only in Germany but also in America. When the parable of the Wicked Husbandmen is read in American Christian contexts, including both church and classroom settings, these settings, too, should be understood as post-Holocaust contexts. I spent much time in this book showing how the difficulties of Holocaust remembrance, the "legacy of an unmourned trauma" (Santner), was transported from German to American scholarship. Scholars in America inherited the anti-Jewish rhetoric that characterized German New Testament scholarship. These scholars were also heirs of many missed opportunities during the postwar decades to let the memory of the Holocaust inform New Testament scholarly practices. In a similar way, the post-Holocaust legacy of the parable of the Wicked Husbandmen with its multiple and complicated aspects has been transported to America and left its traces in scholarly and nonscholarly discourses.

For my American students the crimes of the Holocaust are not as prominent and as present as they are for me. But the parable of the Wicked Husbandmen can raise a number of troublesome issues for my students that would impel me to talk to them about the post-Holocaust times in which they, too, find themselves. My students may not be aware of this, but the parable comes to them not as a tabula rasa but attached to a long and problematic history of interpretation. Several of my students automatically place the parable within Jesus' polemical relationship with his Jewish opponents. Such an interpretive notion is informed not only by the gospel context but also by the work of Jeremias, whose reconstructions of the parables' first historical settings have been passed on from one academic generation to another, influencing Christian education and preaching across national borders. Not all students but some of them are also informed by the age-old anti-Jewish interpretive pattern that Aaron Milavec is concerned with. "God sent many prophets to the Jewish people, the Jewish people rejected and killed them. Then God sent his son to earth. Some people from the Jewish community killed him. This opened the door for Gentile salvation." This is how one of my students summarized how she had learned to read the parable. Again, my students are mostly unaware of the fact that such readings perpetuate a long-standing anti-Jewish history of interpretation and how destructive this interpretation has been. But the fact that these things are unconscious is precisely the reason why I consider the post-Holocaust context an important category that should be introduced also in an American classroom.[8]

Prioritizing a post-Holocaust context for reading Mark 12:1–12 does not invalidate other contexts or interpretive concerns. But in important ways, a post-Holocaust context opens up space for a number of interpretive steps that otherwise would not be possible. Moving from the American classroom back to the German church setting, I would like to bring into closer view the poetic power of Mark 12:1–12.

Attending to the Poetic Powers of Parables

Earlier in this chapter I offered a Ricoeurian reading of the parable that pointed to the poetic transfer triggered by the parable's metaphoric tension. I find this reading valuable because it articulates and opens up for debate something that I suspect usually remains unspoken: the uncanny power of this text to leave images of destruction. A post-Holocaust reading of the Wicked Husbandmen should continue with a thorough attempt to work with these vague impressions evoked by the parable's "extravagance." Within the German church setting, for example, it would be crucial to move from a fleeting thought about Nazi atrocities to a thorough reflection on this metaphoric process. As Des Pres argues, vague impressions of the horror of Auschwitz are not beneficial to Holocaust remembrance (*Survivor* 172). Regardless of how powerful such impressions may be, they do not lead to a real understanding or evaluation of the events. Neither do they lead, I would add, to an adequate post-Holocaust hermeneutics of New Testament parables. The impression of Nazi atrocities in my mind was powerful but shapeless, deprived of even the most basic distinction, the one between perpetrators and victims. It is not enough to trace and verbalize the transfer from the world of the text to the extremity of the Holocaust. It is equally important to then respond to and work with this transfer.

Andreas Huyssen articulates some of the difficulties at stake in this endeavor. Formulating the tasks involved in a "labor of remembrance," Huyssen speaks of the "unimaginable, unspeakable, and unrepresentable horror" (259) that is and will remain the core of all Holocaust remembrance. When I read the parable of the Wicked Husbandmen in the German church I felt myself being referred to this horror. According to Huyssen, however, an acknowledgment of this horror needs to be accompanied by the work of attending to the actual experiences of specific people who suffered, died, or survived the Holocaust. A "labor of remembrance," according to Huyssen, needs to "sustain the tension between the numbing totality of the Holocaust and the stories of the individual victims, families, and communities" (259). Following Huyssen, one may want to consider a hermeneutics that would lead from "the numbing totality of the Holocaust" to the details of Jewish suffering during the Holocaust, a hermeneutics that would prompt a German audience to integrate testimonies of Holocaust survivors into its Christian discourse.

However, Björn Krondorfer makes an important argument against such a step. For him, the move from the parable of the Wicked Husbandmen to Jewish Holocaust testimonies, especially in the context of a German church, would be a move into the wrong direction. In his essay "Of Faith and Faces," Krondorfer criticizes the tendency among German Christian theologians to focus on testimonies of Jewish suffering while eclipsing the question of how to respond to the Holocaust from a *German* perspective. German theologians after Auschwitz, he argues, need to think about the events of the Holocaust as a legacy that concerns their own identity not only as Christians but also, and more important, as Germans. Krondorfer writes: "The problem of German Holocaust theology . . . is rooted in a fundamental blindness to one's cultural location as postwar and post-Shoah Germans" (91). As Krondorfer notes, the narratives of Jewish victims and survivors are often cited in an effort to theologize a shared post-Holocaust faith for Christians and Jews. But in the process, the difference between Jews and Germans are blurred: "No space is left for reflecting on differences between a Christian theology that emerges from the past of a perpetrator culture and Jewish responses that are coming forth from a community severely victimized" (95).

Krondorfer calls for an acknowledgment of the social location and positionality of interpretive discourses. He argues that in their post-Holocaust reflections German Christian scholars need to attend to their own groundedness within the perpetrator culture instead of embracing too easily the discourse coming forth from the victims and survivors of the Nazi crimes. Krondorfer makes the following provocative suggestion: "How dangerous would it be to locate oneself as a German theologian in the cultural tradition of the Auschwitz Kommandant rather than that of the Jewish mother and her children?" (103) The primary reference point for a post-Holocaust German Christian theology, according to Krondorfer, should be the perpetrator culture, not the discourses of Jewish suffering.[9]

Following Krondorfer, I would argue that the parable of the Wicked Husbandmen should refer a German Christian audience to its roots in the social and cultural traditions of the perpetrators. I have argued, in very general terms, that the excessive violence of the parable can cause a transfer to the extreme horror of the Holocaust. However, this horror and its numbing quality result not only from the extremity of the victims' suffering but also from the extremity of the perpetrators' crimes. I believe that the primary reason for the ongoing difficulty of Holocaust remembrance in Germany is not the horror suffered by the victims but the fact that the suffering was caused in the name of Germany. Huyssen writes: "How can we understand when even the witnesses had to say: 'I could not believe what I saw with my own eyes'" (259). It is critical to recognize that this question will have different connotations depending on who raises it. From a non-Jewish German perspective the question is this: how can I understand that these unimaginable, unspeakable, and unrepresentable things were done by Germans, that millions were slaughtered by people whose national, cultural, and religious identity I share; that the violence began and took its course in the German towns and villages where I am at home? The difficulties of Holocaust remembrance for many Germans result from the fact that it is intellectually and emotionally hard to comprehend the systematic murder of millions *from the perspective of the perpetrators.* "How could you," ask the children in Marie Luise Kaschnitz's poem from the 1960s. This question connotes not only moral indignation launched at the older generation but also astonishment, articulating how very difficult it is to imagine that entire Jewish communities were wiped out because of the failures and crimes of one's parents. Notwithstanding the many complicated ways that Germans did and did not become "guilty" during the years of the Nazi regime, for Germans, very generally speaking, Holocaust remembrance involves acknowledging and living with the fact that these unbelievable crimes were initiated, organized, and carried out in the name of one's own country.

To understand the enormity of the German crimes in Germany does not get any easier as time goes by. Quite the opposite—as contemporary German identities are shaped by more recent powerful events and memories, the German crimes of the 1930s and 1940s become more and more alien and the quality of their incomprehensibility increases. In my opinion, phrases such as "Stop dwelling on the past!" and "Enough is enough!" uttered by countless Germans today are by no means a symptom of overeducation in matters of German history. Rather they are sighs of helplessness and exasperation, symptoms of the difficulty of making the link between horrendous crimes and one's own identity.

I would like to suggest that in this situation a text such as the parable of the Wicked Husbandmen may be an important venue for German Christians to try to integrate these crimes into their cultural and religious self-understanding. The parable's capacity to forcefully evoke images of extreme violence could be channeled into an effort to identify and remember the violent acts committed by Germans in the first half of the twentieth century. More specifically, the poetic powers of the parable could lead to an effort to recover and remember the histories of violence that shape the very place where the parable is read. The town where I grew up, for example, used to be the hometown of a number of Jewish families whose names are now buried in the archives. Reading the parable of the Wicked Husbandmen in my home church could lead to the work of exploring the acts of persistent violence that culminated in the deportation of these Jewish families to the death camps in eastern Europe.[10] Krondorfer asks how dangerous it is to locate oneself in the cultural tradition of the perpetrators. Acknowledging the records of anti-Jewish violence in one's hometown is "dangerous" in the sense that it destroys any naive notion of one's home, one's *Heimat*, as an innocent place. It seems to me, however, that the loss of this innocent place is an inevitable aspect of the German Christian labor of remembrance.[11]

How to Live with a Tainted Text?

Once the Holocaust memories evoked by the parable are specified from a Christian *and* German perspective, it is possible to look anew at the problem of anti-Judaism raised by the parable of the Wicked Husbandmen. I have postponed the problem of the anti-Jewish reception history of Mark 12 in order to prevent a premature closure of the interpretive task. By attending to the parable's poetic powers I wished to demonstrate how much more is at stake than correcting an age-old troublesome pattern of interpretation. However, once the full scope of the interpretive challenge is acknowledged, a post-Holocaust hermeneutics must also attend to the biblical story's anti-Jewish legacy. This is how church father John Chrysostom interpreted the parable of the Wicked Husbandmen in the fifth century.[12]

> Many things does he [Jesus, the Lord] intimate by this parable: (a) that God's providence had been exercised towards them [the Jews] from the first; (b) that their disposition was murderous from the beginning; (c) that nothing had been omitted [by God] relative to a heedful care of them; (d) that even when the prophets had been slain, he [YHWH] had not turned away from them, but had sent his very Son; (e) that the God of both the New and of the Old Testament was one and the same; (f) that his death should effect great blessings; (g) that for the crucifixion, their crime, they were to endure extreme punishment: the calling of the Gentiles and the casting out of the Jews.

The tenants' exaggerated violence, which in my mind refers to Nazi atrocities, refers in Chrysostom's homily to the "murderous disposition" of "the Jews." The church father reminds us that the parable carries with it one of the most destructive myths in the history of Christian-Jewish relations: "the Jews killed Christ." Uncannily, the parable of the Wicked Husbandmen evokes Nazi atrocities at the same time it attests to those

Christian notions that have fueled anti-Jewish climates for centuries. The story thus bears both cause and effect of anti-Jewish violence.

How then should a post-Holocaust hermeneutics deal with the anti-Jewish legacy of Christian traditions? Aaron Milavec believes that it is possible to recover an original version of the parable that is free of anti-Judaism. He argues that within Mark's Jewish horizon of understanding the parable was a "*true* Jewish story" (99) about inner-Jewish conflict. The idea of "the Jews" as Christ-killers was read into the parable by later interpreters, according to Milavec's overall claim. I do not intend to challenge Milavec's argument here. But I would like to problematize the desire that I sense behind his argument, namely, to recover an innocent strand behind the layers of Christian scripture. I do not want to engage in a discussion of whether or not anti-Judaism is an "intrinsic" part of the New Testament, but I do want to challenge the quest for a "pro-Jewish" New Testament parable. Even if Milavec's thesis is correct in surmising that the original meaning of this story was "pro-Jewish," this thesis cannot do away with the fact that the parable of the Wicked Husbandmen was very soon turned into a weapon against Jewish communities.

Instead of diffusing the parable's anti-Judaism by recovering an original meaning, I would want to explore the historical roots of this anti-Jewish reading pattern, considering when, where, and why the supersessionist reading emerged. The anti-Jewish reading pattern should not be viewed as a problem to be fixed but as a problem that needs to be historicized. A post-Holocaust hermeneutics of Mark 12 should engage in the work of exploring the historical reasons that made it possible for an anti-Jewish interpretation to establish itself. It should join the important scholarly efforts to explore the complex situation of early Christian communities *before* the split between church and synagogue and to trace the developments that eventually would lead to the antagonistic relationship between the two communities.[13] I would like to think of these efforts as another kind of "labor of remembrance." Working within the parameters of the first century, this labor of remembrance would try to excavate and reflect on the historical circumstances that turned the parable from a "*true* Jewish story" into the anti-Jewish Christian story we find in Chrysostom's hateful homily.

The post-Holocaust hermeneutics I am proposing here will resist the desire to save the parable of the Wicked Husbandmen from its violent legacy. For me, the parable will remain a tainted text. As a German I understand this text as part of a poisoned Christian cultural reservoir (Santner, *Stranded* 45) with which I need to live and to work. I part here not only with Milavec's "fresh analysis" but also with the hermeneutic efforts of the literary scholars of the parables examined in this book. In their various interpretive attempts, Ricoeur, Crossan, and Harnisch, I argued, were driven by the desire to have in Jesus' parables meaningful stories for our time. Their readings were intended to revitalize these ancient texts, to recover their relevance for today. I, too, bring the parable of the Wicked Husbandmen back to life by investing my interpretive energies in this text. But in contrast to Harnisch, Crossan, and Ricoeur, I wish to revitalize the parable not as meaningful scripture but as a cause for trouble. I do not think that the parable, because of its innovative powers, can shed new light on our post-Holocaust situation. The parable is a valuable text, however, because it can compel us to engage in a double work of remembrance. Because of its canonical status, the parable will remain a prominent cultural object. Because of its place in lectionaries, it will continue to be read publicly. A post-Holocaust hermeneutics could channel such readings into explorations of both the anti-Jewish legacy carried by this text and its contemporary resonances with the events of the Holocaust.

In the introduction to *Strange Fire: Reading the Bible after the Holocaust*, Tod Linafelt describes the challenges of a post-Holocaust biblical hermeneutics as follows.

> The goal of this volume certainly is not to show that the Bible provides the theological or ethical resources for "understanding" or "explaining" the Holocaust. The Holocaust is too complex, too massive, and too much the product of the twentieth century for such an approach to have integrity. At the same time the volume is not intended to demonstrate that biblical notions of God and humanity, good and evil, or suffering and survival, are now bankrupt or irrelevant or somehow proven wrong. . . . [T]he Bible is itself at times endlessly complex, massively disturbing, and not so far removed from the concerns of the twentieth century as one might expect of an ancient text. (18)

Likewise, the parables of Jesus offer no resources for understanding or explaining the Holocaust. The interpretive process I propose will not result in a reorientation of disconcerted readers who find themselves faced with the reality of Auschwitz. On the contrary, this process illuminates a tension that no act of interpretation can resolve: the tension between an anti-Jewish Christian story and the crimes committed by Nazi Germany. This is a tension that cannot be resolved but can be addressed and explored. The parable of the Wicked Husbandmen forces us to work with the imbricated legacies of the Holocaust and of Christian anti-Judaism. It can ask us to engage in what Tod Linafelt calls "a sort of uneasy dialectic relationship . . . in which both [the Bible and the Holocaust] must be taken into account but in which neither is finally able to absorb or to nullify the other" (18). It is always possible to contain or avoid the resonances between the Bible and the Holocaust through a focus on the biblical text's first historical setting or through a focus on its literary form. Instead, however, I would like to propose that these contemporary meanings and echoes be spelled out as thoroughly as possible. As long as the parable exists as a living piece of the Christian tradition, the best we can do is to take this tainted text as a venue for exploring the complicated legacies that confront post-Holocaust audiences.

Notes

Chapter 1

All biblical quotes are from the *New Revised Standard Version*.

1. By "ethos" Schüssler Fiorenza means "the shared intellectual space of freely accepted obligations and traditions as well as the praxial space of discourse and action" ("Ethics" 9).

2. My quotation is taken from the published version of the speech: "Ethics" 10–11.

3. In 1920 women's membership reached 20 percent. In 1970 the percentage had dropped to 3.5. The gradual increase in the representation of women in the 1970s and 1980s was influenced by the second wave of the women's movement.

4. She mentioned particularly the work presented by the Women in the Biblical World section of the Society (8).

5. Schüssler Fiorenza described the present moment by referring to "the growth of right-wing political fundamentalism and of biblicist literalism in society, religious institutions, and the broader culture," which, she said, "feeds antidemocratic authoritarianism and fosters personal prejudice" (16).

6. I already had encountered Schüssler Fiorenza's works *In Memory of Her* and *Bread Not Stone* in seminars on feminist theology and New Testament hermeneutics in Germany. But the discussions around her work, as I experienced them, seemed always to be separate from mainstream scholarship. I had never witnessed a real confrontation between the two.

7. An important site for this paradigm shift in biblical studies is *Semeia: An Experimental Journal for Biblical Criticism*.

8. There have been various attempts by biblical scholars to engage in an "ethics of accountability." Daniel Patte, with his *Ethics of Biblical Interpretation*, has devoted an entire book to the question of what it would mean for him to take responsibility for his "male European-American" (1) scholarship, in light of Schüssler Fiorenza's presidential address. See especially 6–12. How a concern with ethics can accompany conventional scholarship can be seen in John Dominic Crossan's 1995 publication of *Who Killed Jesus?* in which he advocates an "ethics of historical reconstruction" that is motivated by a concern with the legacy of anti-Judaism associated with the gospel stories of the death of Jesus. While Crossan's language echoes very much Schüssler Fiorenza's original call, he does not refer to her address. For an explicit use of Schüssler Fiorenza's ethical categories in the context of Pauline studies, see Neil Elliott, *Liberating Paul*. Schüssler Fiorenza herself explicated her presidential address in her 1999 publication *Rhetoric and Ethic*.

9. See especially *Semeia* 51, entitled "Poststructural Criticism and the Bible: Text/History/Discourse." The implications of critical theories for historical criticism are explored in Gary Phillips's contribution, "Exegesis as Critical Practice," and Fred Burnett's essay "Postmodern Biblical Exegesis." A sustained discussion of Schüssler Fiorenza's approach can be found in David Jobling, "Writing the Wrongs of the World."

10. See *The Postmodern Bible* 15. Schüssler Fiorenza discussed poststructuralist approaches to biblical texts in her book *But She Said*. For a critical response, see *The Postmodern Bible* 260–267.

11. Toward the beginning of their book the authors of *The Postmodern Bible* argue: "Historical criticism brackets out the contemporary milieu and excludes any examination of the ongoing formative effects of the Bible. By embracing scientific method as the key in the search for historical truth, modern biblical scholarship has kept faith with the Enlightenment's desire to do away with ambivalence and uncertainty once and for all by effectively isolating text and its criticism from the reader's cultural context, values, and interests" (1–2). This indictment repeats Schüssler Fiorenza's concern.

12. I studied these recent trends in historical criticism with Eckard Rau in Hamburg. See his *Reden in Vollmacht*.

13. In Germany, see especially Harnisch, *Die Gleichniserzählungen*. In Switzerland, see Hans Weder, *Die Gleichnisse* and *Neutestamentliche Hermeneutik*.

14. Even though I had read the early works by John Dominic Crossan and Robert Funk already in Germany, I had never paid much attention to their date of publication. I rather read them with a vague sense that "everything American is new."

15. Hans Weder in Zurich and Wolfgang Harnisch in Marburg were among the first German-speaking scholars to develop the notion of the parables as metaphors. Weder's dissertation on the topic was published in 1978. He developed his work on the parables into a comprehensive New Testament hermeneutics in 1986. Harnisch's book on parables came out in 1985.

16. For example, Daniel Patte and Gary Phillips were participants in a conference on "Semiology and Parables," held in the mid-1970s, that discussed structuralist and other literary theories and their applicability to the parables. In the 1990s Patte has become a proponent of an ethics of biblical interpretation. Phillips is one of the authors of *The Postmodern Bible*. This shift can also be studied in regard to the journal *Semeia*: in the 1970s, the journal published the new literary discussions, while in the late 1980s and 1990s the journal became a major site for what Schüssler Fiorenza called the decentering of biblical scholarship.

17. Rather than offering a clear definition of the term "Holocaust," I wish to deploy the term together with all the vagueness that comes with it. This vagueness will become a major theme in the following chapters. I am aware of the problematic sacrificial connotations of the term that have been pointed out by many. It is interesting to me that in Germany this concern has led to a widespread practice of replacing the term "Holocaust" with the term "Shoah." In the United States, the term "Holocaust" continues to be used in discourses across the disciplines. This also means that taking a course on the "Holocaust" can lead an audience to very different reference points depending on the type and the disciplinary context of the course. For a helpful study of the challenges in naming "the Holocaust," see Young, *Writing and Rewriting the Holocaust* 83–98.

18. This is the subtitle of a collection of essays edited by Saul Friedlander.

19. Friedlander's book, which was published in 1992, gives a good overview of the spectrum of these discussions; so does Geoffrey Hartman, *Holocaust Remembrance*, published in 1994, and Lawrence Kritzman, ed., *Auschwitz and After*, published in 1995. Important instances are John Felstiner's work on Paul Celan, Sara Horowitz's work on ghetto writings and women survivors' testimony, Andreas Huyssen's work on Holocaust memory, Dominic LaCapra's investigations into Holocaust representation, Lawrence Langer's work on Holocaust literature, and Eric

Santner's work on memory and mourning in postwar Germany. James Young, *Writing and Rewriting the Holocaust*, published in 1988, is an early and comprehensive discussion of a literary approach to the Holocaust.

20. I should add that studying the Holocaust in the mid-1990s was a timely thing to do: 1994 initiated the long series of fiftieth anniversaries of the end of the war and the liberation of the death camps. The following years were characterized by widespread commemorative efforts on national and communal levels and by an accelerating proliferation of literature on the Holocaust, not only in the United States but, as I witnessed during my annual visits, also in Germany. Other palpable signs of an increasing public awareness were the release and success of Steven Spielberg's film *Schindler's List* and the opening of the Holocaust Memorial Museum in Washington, D.C., in 1993.

21. My critical reading of New Testament scholarship has a focus similar to that of the kind of analysis presented by Ernst Van Alphen in *Caught by History*. This work traces what Van Alphen calls Holocaust effects in contemporary art, literature, and theory.

22. See especially Des Pres, *The Survivor*, and the works of Lawrence Langer from the 1970s. More recently the limit has become a crucial category in theoretical discussions of the "limits of representation." See Friedlander 1–21.

23. Autobiographical interventions have emerged in much recent literary criticism. A discussion about the advantages and limitations of the personal mode of writing is offered in *Confessions of the Critics*, edited by Aram Veeser. A recent (1995) issue of *Semeia* attests to the increasing interests of biblical scholars in this mode of writing. The issue is entitled "Taking It Personally: Autobiographical Biblical Criticism." Steven Moore's contribution, "True Confessions and Weird Obsessions," gives an overview of autobiographical criticism in literary and biblical studies.

Chapter 2

1. An overview and critical discussion of the frequent use of "the uncanny" in recent discourses are provided by Martin Jay, "The Uncanny Nineties." Jay is particularly concerned with the 1994 publication of Jaques Derrida's *Specters of Marx*.

2. Early attempts are Dominic LaCapra's chapter "The Return of the Historically Repressed" in *Representing the Holocaust*. See also Eric Santner, *Stranded Objects*, particularly chapter 2. Jean-Francois Lyotard interprets the controversy around Heidegger and Nazism by referring to the "economy of the *Unheimlich*" (*Heidegger and "the jews"* 55–56). For a more recent use of "the uncanny," see Van Alphen's chapter "Subliminity in the Home."

3. The poem first appeared under a different title, "Rauch und Nebel:I–IV," in the journal *Die neue Rundschau* in 1964. The issue, according to the journal's general scope, offered a wide spectrum of political and historical discussions. Kaschnitz's poem was placed after an essay by Georg Lukacs, which dealt with socialist realism and the time under Stalin. A year later, the poem appeared under the title "Zoon Politikon:I–VI" in Marie Luise Kaschnitz, *Ein Wort Weiter*.

4. In his essay accompanying a 1995 German edition of Améry's speech, Horst Meier points out that "Resentments," in contrast to other essays by Améry, was not acknowledged by the German public and until the 1990s was hardly known in Germany. Meier also points to the sad irony of this lack of reception, since "Resentments" is the only place where Améry addressed the Germans in such a clear and demanding way (51).

5. The Mitscherlichs' theory is not uncontested. For a critical revision of their account of the postwar decades, see Robert Moeller, "War Stories."

6. In her essay "Wie man da stand," Kaschnitz writes: "Frankfurt im Krieg, und worin soll sie denn bestanden haben, unsere sogenannte innere Emigration? Darin, daß wir ausländische Sender abhörten, zusammensaßen und auf die Regierung schalten, ab und zu einem Juden auf

der Straße die Hand gaben, auch dann, wenn es jemand sah? Daß wir prophezeiten, zuerst den Krieg, dann die Niederlage und damit das Ende der Partei? Nicht heimlich im Keller Flugblätter gedruckt, nicht nachts verteilt, nicht widerständlicherischen Bünden angehört, von denen man wußte, daß es sie gab, es so genau aber gar nicht wissen wollte. Lieber überleben, lieber noch da sein, weiter arbeiten, wenn erst der Spuk vorüber war" (55). I translate: "Frankfurt during the war—what exactly did it mean, our so-called inner emigration? That we listened to foreign radio stations, that we sat together and criticized the regime, that we occasionally shook hands with a Jew on the streets, even when someone was watching? That we prophesied, first the war, then the defeat and therefore the end of the Nazi party? We did not secretly print leaflets in the basement, did not distribute them at night, did not belong to resistance groups, which we knew existed without wanting to know the details. We preferred survival. We wanted to still be there, and work, after the nightmare was over." A study of Kaschnitz's writing and publishing during the war and shortly after is provided in Theodor Eduard Dohle, "Marie Luise Kaschnitz im Dritten Reich und in der Nachkriegszeit." See also David Basker, "Love in a Nazi Climate."

7. Freud's essay "Das Unheimliche," first published in 1919, has a very different historical context from that of Kaschnitz's poem from the 1960s. Nevertheless, Freud's detailed analysis has given me important clues for interpreting what is going on in the German home.

8. The ambivalent meaning of *heimlich* points to the ambivalent function of home (*Heim*), generally speaking. Places that appear to be culturally homogeneous, where people "belong," where they feel at ease and in agreement with themselves, are based on the concealment and exclusion of everything that "does not belong"—people who are "other," local histories of conflicts and violence—everything that would expose the homogeneity and peace within the parameters of the home as an illusion. At stake within the homes in Germany during the postwar decades was the murder of six million Jews, which makes the ambivalent function of *heimlich* particularly charged. Questions of home have been theorized by many cultural and feminist critics. My reading of Kaschnitz is informed especially by Angelika Bammer, *The Question of "Home,"* Michael Geisler, "'Heimat' and the German Left," Laura Levitt, *Jews and Feminism,* and Minnie Bruce Pratt, "Identity: Skin Blood Heart."

9. This exhibition produced the publication *1945: The Year of Liberation,* by the United States Holocaust Memorial Council.

10. Barnouw sharply criticizes what she describes as the specifically American expectation that Germans, confronted with Nazi atrocities, should "see, accept, and repent their complicity in these acts" (xii). Barnouw argues that the images of liberated camps were problematically used by the Allies as evidence for the Germans' collective guilt. Barnouw criticizes the Mitscherlichs for not taking into account the expectations that were imposed on the Germans by the Allies. I do not share Barnouw's, I think, rigid interpretation of the Allied policy. Rather than criticizing the fact that there were expectations being imposed on the Germans, as Barnouw does again and again, it would be important to disentangle and examine the operating concepts, such as "collective guilt" or "atonement," which in Barnouw's analysis ultimately are left intact. What I do find helpful in Barnouw's analysis, however, is her effort to open up for discussion that very decisive moment when the German population was confronted with the outcome of crimes that for many had become known during the war only as vague rumors or, allegedly, not at all. Paying attention to this moment of confrontation and asking questions about its meaning, as Barnouw attempts to do, seems crucial to me in order to understand the ongoing difficulties of Holocaust memory in Germany. For a different reading of the images of confrontation, see Barbie Zelizer, *Remembering to Forget* 104–105.

11. One of the earliest attempts to grapple with these questions is Karl Jaspers, *The Question of German Guilt.* Jaspers writes, for instance: "The guilt question received its universal impact from the charges brought against us Germans by the victors and the world. In the summer of 1945, when in all towns and villages the posters [were] hung[,] with the pictures and stories

from Belsen and the crucial statement, 'You are the guilty!' consciences grew uneasy, horror gripped many who had indeed not known this, and something rebelled: who indicts me there? No signature, no authority—the poster came as though from empty space. It is only human that the accused, whether justly or unjustly charged, tries to defend himself" (47).

12. My English translation fails to capture the subtle historical references of these phrases. The German word *Lade*, for instance, could also be read as a loading device to transport dead bodies. "Ein Rauch / Stinkender" literally means "a smoke of stinking ones" and refers to the notorious smell from the crematoria more directly than my English translation does.

13. This passivity might also be the reason why the forgotten images of 1945 appear not just once, but again and again. Among the many uncanny examples listed and described by Freud there is one that is characterized by the "factor of involuntary repetition": the "unintended recurrence of the same situation" (237). An experience is uncanny when it repeats itself independent of my own doing.

14. Améry suggested, for example: "At best, he [the author] is able to imagine vaguely a national community that would reject everything, but absolutely everything, that is accomplished in the days of its own deepest degradation, and what here and there may appear to be as harmless as the Autobahns" (78). Horst Meier has discussed this quite far-ranging suggestion in terms of an anti-Nazi imperative.

15. This passivity raises questions about the title of the larger poem. "Zoon Politikon" as a reference point for the people in the home sounds ironic, since these people seem to be unable to take up the vocation implicit in the phrase: the shaping of a society.

16. So it seems if one reads the introductory "wenn" as building a causal connection between the children's protest and the events in the home.

17. The student movement has also been criticized for assuming an innocent and self-righteous position vis-à-vis the German past. Michael Geisler, for instance, problematizes the unwarranted self-exemption from responsibility that characterizes the German Left during these years. "The children," as they are portrayed in Kaschnitz's poem, bring this attitude to my mind.

18. I am following the definition of the "third generation" provided by Björn Krondorfer in his book *Remembrance and Reconciliation*. With regard to both German and Jewish third generations, Krondorfer explains: "The third generation, generally speaking, are the grandchildren of the first generation. They were born in the 1960s and 1970s. They have, with a few exceptions, not yet articulated a distinct discursive practice but have certainly been influenced by a communal ethos and public discourse" (12). Krondorfer's book offers attempts to articulate both ethos and discourse of the third generation. With respect to young Germans, see especially 29–37 and 56–70. My next chapter can be understood as a similar attempt to identify the particular challenges of Holocaust remembrance for "third-generation" Germans.

Chapter 3

1. Harnisch is influenced by Ricoeur's major work on metaphor theory, *The Rule of Metaphor*, and by Ricoeur's own attempt to apply his concept of metaphor to the parables of Jesus, "Biblical Hermeneutics," which I discuss in chapters 10 and 11.

2. With this argument Harnisch diverges from Ricoeur, for whom the criteria to distinguish religious from poetic discourse is the degree of "extravagance" (158–167). Harnisch, in contrast, theorizes a difference in content; see also Harnisch 151.

3. Harnisch's interpretation draws from the work of the German Kafka scholar Heinz Politzer. The appropriation of Kafka and Politzer by parable scholars will be a central issue in chapter 9.

4. See Harnisch's full sentence: "By cleverly ignoring the interest of the opponents, the landlord's question opens up for them the possibility to perceive goodness as something irresistible, as an indisputable value, as something that cannot be disapproved." "Durch eine raffinierte

Nichtbeachtung des Argumentationsinteresse der Gegenpartei eröffnet sie [the landlord's question] dieser die Möglichkeit, die Güte als etwas Unwiderstehliches, als ein unbestreitbares Gut wahrzunehmen—als etwas, das sich gar nicht mißbilligen läßt."

5. *"Die Wahrnehmung einer im Licht der Liebe wunderbar verwandelten Welt"* (his emphasis).

6. Harnisch talks about "ein Beispiel moderner Lyrik."

7. My critical concern was partly informed by a changed sensitivity toward literature that has shaped a general academic climate in recent decades, especially in the United States. Harnisch's approach to the poem is typical of the effects of a particular strand within literary theory, usually associated with structuralism or the New Criticism, which puts emphasis on the formal qualities of literature and seeks to block out a text's historical referent. Today these dehistoricizing tendencies have given way to an emphasis on the embeddedness of literature in a specific historical reality. Today a formalist approach would not seem to do justice to Kaschnitz's poem.

8. In his essay "Sprache des Möglichen," Harnisch explains his hermeneutics by means of another historically charged piece: Art Spiegelman's cover for the *New Yorker* that depicted an orthodox Jew and an African-American woman kissing. Harnisch calls this picture "the revelation of a dream which suspends reality through offering the unimaginable possibility of a relationship between the two hostile ethnic groups." "die Veröffentlichung eines Traums, der das Wirkliche in die unfaßliche Möglichkeit einer versöhnten Beziehung der beiden verfeindeten Volksgruppen aufhebt" (29). In contrast to his use of Kaschnitz, Harnisch puts his hermeneutics here in explicit relation with contemporary history and thus opens it up for debate.

9. "Life is complicated" is the slogan with which Avery Gordon opens her book *Ghostly Matters* (3).

10. I offer the original German paragraph: "Durch ein wiederholtes 'wenn' gegliedert, beschwört die Satzfolge der *mittleren Gedichtpartie* das Ambiente bürgerlicher Geborgenheit: die 'Wand Rosentapete' und den 'versiegelten,' 'schön glänzenden Estrich.' Im Kontext des Gesagten erscheint beides freilich als brüchige Fassade, die das Grauen der Vergangenheit nicht verdecken und das von außen andrängende Unbehagen nicht abschirmen kann. Denn aus geblümter Wand und Glanzparkett, den Wertzeichen privaten Glücks, quellen Totenschädel und Krematorienrauch. Es ist diese Zusammenfügung des Vertrauten mit dem Ungehörigen und Unpassenden, auf der die abgründige Ironie der Mitteilung beruht: Der Raum behaglichen Sonntagsfriedens wird zum Ort des Schreckens, angefüllt mit den Indizien eines unvorstellbaren Verbrechens. Das Ganze kulminiert im Akt der von langer Hand vorbereiteten Bekleidung, die sich nun an 'uns,' den Hausbewohnern, vollzieht. Wieder durch ein unscheinbares 'so' eröffnet, gibt sich die Aussage als Folge des soeben Beschriebenen zu erkennen. Kann die Rede von dem Kleid, das 'uns' zukommt,' etwas anderes meinen als ein Totenhemd? Dann bringt 'uns' die unerwartete Präsenz des Verdrängten um den Genuß der Gegenwart. Die Opfer von Auschwitz klagen das Leben der Henker und aller Mitwisser ein."

11. If I were to debate with Harnisch I would argue that his invocation of skulls (*Totenköpfe*) mistranslates "the emaciated Jewish heads." In my opinion, Kaschnitz refers to the 1945 images and photographs from the death camps. What was seen there were not skulls but decaying bodies.

12. "Das Gedicht wiederholt ex eventu die grauenvolle Vision vom Schicksal der Juden, die Franz Kafka in zynischer Selbstironie einem der Briefe an Milena anvertraut hat. Auf diesen Zusammenhang verweist das im Kaschnitz-Gedicht begegnende Motiv der 'Bettlade.'"

13. I should specify here: these question do not matter if one is solely interested in the function of metaphor in the Ricoeurian sense. For a powerful account of how metaphors and their historical referents matter in regard to the experience of the death camps, see John Felstiner, "Translating Paul Celan's 'Todesfuge,'" and Sidra DeKoven Ezrahi, "'The Grave in the Air': Unbound Metaphors in Post-Holocaust Poetry."

14. I thank Harnisch for letting me know that the connection between Kafka and Kaschnitz is based on his own reading of these literatures (letter January 1997).

15. My second thoughts on Harnisch's quotation of Kaschnitz are partly inspired by a vivid memory. On the morning of November 10, 1989, I went to school to attend Harnisch's lecture on Paul's first letter to the Corinthians. Everybody was moved by the astonishing events that had happened the day before, the coming-down of the Berlin Wall. Harnisch started his lecture by asking us not to forget—over the enthusiasm of these days—that the ninth of November was also the anniversary of the so-called Kristallnacht, the most violent pogrom in prewar Germany. I am still deeply impressed by this reminder. Harnisch was the only person I know who had so immediately pointed out this jarring coincidence.

16. This thought became first clear to me through Claudia Schippert, "Ruining the Entire Afternoon: Memory in Bergen Belsen."

17. I have in mind here several of Huyssen's thoughts. Huyssen describes the core of all Holocaust representation as "unimaginable, unspeakable, and unrepresentable horror." He writes: "Post-Holocaust generations can only approach that core by mimetic approximation, a mnemonic strategy which recognizes the event in its otherness and beyond identification or therapeutic empathy, but which physically innervates some of the horror and the pain in a slow and persistent labor of remembrance" (259). For a helpful discussion of this quotation see Michelle Friedman's dissertation on second-generation Holocaust Literature, "Reckoning with Ghosts."

18. As other students of Harnisch's book have told me, this seems to be the standard reaction to his quotation of Kaschnitz's poem.

19. In the context of Argentina, Gordon argues, the facts and figures of state-sponsored terror "can be isolated and laid bare, and they can be put to the political task of exposure, but it seems as if in that very act the ghosts return, demanding a different kind of knowledge, a different kind of acknowledgment" (64).

Chapter 4

1. The first publisher was Zwingli in Zurich, Switzerland. My opening quotation is based on the book's first English translation, published in 1955, 19.

2. See their essay "The Holocaust as Interruption and the Christian Return into History," published in a 1984 issue of *Concilium*. In other contexts both authors have developed this argument in different ways. See Schüssler Fiorenza, "The Ethics of Biblical Interpretation," and David Tracy, "Christian Witness and the Shoah."

3. See Rudolf Mack, and Dieter Volpert's high school textbook *Der Mann aus Nazareth–Jesus Christus* 13–14. The authors present here an interpretation of the parables of Jesus that is clearly based on Jeremias's scholarship. In an overview of modern parable interpretation, Normal Perrin writes that Jeremias's book "became the most widely read book on the parables, and today is the essential starting point for parable research" (91–92).

4. This notion about the parables and their effects goes back to the gospels themselves, specifically to the "hardening" theory in Mark 4:10–12. Jülicher writes emphatically: "what a horrible thing to imagine: a savior who deliberately invents ways to prevent his numb people from coming back to life, who presents the truth so that it does not have any effects!" "welche schauerliche Vorstellung von einem Heilande, der extra Mittel erfindet, um seinem stumpf gewordenen Volke die Belebung unmöglich zu machen, der ihnen die Wahrheit in einer Form bietet, die sie wirkungslos macht!" (140–141).

5. In her book *Abraham Geiger and the Jewish Jesus*, Susannah Heschel critically examines the ways this image of the historical Jesus is tied up with a negative image of Judaism. While my own study focuses rather strictly on the scholarly discourse as it pertains to Jeremias's post-Holocaust parable interpretation, it should be noted that Jülicher's nineteenth-century scholarship has its own problematic legacies after the Holocaust. Heschel's study helpfully explores the

wider scholarly context in which Jülicher's work is situated: German Christian liberal theology and its strong anti-Jewish trends.

6. The basic forms underlying "allegories" on the one hand and "parables" on the other are, according to Jülicher, "metaphor," the replacement of one word by another, and "comparison," a sentence construction that points out the similarity between two things. One of the idiosyncrasies of parable scholarship is that several decades later, the concept of "metaphor," vehemently rejected by Jülicher, was rediscovered as the main model for parable interpretation. See chapter 11.

7. "We will never get over the fact that many of his precious figurative sayings are transmitted to us only as fragments. We often know neither the occasion nor the atmosphere nor the audience to which he spoke, not to mention the place where he was or the preceding events that were still on his and his disciples' minds. We also do not know what Jesus said to introduce his parables or what he added to them as he walked on the sunny street of his contemplation." "Nimmer verschmerzen wir's, dass viele seiner köstlichen Aussprüche bildlicher Art . . . nur fragmentarisch uns überliefert worden sind, dass wir häufig weder die Veranlassung kennen, bei welcher, noch die Stimmung, in welcher, noch die Hörer, zu welchen er sie sprach, geschweige die Örtlichkeit, in der er sich gerade befand, die letzten Erlebnisse, die in seinem und der Seinigen Herzen noch nachklangen, sowie was Jesus solch einem Ausspruch vorbereitend vorausgeschickt, was er weiterschreitend auf der sonnigen Strasse seiner Kontemplation daran angeknüpft haben mag" (91).

8. The most blatant example is the parable of the Sower, Mark 4:3–9, which is accompanied by an allegorical interpretation (verses 14–20) that, according to Jülicher, goes back not to Jesus but to the writers of the gospel.

9. "Only by lovingly immersing ourselves into the mind of Jesus will we be able to fill the gap left by tradition and to regain the full value of Jesus' parables." "Nur durch ein liebevolles Versenken in den Geist Jesu . . . können wir diese Lücke, die die Tradition lässt, einigermassen ausfüllen und so den vollen Wert der Reliquien von Jesu Gleichnissen zurückgewinnen" (92).

10. Throughout this section I refer to the English edition of Jeremias's book of 1963. From 1947 on, Jeremias revised and greatly extended his work. I explicitly refer to the 1947 edition in chapter 5, where I also note the differences between the early and late editions.

11. This was done by Albert Schweitzer in his famous book *Geschichte der Leben-Jesu-Forschung*, the first edition of which appeared in 1906 under the title *Von Reimarus zu Wrede: Eine Geschichte der Leben-Jesu-Forschung*.

12. Jeremias's departure from Jülicher has been told and interpreted numerous times over the decades. For an American perspective, see Perrin, *Jesus* 97–106.

13. Thereby Jeremias made first steps in the direction of what later would be called "the new quest for the historical Jesus."

14. Perrin writes: "Jeremias assumes that one must come to the parables of Jesus from an intensive study of the use of parables in ancient Judaism, especially from an intensive study of the use of parables by the rabbis representing the earlier phases of the Jewish rabbinical literature, those most nearly contemporary with Jesus. Jeremias has conducted such a study himself; that much is evident from every page of his book, and this is an important aspect of his historical approach to the parables" (*Jesus*, 101). As I will discuss shortly, Jeremias's treatment of rabbinical literature has come under sharp criticism in recent years.

15. In critical interaction with Jülicher's work, Jeremias writes: " We are told [by Jülicher] that the parables announce a genuine religious humanity; they are stripped of their eschatological import. Imperceptibly Jesus is transformed into an 'apostle of progress,' a teacher of wisdom who inculcates moral precepts and a simplified theology by means of striking metaphors and stories. But nothing could be less like him" (19). The importance of eschatology for parable interpretation was pointed out already in C. H. Dodd, *The Parables of the Kingdom*, published in 1936. Jeremias replaced Dodd's notion of a "realized eschatology" with a more nuanced concept: an "eschatology in the process of realization."

16. In my earlier use of this parable I highlighted Harnisch's interest in the metaphorical tension of parables. I showed that Harnisch bases his interpretation on the interplay between a usual and an unusual story whose incongruity poses a challenge for the hearer. In Matthew 20:1–15 the tension is between the equal payment and the hearer's expectation that the workers who were first employed would receive a higher wage. This means that Harnisch finds the interpretive clue within the realm of the narrative itself, with everything external being irrelevant. The parable's first audience and the particular debate or discussion during which the parable was told by Jesus do not matter to Harnisch. For Jeremias, these things are crucial.

17. In my earlier quotation I left out verses 1a and 16. Verse 1a, the introductory formula, according to Harnisch, is secondary, a response to the parable by the early Christian community (174–176). Verse 16, according to a general scholarly agreement, does not belong to the original parable. I also omitted the verse numbering in order to simulate a parallel between Kafka's and Jesus' parables.

18. Jeremias further points out that in the gospel context the parable is directed at Jesus' disciples. Originally, however, the parable was directed against Jesus' opponents: "Many parables which the primitive Church connected with the disciples of Jesus, were originally addressed to a different audience, namely, to the Pharisees, the scribes, or the crowd" (38). Matthew 20:1–16, according to Jeremias, underwent a change in audience and a change in function: "The change of audience has resulted in a shift of emphasis; an apologetic parable has assumed a hortatory character" (40). Verse 16, according to Jeremias, is also a creation of the early church. It is an instance of what Jeremias calls generalizing logia, which are attached at the end of a parable and usually offer misleading interpretations of the parables (107–117). Jeremias points to the importance of freeing the parables from this generalizing interpretation: "the recognition of its secondary nature is significant, since, through the addition of such generalizations, the parables concerned have acquired a moralizing sense which obscures the original situation and blunts the sense of conflict, the sharp edge of the eschatological warning, the sternness of the threat" (112). Numerous interpreters have followed Jeremias in his reconstruction of the original length of the parable. See, for instance, Harnisch 198–200. Perrin writes: "It is to Jeremias above all others that we owe our present ability to reconstruct the parables very much in the form in which Jesus told them. Indeed, when we talk of interpreting the parables of Jesus today we mean interpreting the parables as Jeremias has reconstructed them, either personally or through his influence on others who have followed the method he developed" (101).

19. According to Jeremias, the laborers' comment that no one had hired them is a false excuse: the landlord pities them "[e]ven if, in the case of the last labourers to be hired, it is their own fault that, in a time when the vineyard needs workers, they sit about in the market-place gossiping till late afternoon" (37).

20. Jeremias writes: "The pay for an hour's work will not keep a family; their children will go hungry if the father comes home empty-handed. It is because of his pity for their poverty that the owner allows them to be paid a full day's wages. In this case the parable does not depict an arbitrary action, but the behavior of a large-hearted man who is compassionate and full of sympathy for the poor" (37). In a later discussion of the parable, Jeremias describes the workers as victims of "the spectre of unemployment" that plagued people's lives at the time of Jesus (139).

21. This is indicated by the introductory formula.

22. Compare Jülicher 466–467. Jülicher's and Jeremias's interpretations of Matthew 20 are, in fact, quite similar to each other. Like Jeremias, Jülicher contextualizes the parable within a situation of conflict between Jesus and the Pharisees. What distinguishes Jeremias's interpretation, I would argue, is a more violent interpretive language. If Jülicher talks about a theological dispute, Jeremias tends to talk about a mortal conflict between Jesus and his enemies.

23. The appearance of a king instead of a landowner, according to Jeremias, is another proof for the secondary character of the rabbinical story.

24. In later German editions, Jeremias claims the dependency of rabbinical parables on Jesus as early as his introduction. He asks "if Jesus' example was perhaps a main factor leading to the rise of the genre of rabbinical parables." "ob Jesu Vorbild nicht . . . massgeblich an der Entstehung der Literaturgattung der rabbinischen Gleichnisse beteiligt ist?" (8) As I will discuss later, this claim has been refuted in recent works on the parables.

25. This point needs to be applied to the parable's Sachhälfte, the death of a twenty-eight-year-old rabbi. The parable suggests that God has taken the rabbi from the living because he already had accomplished more than many scholars who lived much longer. Jeremias points out that the element of the complaints of the coworkers in the rabbinical story is not anchored in an actual historical situation as Jesus' parable is.

26. At several places in his work, Jeremias uses ancient Jewish and rabbinical literature in order to highlight the qualities of Jesus' parables. He talks for instance about "wearisome length" of a pre-Christian allegory in contrast to the "vivid" nature of Jesus' parables and claims that "in the rabbinic use of the masal, by far the most common form is that of the parable which contains traditional metaphorical elements" (89)—clearly a disapproving assessment within Jeremias's hermeneutics. He refers to the notion of retribution, which, as he argues, characterizes "the outlook of late Judaism" (184) and opposes it to Jesus' parable of the Rich Man and Lazarus. The contrast between law and grace is a recurrent theme. In relation to the parable of the Guest without a Wedding Garment, as he calls it, Jeremias uses rabbinical material as a negative foil: the call for repentance is contrasted with Jesus' announcement of redemption. In his interpretation of the passage about The Last Judgment in Matthew 25:31–46, Jeremias again draws a contrast between Jesus' teachings and rabbinical parallels. In the latter, the protagonists self-confidently proclaim their good deeds, says Jeremias. "How differently sounds the surprised question of the righteous in vv. 37–39 of our passage, who are unconscious of having rendered any service, to say nothing of the conception that in the persons of the poor and the wretched, men are confronted by the hidden Messiah" (208). And, using a quote by T. W. Manson, Jeremias continues: "Our pericope . . . contains, in fact, 'features of such startling originality that it is difficult to credit them to anyone but the Master himself'" (208–209). A few pages later Jeremias writes: "Judaism taught that God rules the world by the two measures of Mercy and Judgment; but at the last Judgment he only makes use of the measure of Judgment. . . . On the other hand, Jesus taught that the measure of Mercy is in force at the Last Judgment also" (213–214).

27. See Sanders's discussion of the work of W. Bousset, R. Bultmann, G. Bornkamm, M. Dibelius, E. Kaesemann, E. Fuchs, W. G. Kümmel, E. Schweizer, and J. Jeremias, Jesus 23–58. As Sanders shows, all of these scholars center their works on the historical Jesus around what they believe to be a fundamental difference between Jesus and other contemporary teachers. Many of these scholars are participants in what is called the "new quest for the historical Jesus." Gerd Theissen has responded to Sanders's reading of Bornkamm's work in his essay "Theologie and Exegese in den neutestamentlichen Arbeiten von Günther Bornkamm" (see 320 n. 40). In this essay, Theissen helpfully contextualizes Bornkamm's work within the debates between the Confessional Church (Bekennende Kirche) and the German Christians (Deutsche Christen) during the Nazi era as well as within the postwar landscape of German theology. Susannah Heschel shows that these debates are not new but had taken place already in the nineteenth century between the Jewish historical critic and theologian Abraham Geiger and his Christian colleagues. See her book Abraham Geiger and the Jewish Jesus, especially the chapter entitled "Reconceiving Early Judaism."

28. In biblical scholars' vocabulary, this rule is part of the criterion of double dissimilarity. Perrin defined it thus: "the earliest form of a saying we can reach may be regarded as authentic if it can be shown to be dissimilar to characteristic emphases both of ancient Judaism and of the early Church," as quoted by Evans in his critical discussion on "dissimilarity" (Jesus 19).

29. The "third quest" distinguishes itself from the "old" and the "new quest": the "old quest" was characterized by the optimism of liberal theologians of the last century who thought them-

selves capable of reconstructing the personality of Jesus. Jülicher's work on the parables falls in this phase. As I noted earlier, the movement broke down with Albert Schweitzer's work. "The new quest" was initiated in the 1950s and searched for relations between the "kerygmatic Christ" and "the historical Jesus." Jeremias was a major proponent of this movement. As James Robinson points out, Jeremias's work on the parables effectively demonstrated the possibility for historical Jesus research (24). For an overview of the different phases of research see Theissen and Merz 1–15. For a general discussion of "the third quest," see Evans 1–49. Not everybody agrees on the terminology, however. See, for example, Crossan, "Our Own Faces" 18.

30. The criterion of dissimilarity has consequently come under critical scrutiny; see Evans 19–21, Sanders 16–17. Theissen and Merz talk about the shift from the "criterion of difference" to a "historical criterion of plausibility." They write: "What is plausible in the Jewish context and makes the rise of Christianity understandable may be historical" (11).

31. How much some American third-quest scholars, despite the recent methodological revisions, hold on to a contrast between Jesus and Judaism is pointed out by Heschel: "Yet despite Sanders's work, an important trend within American scholarship continues to de-Judaize Jesus" (234). Heschel mentions the work of Burton Mack, John Dominic Crossan, and Marcus Borg.

32. Sanders adopts J. Klausner's formulation of the task: "a good hypothesis with regard to Jesus' intention and his relationship to Judaism should meet Klausner's test: it should situate Jesus believably in Judaism and yet explain why the movement initiated by him eventually broke with Judaism" (18).

33. One of Sanders's efforts is to differentiate between "the poor" and "the sinners," which many New Testament scholars slide together. See 177–182.

34. According to Sanders, much more serious was the conflict that was caused by Jesus' aggressive action in the Temple. This conflict, Sanders argues, eventually led to Jesus' crucifixion.

35. At some other point, Sanders talks about a lack of historical imagination: scholars such as Jeremias "cannot imagine the crowded streets of Jerusalem, the villages of Galilee, the farms in the valley of Jezreel. If they did, they would know that no small group of super-pious, super-educated bigots (in case there were actually such a group) could in any way effectively exclude from religious and social life those who did not meet their standards; much less would such a group have any reason for taking umbrage at a wandering Galilean healer and preacher who associated with the common people" (199).

36. This is emphasized in John Koenig, "In His Time and in History." Sanders and Ben Meyer have exchanged views on Jeremias's use of sources. See Sanders, "Jesus and the Kingdom," and Ben Meyer's answer to Sanders in "A Caricature of Joachim Jeremias and His Scholarly Work." This discussion is embedded in a nasty debate over what Meyer calls "Sanders's insinuation that Jeremias was an anti-Semite" (451). Let me emphasize at this point that my discussion of Jeremias's anti-Jewish tendencies in this and the following chapters is distinct from the debate over whether or not Jeremias was an anti-Semite. I believe that in the context of German New Testament scholarship it is useful to distinguish between anti-Judaism and anti-Semitism, or more specifically, between anti-Jewish Nazi propaganda and a scholarly discourse that produced degrading images of first-century Judaism. The complicated relation between these two trends or discourses is expressed in a question Theissen asked in regard to the tendency of German New Testament scholars to draw a contrast between Jesus and Judaism: "How could such an [anti-Jewish] image of Jesus emerge at a time when New Testament scholars opposed the anti-Semitism of National Socialism with great personal investment?" "Wie konnte es zu diesem kontrastierenden Jesusbild kommen—und das in einer Generation von Neutestamentlern, die unter großem persönlichen Einsatz dem Antisemitismus der Nationalsozialisten widersprochen hatten?" ("Theologie und Exegese" 321).

37. See also Sanders 25 and 278–279. This argument is a repeated critique launched by "the third quest" against "the new quest." See Evans 11–12; Theissen 28.

38. According to Sanders, the sayings material in general is not a viable starting point for Jesus research. He bases his work on what he calls "the facts about Jesus."

39. Rau quotes from Jeremias's introduction. Jeremias 10; Rau 231.

40. Rau tentatively proposes that Jesus was taught by John the Baptist. See 240.

41. Against the notion of a superior literary quality of the parables of Jesus, Hezser writes: "Derartige ästhetische Werturteile liegen ausserhalb des Zuständigkeitsbereichs des historisch-kritischen Forschers und zeugen von der antijüdischen Einstellung von Neutestamentlern der damaligen Zeit" (164). "Such aesthetic value judgments are beyond the competence of historical critics and reveal the anti-Jewish attitudes of New Testament scholars at the time." Hezser is here concerned with P. Fiebig's work on rabbinical and New Testament parables. A more general indictment can be found in the epilogue of her book: "For most Christian New Testament scholars, anti Jewish bias and a lack of Hebrew language competence made it impossible to access the Jewish sources without prejudice." "Dem weitaus größten Teil christlicher Neutestamentler war durch antijüdische Vorurteile und mangelnde Kenntnis der hebräischen Sprache der unvoreingenommene Zugang zu den jüdischen Quellen verstellt" (300). I will discuss the second quotation in chapter 6.

42. In this part of her work, Hezser is interested not in a possible interdependence of the different parables but in the available cultural imagery and the different possibilities of plot development.

43. Hezser disagrees with Jeremias, who thinks that it is the workers' own fault to be hired only late in the day. See Hezser 238 and Jeremias 37.

44. Hezser does not discuss Jeremias's use of the rabbinical parable. In a brief discussion of Jeremias's overall interpretation of Matthew 20:1–16, she dismisses his claim that Jesus, by telling the parable, posits a relationship between God's and his own action. This argument, Hezser says, is theology, not history (16).

45. Hezser suggests that the parable's Sitz im Leben is a discussion between Jesus and the Pharisees in which Jesus argues that God accepts also the many people who do not meet Pharisaic requirements. This definition, at first sight, might seem to be not much different from Jeremias's reconstruction of the parable's first historical setting. However, Hezser goes on to say that thereby Jesus reminds the Pharisees of the theology they share with him (298).

Chapter 5

1. The English translation renders the heading "The Imminence of Catastrophe," which does not preserve the visual aspect of the German expression. As I will discuss hereafter, the German expression became important for my reading of Jeremias.

2. I am quoting here from the 1947 edition, whose wording in the second quotation slightly differs from the later editions. I also use the 1955 English edition for the translations. I give priority to the German quotations in my text because I had worked with the German text in 1994. In general, I am concerned in this chapter with the resonances and nuances of Jeremias's original language.

3. This makes the case of Jeremias different from Crossan's *Raid on the Articulate* and its rich web of allusions to the horrors of this century, discussed in chapter 8.

4. Jeremias writes that the parables "shock into realization of its danger a nation rushing upon its own destruction, more especially its leaders, the theologians and priests." This last specification also played into what I call the overdetermination of Jeremias's language: it evoked for me the painful debate over the partial responsibility of the leaders of Jewish organizations as it was triggered, for instance, by Hannah Arendt's book *Eichmann in Jerusalem*. Let me stress again that I trace these evocations back to my own receptivity and mindframe in 1994. I am concerned here with aspects of my own reading during that time, not with Jeremias's authorial intentions.

5. Bernstein argues instead for the importance of sideshadowing: "Sideshadowing's attention to the unfulfilled or unrealized possibilities of the past is a way of disrupting the affirmations of a triumphalist, unidirectional view of history in which whatever has perished is condemned because it has been found wanting by some irresistible historico-logical dynamic" (3).

6. I eventually found out that this heading was not part of the 1947 edition. The heading in 1947 is "Die bevorstehende Krise," which is equivalent to the English "The Imminence of Catastrophe."

7. In this chapter I obviously work with many layers of meaning. My reading includes at least two interpretations of "the catastrophe" in Jeremias's discourse. In my first and less-than-conscious reading of the phrase, I took the catastrophe to be the threat of the extermination machinery that was about to destroy European Jews in the early 1940s. Here I am interpreting the catastrophe from an immediate postwar and non-Jewish German perspective.

8. I did not know at the time that most of Jeremias's work with rabbinical material appeared only in later editions. The degradation of rabbinical parables is not yet to be found in the 1947 edition. This raises important questions about the historical context of Jeremias's later editions. What does it mean that the anti-Jewish trends became stronger rather than weaker during the postwar decades? I discussed this time period in chapter 2. In this chapter I am focusing on Jeremias's first publication of 1947.

9. A differentiated post-Holocaust discussion of Kittel's contested *Theologisches Wörterbuch zum Neuen Testament* is provided by Alan Rosen in his essay "'Familiarly Known as Kittel': The Moral Politics of the Theological Dictionary of the New Testament."

10. Following this argument, one may wonder whether the German inability to mourn for the Nazi victims was a continuation of an earlier and more disastrous inability, namely the failure of many Germans to be concerned about and resist the persecution of Jews and others.

11. Moeller argues against the Mitscherlichs: "The apparent failure of West Germans to pay the high psychic costs demanded by the Mitscherlichs did not mean that they fled headlong from the past or suffered from collective amnesia. There were many accounts of Germany's 'most recent history' that circulated in the 1950s; remembering selectively was not the same as forgetting" ("War Stories" 1012–1013).

12. However, I also want to provide the next sentences: "And yet, though aware of our helplessness in the face of extremity, we feel at moments an urgent longing for the calm truth. The aggravation of distress by the indictment (of the German people) is not irrelevant, or a mere cause of anger. We want to see clearly whether this indictment is just or unjust, and in what sense" (27–28).

Chapter 6

1. I quote again from the 1962 English edition.

2. See, for instance, Jülicher 406.

3. Jeremias concedes that the "parable, linked up as it is with the Song of the Vineyard in Isa 5.1–7, exhibits an allegorical character" (70). As Jeremias continues to argue, however, the resonances between the parable and Isaiah 5 should not be overestimated. The story can be understood without these references.

4. In the context of the gospels, Jeremias argues, "the son" is applied to Jesus Christ "first in the words *hion agapeton* (12.6) [beloved son], an echo of the voice from heaven in I.II and 9.7, and then in vv. 10–11, where in the form of the Old Testament symbol of the rejected stone which God made the key-stone (Ps. 118) there is introduced one of the primitive Church's favorite proof-texts for the resurrection and exaltation of the rejected Christ" (73–74). For Mark, the owner's son thus has a deeper meaning: it is applied to Jesus Christ, the son of God. However, Jeremias emphasizes that in the parable's first historical setting these christological allusions were not self-evident, at least not for Jesus' audience. "There can be no doubt that in the sending of the son Jesus

himself had his own sending in mind, but for the mass of his hearers the Messianic significance of the son could not be taken for granted, since no evidence is forthcoming for the application of the title 'Son of God' to the Messiah in pre-Christian Palestinian Judaism" (72–73).

5. Besides Milavec's essay, the volume includes a second essay that deals with the parable of the Wicked Husbandmen: "Jesus' Parables from the Perspective of Rabbinic Literature: The Example of the Wicked Husbandmen," by the Jewish scholar David Stern. Stern, like Milavec, critically addresses Jeremias's work on the parables. However, Milavec's essay is more relevant to my concerns because of its use of the category "post-Holocaust."

6. Understood within the Jewish horizon of understanding, Milavec emphasizes, there are no indications that Mark identified the owner's son with Jesus. Jeremias's argument that the christological allusion is given, for instance, with Mark's reference in v. 6 to the "beloved son" can easily be refuted: Matthew, who used the gospel of Mark and who had "finely developed Jewish instincts" apparently did not perceive this reference as a christological clue; otherwise he would not have removed it. When Jeremias and others assume that the gospel writers identified "the son" with Jesus, they are not guided by the original horizon of understanding but by their own Christian training (102).

7. This is what Milavec hopes for. His last footnote ends with the following sentence: "The contemporary Church, having abandoned its teaching of contempt, is now once again in a favorable situation for rediscovering some lost meanings and even for pioneering new understanding which harmonize with the recently recovered sense that there exists a common heritage which unites Christians and Jews" (117).

8. I do not know about Sanders's motivations. From Rau's seminar I remember a deep concern with anti-Judaism, although Rau does not use the category in his book. Generally, I believe that historical scholars who recover any kind of Jewish aspect of Jesus and his message do this work in recognition of the Holocaust and of its challenge for Christianity, even if this recognition is not explicated.

9. "Dem weitaus größten Teil christlicher Neutestamentlicher war durch antijüdische Vorurteile und mangelnde Kenntnis der hebräischen Sprache der unvoreingenommene Zugang zu den jüdischen Quellen verstellt. An diesem Zustand hat sich leider auch nach dem Zweiten Weltkrieg und der Vernichtung eines großen Teiles des jüdischen Volkes nicht viel geändert. Während jüdische Neutestamentler beginnen, Jesus ins Judentum 'heimzuholen,' gibt es noch immer christliche Neutestamentler, die versuchen, Jesus vom Judentum abzugrenzen. Nur bei einigen Wenigen hat ein Umdenken stattgefunden. . . . Wenn wir lernen, die jüdischen Texte mit anderen Augen zu sehen, können wir viele Gemeinsamkeiten zwischen ihnen und der Lehre Jesu entdecken und erkennen, daß die Lehre Jesu Juden und Christen verbindet. Vieleicht kann Jesus auch bei uns eine Umstrukturierung der Wahrnehmung bewirken. Anstatt die jüdischen religiösen Traditionen herabzusetzen, um unsere eigenen Traditionen höher zu bewerten, sollten wir uns mitfreuen über die religiösen Wahrheiten und ethischen Lehren, die in den rabbinischen Schriften enthalten sind" (300).

10. The authors ask: "And if Christian theologians do face that historical *caesura*, can any of us any longer easily retrieve the 'fulfillment' theme always in danger of becoming a supercessionist theme, the lack of theological anger at Matthew 25 or the use of 'the Jews' in John's gospel, the uninterrupted use of traditional law-gospel motifs?" (85) Hezser and Milavec, it seems to me, are scholars who have faced that historical caesura and decided that they are no longer able to hold on to these things.

Chapter 7

1. The interpretive challenge to develop a new understanding of "context" could be witnessed during a discussion over a paper given by John Dominic Crossan at the conference "Semi-

ology and Parables" held in 1975. One of the major points in this discussion was the question of the particular understanding of "context" underlying Crossan's presentation. As Crossan eventually, and perhaps a little impatiently, replied: "The context I am taking seriously at the moment is the context of the genre parable. You have used the term 'genre.' That is the context" (Patte, *Semiology* 312).

2. Interesting explorations of this shift include William Doty, "The Parables of Jesus, Kafka, Borges, and Others with Structural Observations," and Robert Funk, *Jesus as Precursor*. Wolfgang Harnisch's work on the parables represents a German response to these American endeavors.

3. In the mid-1980s John Dominic Crossan turned away from the literary study of parables and toward more conventionally historical questions. Today he is well known for his numerous publications, popular and scholarly, on the historical Jesus and early Christianity.

4. See Perrin 105–106 and 123–127. According to Perrin's account, this insufficiency characterized not only historical criticism but also the work of the "New Hermeneutic," a strand in German scholarship that developed the notion of the parables as "language events." Representative of this strand are the works by Eberhard Jüngel and Ernst Fuchs. The "New Hermeneutic" and its appropriation of Heideggerian philosophy has informed what I call here the American endeavor and is also a major influence of Harnisch's work.

5. "One of the most interesting observations made in recent reviews of the history of biblical criticism is that some of the pioneers like Herder, Overbeck, Gunkel and Norden had wider concerns with language-forms and 'how language works' than were pursued by their followers. Their widely humanistic scope and curiosities were narrowed in the sequel" (Wilder 4). I would add that Adolf Jülicher's work represents precisely such an open, humanistic, and curious approach to the parables. Jülicher's investigations into the form of parables were narrowed by Jeremias, who was not concerned with questions of language.

6. For a thorough discussion of several of these early essays, see Perrin 168.

7. This first becomes apparent during Crossan's discussion of the "Kingdom of God" and of what he calls "permanent eschatology": What is God? God is the "one who challenges world and shatters its complacency repeatedly" (28). And what is the Kingdom? The "Kingdom is that which in shaking man's world at its foundations establishes the dominion of God over and against all such worlds" (27). These definitions bring into focus the central theme of Crossan's thoughts on parables: "shattering" and "shaking" as permanent divine activities against all human establishment; God's challenge to everything that is humanly made up but has become absolutized and turned into supposedly secure foundations of reality. "Permanent eschatology" is the term Crossan creates for this challenge. And he identifies "paradox" as its linguistic counterpart, the form of language in which the challenge has been proclaimed by Jesus: "Jesus" announces God as the shatterer of world, as the One of permanent eschatology, and so his language is sharpened necessarily into paradox, for paradox is to language as eschaton is to world" (76).

8. This reading depends on the parable's version in the gospel of Thomas, which leaves out the final act of the story, the destruction of the tenants.

9. This is proposed, for example, by Tim Schramm and Kathrin Löwenstein, *Unmoralische Helden* 36.

10. It is precisely this sort of reading of Jesus' parables that hit a nerve with several of Crossan's colleagues. For example, in a 1985 consideration of Crossan's work, Lynn Poland complained that Crossan reduces the parables to a mere function stripped of all content. With the shift from metaphor to paradox Crossan indeed rejects what for many biblical scholars was so attractive about the possibility of understanding the parables of Jesus as poetic metaphors: its capacity to discover something new about reality. "Crossan empties the parables of disclosive power," Poland writes. Consequently, it would appear that "Jesus may be one who overturns established meanings, but he offers no positive vision of the Kingdom he proclaims" (112). For a similar critique, see John B. Cobb, "A Theology of Story" 153–155.

11. Crossan himself does not use the label "postmodern" for his work. I find the term helpful because it can highlight the recognition of the loss of Western master narratives, the valorization of short stories, and the emphasis on play in Crossan's thought. I will explicate hereafter how this rendition of "postmodernism" would be challenged by biblical scholars today.

12. Playing with a famous quotation from Paul, he says: "we do not mourn that we see through a glass darkly, we now rejoice in the dark loveliness of the glass" (*Dark* 24).

13. In contrast to both prophetic and apocalyptic eschatology, Crossan's comic eschatology challenges any kind of tragic vision about the ending of the world (*Raid* 30-33).

14. This unresolved tension has been pointed out, for example, by Moore 144-145 and Brown and Malbon 534.

15. In contrast, see his 1995 book *Who Killed Jesus?* a historical-critical study of the passion narratives that is motivated, Crossan says, by an ethics of historical reconstruction and public discourse (35).

16. See, for example, the contributions to *Semeia* 51 and 54, especially Gary Phillips, "Exegesis As Critical Praxis: Reclaiming History and Text from a Postmodern Perspective," as well as the introduction to *The Postmodern Bible* by the Bible and Culture Collective.

17. The literature is too vast as to mention here. I am thinking especially of feminist readings of French theory. Early examples include the essays collected in Judith Butler and Joan Scott, *Feminists Theorize the Political*, and Teresa de Lauretis, *Feminist Studies/Critical Studies*.

18. Consequently, the field of study to which *Raid* would belong is strikingly unclear. *Raid* does not necessarily belong to the field of New Testament parable hermeneutics because it lacks a clear interpretive focus on the parables of Jesus as the primary object of interest. At Temple University's library I found it not among the books on the parables of Jesus but among the critical literature on Jorge Luis Borges. But it could have been just as well be classed with books on theology and literature or on literature and the comic.

Chapter 8

1. This indictment is directed against "the apodictic claim of Enid Welsford that, 'the facts of life are tragic, and the human heart is proof against the comic spirit.'" (11) It is left open what Crossan is thinking of in relation to the "mid-thirties of this century." For me, this time period is closely associated with the Nazi rise to power and the installment of anti-Jewish legislation.

2. "Helmut Plessner might be expected to sympathize with a circular theory of time since the Nazis who had dismissed him from his philosophy chair at Göttingen in 1933 did it again in 1943 from Groningen in Holland" (136). This biographical information is offered by Crossan as an amusing observation in passing.

3. The context is Crossan's question whether the Greek epic Antigone is comic or tragic. "Looking back at the horrors of this century," Crossan suggests, "one sympathizes fully with Antigone and judges her completely, if tragically, in the right" (15). This suggestion, however, is not explained. Which horrors does Crossan have in mind? And how exactly would they inform a (re)evaluation of Antigone's decision?

4. At the 1997 conference "Religion and Postmodernism" at Villanova University I heard Crossan distinguish himself from a German colleague in regard to their different assessments of historical Jesus research: "I am deeply aware of divergent sensibilities between somebody like Koester and myself. I am Irish and Roman Catholic, he is German and Lutheran. Furthermore, we lived in very different worlds in the 1940s and I was in the far safer but not necessarily the more honorable location, the protected lee of a rejected empire. That does not make either of us right and the other wrong but it gives us different religious, political, and autobiographical sensitivities. . . . I do not see the specter of Hitler as inevitably haunting such study [i.e., historical

Jesus research]" ("Our Own Faces" 289). I suspect that Crossan, too, would trace my reading of his 1976 book back to my own "autobiographical sensitivities."

5. This also means that in my reading I have neglected the most central aspect of *Raid*: Crossan's treatment of Borges's writings. Instead I have focused my attention on Crossan's engagement with texts and writers that are more closely linked to the history of the Holocaust. A historicized reading of Borges's work has been offered by Daniel Balderston in his book *Out of Context*. As Balderston suggests, the mainstream of Borges criticism has tended to dehistoricize Borges's literature on the assumption that Borges was an "irrealist" or "escapist" writer. Against this tendency, Balderston proposes to "show how an imaginative reading of Borges's texts that is attentive to historical and political context can discover implications in those texts that considerably complicate the picture we have had up to now of the 'postulation of reality' in Borges" (5). Balderston positions his project within a more general endeavor to recover the historical context not only of Borges but also of writers such as Kafka or Beckett (16). As Balderston makes clear, these efforts are quite recent—"we are only beginning to be able to read what is under erasure" (16). Balderston's work would be able to throw critical light on Crossan's reduction of Borges's writings to a phenomenon of form.

6. Comedy and tragedy are familiar concepts for parable interpreters in the 1970s. They have been introduced into scholarship especially by Dan Otto Via as technical terms to theorize the different plot developments of the parables: "comic" parables describe an upward movement that leads to the protagonist's well-being and integration into society; the plot of "tragic" parables moves downward to catastrophe and isolation. Crossan's discussion of comedy and tragedy, however, is distinct from this technical use of the terms. For Crossan, these terms imply much more than two different kinds of narrative structure. He writes: "I intend to view comedy and tragedy, in the words of Robert Martin, not as 'forms of literature or genres, but formulations of modes of thought, attitudes toward the world, ways of coming to terms with the meaning of its triumphs and vicissitudes'" (17).

7. As my review explained, "comedy" plays a key role in Crossan's postmodern vision of language and reality. According to Crossan, comedy reminds us that reality is made up of human language and storytelling, an activity that he finds especially in the language of Jesus and Borges and that he further defines as comic eschatology.

8. I would argue that Crossan's discussion of tragedy and comedy actually circumvents the confrontation with "real suffering and actual pain." For a helpful reflection on the role of the comic that does not circumvent the issue, see Terrence Des Pres's essay "Holocaust Laughter."

9. I am sure that Crossan upon the slightest impulse would have been able to rethink his argument, even in the 1970s, and let it be said at this point that in the 1990s Crossan had thought through these matters enough to address the legacy of the Holocaust as motivating factor of his scholarship. See his 1995 book *Who Killed Jesus? Exposing the Roots of Anti-Semitism in the Gospel Story of the Death of Jesus*.

10. As Crossan points out, Borges wrote a number of stories that attack biblical time by means of the circle. "Circularity," Crossan explains, "serves as a comic and parabolic critique of our presumption that linear and progressive time . . . is an obvious and self-evident datum of objective reality" (142). Borges does not replace time with circular time; he rather subverts any positive notion of stable, meaningful time. The symbol for this is the labyrinth, commonly associated with Borges, which Crossan does wants to take as a symbol not of doom and dread, as most critics do, but of play and playful human world-building.

11. Crossan's first example is presented in Gerald T. Hurley, "'Buried Treasure Tales in America' for *Western Folklore* in 1951, in which he claimed that the characteristic sequence of such stories is Hiding, Seeking, NOT Finding" (157). Crossan's second example is a story from T. Roszak, *Where the Wasteland Ends*.

12. I thank Marian Ronan for this information. I also would like to thank Tim Schramm for pointing me to a German essay that offers a powerful indictment of the habit of Christians, and specifically pastors, of telling rabbinical stories to their congregations. In "Bedingungen einer Erzählkultur," Karlheinz Müller makes the following appeal to a Christian audience: "Stop using Jewish stories as an opener, so to speak, for your sermons! For it is dishonorable, even unethical, to present Jewish stories from the perspective of those who belong to the triumphant religion, for whom there is nothing at stake, and to ignore the struggle for survival that is an element in almost all good Jewish stories." "Hören Sie auf, von den Kanzeln herunter jüdische Geschichten zu erzählen—als 'Aufhänger' gewissermaßen! Denn es ist unschicklich, ja unmoralisch, jüdische Geschichten im Bewußtsein der Siegerreligion zum Besten zu geben, für die nichts mehr auf dem Spiel zu stehen braucht—und dabei das meistens knappe Überleben zu übersehen, das fast an allen guten jüdischen Geschichten hängt" (49). Against Crossan's practice Müller would say that a rabbinical story "receives its dignity only through the historical context in which it was told and from which it ought not to be separated." "erhält ihre Würde erst durch den zeitgeschichtlichen Kontext, in dem sie erzählt wurde und aus dem man sie niemals lösen sollte" (50).

13. The second example is taken from J. D. Kingsbury, *The Parables of Jesus in Matthew 13*: "To what is the matter like? To one who received a large field in a province of the sea [i.e., in the far distance, in the remote West] as inheritance. And he sold it for a triffle. And the buyer went there and dug it up and found in it treasures of silver and treasures of gold and precious stones and pearls. Then the seller began to choke himself [for anger.] This is what the Egyptians did; for they sent away and did not know what they sent away; for it is written, 'And they said: What is this we have done, that we have let Israel go from serving us?' (Exodus 14.5)" (as quoted by Crossan 154).

14. I will not recapitulate here the critical voices against the contrasting and degrading treatments of Jewish traditions that have emerged since the mid-1980s. Let me just refer back to Catherine Hezser's work on Matthew 20. Hezser's strategies would probably apply as well to the rabbinical material Crossan deals with here.

15. These differences can be studied at a later point in Crossan's discussion. There, Crossan explicitly takes up and develops Jeremias's comparison between Matthew 20 and the rabbinical story. See *Raid* 161.

16. Crossan quotes Jeremias's phrase about "weapons of warfare" at the beginning of his book *In Parables*, in order to refute it. This refutation serves the shift from a historical to a literary paradigm. What remains, however, is the notion of a basic conflict between Jesus and his contemporaries. The violent interpretive language of *Raid on the Articulate*, especially, is not too far from reconfiguring Jesus' parables as "weapons of warfare"—albeit a playful kind of warfare.

17. See, for example, *In Parables* 20. Crossan distances himself here from any "attempt to exalt Jesus above the rabbis as an exercise in Christian chauvinism" (29). For similar gestures in *Raid*, see 65 and 177.

18. See also Eckard Rau's assessment of Crossan's distinction between didactic and poetic metaphors. Rau writes: "It is true that Crossan emphasizes: 'This is not simply an attempt to exalt Jesus above the rabbis as an exercise in Christian chauvinism.' But Crossan does not keep the promise implied in this sentence. Instead he undermines the promise through his discussion of poetic experiences." "Crossan betont zwar: 'This is not simply an attempt to exalt Jesus above the rabbis as an exercise in Christian chauvinism.' Doch wird das Versprechen dieses Satzes nicht eingelöst und durch die Ausführungen über die poetische Erfahrung mehr als relativiert" (229).

19. In 1974 Rosemary Redford Ruether published *Faith and Fratricide*, an early critical reflection on the problem of anti-Judaism in the Bible and its scholarship.

Chapter 9

1. Bernstein develops the argument in relation to readings not of Kafka but of Hitler. In the case of reading Kafka as a Holocaust prophet, the intellectual and moral discriminations Bernstein calls for have been made, for example, by Lawrence Langer in his essay "Kafka as Holocaust Prophet" (In *Admitting the Holocaust*). The essay ends by drawing the following distinction: "Kafka's victims, like his readers, face a world full of lonely lives and lonely deaths, shrouded by spiritual and intellectual confusion and misunderstanding. It is a painful heritage, but with courage and the help of Kafka's art, which was adequate to its task, we can confront it. At this point in time, Holocaust literature must face a violation, not an expression, of man's fate in the modern era; vision pursues valiantly but in vain a vocabulary sufficient to the doom of mass extermination. Kafka never knew how fortunate he was to have suffered such a manageable challenge" (124).

2. In her essay "Protecting the Dead" Francine Prose describes a similar phenomenon. Born as a Jewish child in Brooklyn two years after the war, she grew up with the memory of the Holocaust. Prose describes the difficult process through which she gained what she calls a "real" understanding of suffering and of evil. As a child, she writes, "the Holocaust became invested with an air of the romantic. It was terrible and glamorous, dark-toned and nostalgic, a black-and-white or sepia film in which it was always raining. . . . It was emotionally high-charged but historically abstract" (49). Prose recalls that she looked at the photographs of atrocity with a "mixture of distance, horror, pity, curiosity, and titillation" (51). She also recounts that it was only through her own grief over the death of her father "that suffering no longer seemed to me abstract, romantic, desirable, or voluptuous, but rather ugly, terrifying, deeply moving, and entirely real" (126).

Chapter 10

1. I am paraphrasing the back cover of *Figuring the Sacred*, published in 1995. This collection of essays illustrates Ricoeur's ongoing contribution to Christian theological and hermeneutic thought.

2. Among parable scholars see, for example, McFague TeSelle 40; Crossan, *In Parables* 11; Harnisch 56.

3. Dan O. Via's work on the parables is probably the first well-known structuralist approach.

4. Ricoeur is less articulate about how a historical-critical approach could be integrated into his interpretation theory. I discuss the tensions and continuities between Ricoeur's and Jeremias's work toward the end of this chapter.

5. Ricoeur's argument against what he calls structuralist ideology is based on a recovery and elaboration of the notion of discourse as opposed to that of "langue." He writes: "If language is closed upon itself, discourse is open and turned toward a world which it wishes to express and to convey in language" (82).Whereas signs are the basic entities of the structuralist model, sentences are the units of discourse. The sentence is not reducible to the sign. It is not comprehensible by the structuralist view but requires its own field of study. Crucial for Ricoeur's notion of discourse, including its basic unit, the sentence (and, consequently, metaphor), is what he calls the dialectic of event and meaning. Discourse is an event insofar as it is actual; it happens once and then it is over, it appears and disappears. At the same time, the event-character of discourse is relativized by a dialectical counterpart: the meaning of discourse. The sentence is the bearer of meaning—but not in the structuralist sense, according to which meaning is the effect of the differential relations between the signs within a system. Rather the sentence bears meaning thanks to its predicative structure, which is distinct from the structure of signs. It consists of the identifying function (the subject-function, which identifies something particular and singular) and the predicative function of the sentence (the function of the predicate, which assigns universalizable

qualities to the subject). The polarity between the two results in a propositional content, the meaning of the sentence, and this meaning counteracts discourse's character as an event. Discourse might occur and vanish, but what has occurred is something objective, something that can be identified and repeated.

6. It is in this respect that the traditional rhetorical (and structuralist) focus on the single word or sign is justified to a certain degree. Indeed, a metaphor effects a change of meaning and can be identified on the level of the word. However, this change in meaning is merely a result of and an answer to the semantic impertinence presented by the metaphorical statement.

7. Let me emphasize here that I am concerned with Ricoeur's contribution to parable studies, not to the theory of metaphor in general. For Ricoeur's position within the spectrum of other approaches to metaphor, see, for example, Sacks, ed., *On Metaphor*, a collection of essays that grew out of a symposium on the theme held in 1978. Specifically, Wayne Booths, essay "Metaphor as Rhetoric," takes issue with Ricoeur and may serve to exemplify the many ways that Ricoeur's theory of metaphor was contested in the 1970s. According to Booth's definition, a metaphor is "part of an intended communication"; it is "context-dependent," that is, "the full meaning of the metaphor cannot be determined without reference to the rhetorical situation. . . . That context reveals . . . a clear persuasive purpose" (51). By insisting on the context, the intention, the communicative situation and the purpose behind the production of metaphors, Booth effectively widens Ricoeur's theoretical scope.

8. Ricoeur has affirmed this possibility in his essay "The Bible and the Imagination," first published in 1981. However, I wish to emphasize that in his 1976 essay the metaphorical tension remained ambiguous. In fact, scholars who have appropriated Ricoeur's work have focused on the metaphorical tension *within* the narrative. See, for example, Harnisch, Maurer, Weder.

9. Like the precise location of the metaphorical tension of parables, the role of extravagance remains ambiguous. In the middle part of the essay Ricoeur suggests that the extravagance of a parable, taken in isolation from its context, can be the cause for a metaphorical tension and thus can initiate the transfer from narrative to referent. Later on in the essay, Ricoeur argues that the feature of extravagance constitutes the religious moment in the parables. But if the element of extravagance simultaneously is responsible for the parables' metaphorical tension *and* their religious specificity—is then not every metaphorical discourse religious discourse, in Ricoeur's sense? At the same time, however, Ricoeur emphasizes "that it is not so much the metaphorical function as such which constitutes religious language as it is a certain intensification of the metaphorical function." (108). According to this statement, the religious moment of the parables would not lie in the moment of extravagance as such but in the intensification of extravagance. The parables would be religious insofar as the extraordinary traits displayed in their narratives are particularly intense. But this definition would lead into aporias as well, since there are certainly parables to be found within world literature that surpass the Jesus parables in regard to the degree of extravagance but which resist the label of "religious." As Wolfgang Harnisch has pointed out, Ricoeur's argument would imply that the parables of Kafka have to be called the "non plus ultra" of religious discourse (Harnisch 165). Consequently, there is a third point, which remains unclear (apart from the metaphorical tension and the role of extravagance), namely, what exactly distinguishes the parables of Jesus from nonreligious parables. On the surface, Ricoeur seems to give much room to the distinction between "religious" and "poetic" discourse. In fact, by raising the question of the religious quality of the Jesus parables he counteracted the tendency of progressive American scholars (such as Crossan) to simply equate the parables with world literature. He thereby introduced a new discussion into the discourse on parables, which was taken up by several scholars after the publication of "Biblical Hermeneutics." But these scholars had to find a different answer to the question of the religious character of the parables of Jesus. Wolfgang Harnisch, for example, based his own distinction on content, not formal criteria (Harnisch 151).

10. Ricoeur also suggests that Jeremias would not have missed the trait of extravagance if he had placed a "literary analysis" between historical critique and theological interpretation. See 115.

11. Ricoeur writes that "the ultimate referent of the parables, proverbs, and eschatological sayings is not the Kingdom of God, but human reality in its wholeness" (127). He speaks of a "discernment worked by this language at the heart of this ordinary experience" (123).

12. Ricoeur's critique of Jeremias is based on his vital role in the scholarship. At several places in his essay, Ricoeur acknowledges Jeremias's contribution to parable research in an appreciative manner. See, for example, 71, 97–98, 102, 114.

13. Responsible for this autonomy is the form or literary genre of parables, which "secures the survival of the meaning after the disappearance of its *Sitz im Leben* and in that way starts the process of 'decontextualization' which opens the message to fresh reinterpretations according to new contexts of discourse and of life" (71). From this follows also that the given literary context of the parables, namely, the gospel, needs to be taken into account in the process of interpretation. "An isolated parable," Ricoeur writes, "is an artifact of the historico-critical method" (100).

14. At the same time, Ricoeur concedes that historical interpretation, as performed by Jeremias, should also control the process of reinterpretation. "Our interpretations have only to be related to our particular situation as the original one was to the initial situation. It is in this *analogical* way (A is to B what C is to D) that the original import, i.e., the historical interpretation, is controlling with respect to reinterpretation" (134). How exactly this analogy would be reflected in an actual reinterpretation remains unclear. I would argue that in spite of Ricoeur's concessions to historical criticism, his theory, in practice, would preclude the historical approach.

Chapter 11

1. Catastrophes appear also in Crossan's *Raid on the Articulate*. As I show in chapter 8, they are part of an uncanny subtext that serves as an unexplored background for Crossan's comic interpretations of the sayings of Jesus. In contrast, Ricoeur explicates "catastrophe" and "distress" as possible reference points of Jesus' parables. With regard to Harnisch's argument that the parables disclose absolute, unlimited, and boundless possibilities not to be derived from our reality and unheard-of before, Ricoeur would argue: "the *eruption of the unheard in* our discourse and *in* our experience constitutes precisely one dimension *of* our discourse and *of* our experience" (127).

2. It seems significant to me that of all the possible limit-experiences, which, for instance, also include love, Jaspers chooses to focus on the theme of "disaster and evil." This choice, I believe, is not arbitrary but a reflection of the post-Holocaust time in which Jaspers was writing.

3. In the following I will study Ricoeur's and Des Pres's limit-terminology as rhetorical agents within two different hermeneutic endeavors. In making this "rhetorical turn" I am informed by Steven Mailloux's *Rhetorical Power*. Mailloux argues that every act of interpretation has a rhetorical function in a specific communicative situation.

4. In his study of the experience of survival Des Pres also includes accounts from Soviet camps. He writes: "although the survivor is anyone from any corner of Europe or the Soviet Union (and often far beyond), this book is very much about the fate of the Jews, who fared worst in both German and Russian camps" (viii).

5. I offer here a slightly shortened version of Des Pres's quotation from Weiss's memoir. See Des Pres 44–45.

6. The term "extremity" covers the pages of Des Pres's entire book. For example: "Existence in extremity is not an easy subject" (6); "some margin of giving and receiving, is essential to life in extremity" (37); "survivors discovered that in extremity a sense of dignity is something which men and women cannot afford to lose" (64); "The essential paradox of extremity is that life

persists in a world ruled by death" (99); "In extremity life depends on solidarity" (121); "when conditions become extreme a *need to help* arises" (132); "to speak of *owing life* is not, in extremity, mere metaphor" (133–134); "The purpose of action in extremity is to keep life going" (156); "behavior which does not support day-to-day existence tends to vanish in extremity" (191); "the will to bear witness . . . is an involuntary reaction to extreme situations" (199).

7. Des Pres quotes Primo Levi (64): " In this place it is practically pointless to wash every day in the turbid water of the filthy wash basins for purposes of cleanliness and health; but it is most important as a symptom of remaining vitality, and necessary as an instrument of moral survival" (Levi, *Survival* 40).

8. Des Pres traces this "bias against 'mere survival'" back to the basic split between mind and body, which he believes underlies the workings of civilization. Spiritual realms, symbolic forms, or "higher" activities are superimposed on the concrete, physical, bodily aspects of human existence (165). Very often, Des Pres adds, these supposedly "higher" practices are strategies to hide or displace the often dreadful facts of concrete existence. "One of the functions of culture," Des Pres suggests, "is to provide symbolic systems which displace awareness of what is terrible" (5). The widespread cultural habit of seeking meaning and significance in otherwise senseless death through notions of martyrdom or sacrifice is one example.

9. "The trouble with survivors, in our eyes, is that they do not live by the rules. Their needs cannot be delayed, cannot be transformed or got out of sight. Nor do they seek ideal justification for their struggle. Survivors fight merely to live, certain that what counts is life and the sharing of life" (166). Des Pres worries that the experience of survival during the Holocaust clashes with our usual values and views of the world. The many ways in which we have sublimated and distanced ourselves from our bodily needs, he argues, make it hard to really approach and engage with a realm where the whole point of existence was to stay alive, where death had no other meaning than having lost the struggle to survive against the Nazi attack. Survivors are suspect because their experiences have laid open the physical facts of life that our culture usually covers over.

10. Sara Horowitz discusses the issue of publication in regard to the Warsaw Ghetto "Oneg Shabbes," a collective project that collected vast written information about daily life in the ghetto in all its different aspects. A large part of the archive has yet to be translated into English. See Horowitz, "Voices" 44.

11. Young also critically points to the problematic implications of the organization of Des Pres's book. By centering his own arguments around accounts of victims and survivors printed in bold type, Young suggests, Des Pres reinforces the dichotomy between his commentary and survivors' testimonies, between his own exegetic activity and supposedly transparent and normative, quasi- "sacred" texts (22). Thereby, Young points out, Des Pres precludes the possibility that victims and survivors themselves have created meaning in their texts and have recounted the events and experiences from specific cultural standpoints.

12. Ricoeur goes on: "Nevertheless, they [i.e., traditional stories] do not seem to die in the same way, or at least as soon as might be expected on the basis of this theory. Therefore they seem to rely on some other kind of 'tension' . . . ; it may be that this other kind of tension offers other means of regeneration than just verbal rejuvenation" (93). Indeed, Ricoeur suggests, if the semantic innovation of narratives would depend on the tension between words, parables would be analogous not to living but to dead metaphors, because their word combinations are deeply engraved in Christian memory. There is nothing original or innovative about the sequence of words in the parables of Jesus. The life of parables depends on whether or not the capacity to create new meaning can persist despite the sedimentation of a narrative within culture. The tension of parables must be one that prevents parables from dying and ensures that they regularly recover or regenerate. I find it ironic that the life of parables depends on precisely that part of Ricoeur's hermeneutic theory that, as I showed earlier, is most unclear.

13. To add to Stern's critique, there is a frequent discrepancy between the interpretation theory developed by parable scholars and the actual readings of parables, which often do not live up to the promises of the theory. See Perrin's critique of Funk's work in "The Parables of Jesus as Parables, as Metaphors, and as Aesthetic Objects" 34. One could argue, however, that this discrepancy is an inevitable part of a hermeneutics that takes metaphor as its model: As has been stressed by many interpreters, it is impossible to translate metaphorical language into descriptive discourse without a substantial loss in meaning.

14. Ricoeur wrote on Jaspers's work early on in his career. Like Jaspers, Ricoeur's *Symbolism of Evil* raises questions about fundamental human experiences, particularly the experience of fault. Ricoeur does not offer contemporary examples but focuses on the symbolic language of ancient religious traditions in which he finds the experiences of fault expressed. I cannot help but wonder whether Ricoeur's intensive writings on notions such as "human fallibility," "guilt," or "sin" are not also informed by the twentieth-century "facts of evil" mentioned by Jaspers. How did Ricoeur, a Frenchman who in his turn was very much affected by the war—he spent the years between 1940 and 1945 in a German POW camp—integrate the horror of the German extermination machinery into his philosophical thinking? Did the events of the Holocaust possibly shape the themes of his own work?

Chapter 12

1. Once more I refer to Schüssler Fiorenza and Tracy's essay "The Holocaust as Interruption and the Christian Return into History." See my use of this essay in chapter 6.

2. I am repeating here language used by Ricoeur's interpreter Mark Wallace, critically examined in chapter 11.

3. I read from *Die Bibel. Nach der Übersetzung Martin Luthers.*

4. Mark 12:1–12 is read every second Sunday in Lent, according to the *Agende* of the Protestant Church of Baden (*Lektionar für evangelisch-lutherische Kirchen und Gemeinden mit Perikopenbuch*).

5. In his essay "The Bible and the Imagination," Ricoeur offers a reading of the parable of the Wicked Husbandmen that follows another suggestion, according to which the metaphorical tension can be found in the gospel context. On the basis of two parables, those of the Wicked Husbandmen and the Sower, Ricoeur explores the intertextuality through which these stories refer to each other as well as to other parts of the gospel. In this essay, Ricoeur also critically comments on his earlier suggestion in "Biblical Hermeneutics," according to which the metaphorical tension lies *within* the narrative (149). I am more interested in the earlier suggestion, however, because I am dealing with the parable as an isolated Gospel reading.

6. At the same time, this epilogue opens up a new story with new possibilities: Will "the others" behave more respectfully towards the landlord? Will they conform to the contractual agreements? Or will they eventually break the contract as the previous tenants did?

7. Ricoeur never specifies a historical context in his essay "Biblical Hermeneutics." For an example of Ricoeur's reflections on the events of the Holocaust, see his essay "The Memory of Suffering," which was originally an address given at an Interfaith Memorial Service on Yom Ha-Shoah in 1989.

8. I thank the students of my course "Biblical Literature and Religion" (spring 2001) for their thoughts on the parable.

9. In his book *Writing and Rewriting the Holocaust*, James Young describes the "reciprocal exchange" between the Bible and the Holocaust that I am interested in. He writes: "Experiences, stories, and texts of the ancient past remain the same in themselves; but their meanings, their echoes, causes and effects, and their significance all changed with the addition of new

experiences in the lives of these texts' interpreters" (109). Young refers here to several attempts by Jewish survivors of the Holocaust to reread biblical stories, the most well-known of which is probably Elie Wiesel's rereading of the Akedah, the binding of Isaac. What Young argues with respect to Holocaust survivors is true also for German interpreters of ancient Christian stories. After the Holocaust, the meaning, the echoes, causes and effects, and significance of the parable of the Wicked Husbandmen have changed. However, I find it crucial to differentiate between the interpretive challenges that result from a Jewish turn to the Bible "after Auschwitz" and the challenges of such a turn from a non-Jewish German perspective.

10. In 1940 the Jews of Baden were deported to camps in the South of France. Many died there. Others were deported from France to eastern Europe and were murdered in the death camps (Baumann 9).

11. Within the context of an American classroom, working with the parable's extravagance would take different directions. For example, the parable could refer students to the histories of violence against Native Americans and African Americans that shape the places where they are at home.

12. The homily is quoted in Milavec's essay. See Milavec 83.

13. The historical-critical works reviewed in chapter 4 belong to this effort.

References

Adam, A. K. M. *What Is Postmodern Biblical Criticism?* Minneapolis: Augsburg Fortress, 1995.

Alphen, Ernst van. *Caught in History: Holocaust Effects in Contemporary Art, Literature, and Theory.* Stanford: Stanford University Press, 1997.

Améry, Jean. *At the Mind's Limits: Contemplations by a Survivor on Auschwitz and Its Realities.* Trans. Sidney Rosenfeld and Stella P. Rosenfeld. Bloomington: Indiana University Press, 1980.

——. *Ressentiments. Rede im Süddeutschen Rundfunk am 7. März 1966. Mit einem Essay von Horst Meier.* Ed. Sabine Groenewold. Europäische Verlagsanstalt. Eva Reden, band 18, 1995.

Arendt, Hannah. *Eichmann in Jerusalem: A Report on the Banality of Evil.* New York: Viking Press, 1964.

Arens, Edmund. "Metaphorische Erzählungen und kommunikative Handlungen Jesu. Zum Ansatz einer Gleichnistheorie." *Jahrbuch für biblische Theologie* (1987): 52–71.

Balderston, Daniel. *Out of Context: Historical Reference and the Representation of Reality in Borges.* Durham, N.C.: Duke University Press, 1993.

Bammer, Angelika. *The Question of Home. New Formations* 17 (1992).

Barnouw, Dagmar. *Germany 1945: Views of War and Violence.* Bloomington: Indiana University Press, 1996.

Basker, David. "Love in a Nazi Climate: The First Novels of Wolfgang Koeppen and Marie Luise Kaschnitz." *German Life and Letters* 48 (1995): 184–198.

Baumann, Ulrich. *Zerstörte Nachbarschaften. Christen und Juden in badischen Landgemeinden 1862–1940.* Hamburg: Dölling und Galitz, 2000.

Bernstein, Michael. *Foregone Conclusions: Against Apocalyptic History.* Berkeley: University of California Press, 1994.

Die Bibel. Nach der Übersetzung Martin Luthers. Stuttgart: Deutsche Bibelgesellschaft, 1985.

Booth, Wayne. "Metaphor as Rhetoric: The Problem of Evaluation." In Sacks, 47–70.

Borowski, Tadeusz. *This Way to the Gas, Ladies and Gentlemen.* Trans. Barbara Vedder. New York: Viking Press, 1967.

Breech, James. *The Silence of Jesus: The Authentic Voice of the Historical Man.* Philadelphia: Fortress Press, 1983.

Brown, Frank Burch, and Elizabeth Struthers Malbon. "Parabling as a *Via Negativa*: A Critical Review of John Dominic Crossan." *Journal of Religion* 64 (1984): 530–549.

Burnett, Fred. "Postmodern Biblical Exegesis: The Eve of Historical Criticism." *Semeia* 51 (1990): 51–75.

Butler, Judith, and Joan E. Scott, eds. *Feminists Theorize the Political*. New York: Routledge, 1992.

Camus, Albert. *The Plague*. Trans. Stuart Gilbert. New York: Knopf, 1957.

Castelli, Elizabeth. *Imitating Paul: A Discourse of Power*. Louisville, Ky.: Westminster / John Knox Press, 1991.

Cobb, John, Jr. "A Theology of Story: Crossan and Beardslee." In *Orientation by Disorientation: Studies in Literary Criticism and Biblical Literary Criticism*, ed. Richard A. Spencer. Pittsburgh: Pickwick Press, 1980, 153–160.

Crossan, John Dominic. *Cliffs of Fall: Paradox and Polyvalence in the Parables of Jesus*. New York: Seabury Press, 1980.

——. *The Dark Interval: Towards a Theology of Story*. Sonoma, Calif.: Polebridge Press, 1988.

——. *Finding Is the First Act: Trove Folktales and Jesus' Treasure Parable*. Philadelphia: Fortress Press, 1979.

——. *A Fragile Craft: The Work of Amos Wilder*. Society of Biblical Literature Centenniel Series 3, Biblical Scholarship in North America 3. Missoula, Mont.: Scholars Press, 1981.

——. *The Historical Jesus: The Life of a Mediterranean Jewish Peasant*. San Francisco: HarperCollins, 1992.

——. *In Parables: The Challenge of the Historical Jesus*. New York: Harper and Row, 1973.

——. "Our Own Faces in Deep Wells: A Future for Historical Jesus Research." In *God, the Gift, and Postmodernism*, eds. John D. Caputo and Michael J. Scanlon. Bloomington: Indiana UP, 1999, 282–310.

——. *Raid on The Articulate: Comic Eschatology in Jesus and Borges*. New York: Harper and Row, 1976.

——. *Who Killed Jesus? Exposing the Roots of Anti-Semitism in the Gospel Story of the Death of Jesus*. San Francisco: Harper, 1995.

Dekoven Ezrahi, Sidra. "'The Grave in the Air': Unbound Metaphors in Post-Holocaust Poetry." In Friedlander, 259–276.

De Lauretis, Teresa, ed. *Feminist Studies/Critical Studies*. Bloomington: Indiana University Press, 1986.

Delbo, Charlotte. *Auschwitz and After*. Trans. Rosette C. Lamont. New Haven: Yale University Press, 1995.

——. *Days and Memory*. Trans. Rosette C. Lamont. Marlboro, Vt.: Marlboro Press, 1990.

Derrida, Jaques. *Specters of Marx: The State of the Debt, the Work of Mourning, and the New International*. Trans. Peggy Kamuf. New York: Routledge, 1994.

Des Pres, Terrence. "Holocaust Laughter." In *Writing into the World: Essays 1973–1987*. New York: Penguin Books, 1991, 277–286.

——. *The Survivor: An Anatomy of Life in the Death Camps*. New York: Oxford University Press, 1976.

Dodd, Charles Harold. *The Parables of the Kingdom*. Rev. ed. New York: Scribner's 1963.

Dohle, Theodor Eduard. "Marie Luise Kaschnitz im Dritten Reich und in der Nachkriegszeit. Ein Beitrag zu den Publikations- und Wertungsbedingungen der nicht-national-sozialistischen Autorin." diss., Ludwig-Maximilians-Universität München, 1989.

Dornisch, Loretta. "Symbolic Systems and the Interpretation of Scripture: An Introduction to the Work of Paul Ricoeur." *Semeia* 4 (1975): 1–21.

Doty, William. "The Parables of Jesus, Kafka, Borges, and Others with Structural Observations." *Semeia* 2 (1974): 152–193.

Elliott, Neil. *Liberating Paul: The Justice of God and the Politics of the Apostle*. Maryknoll, N.Y.: Orbis Books, 1999.

Evans, Craig. *Jesus and His Contemporaries: Comparative Studies*. Leiden: Brill, 1995.

Felman, Shoshana. *Testimony: Crises of Witnessing in Literature, Psychoanalysis, and History*. New York: Routledge, 1992.

Felstiner, John. "Biography of a Poem." *New Republic* (April 1984): 27–31.

——. "Translating Paul Celan's 'Todesfuge.'" In Friedlander 240–258.

Freud, Sigmund. "The "Uncanny.'" In *The Standard Edition of the Complete Psychological Works of Sigmund Freud*. Vol 17. Trans. James Strachey. London: Hogarth Press, 1955.

Friedlander, Saul, ed. *Probing the Limits of Representation: Nazism and the 'Final Solution.'* Cambridge: Harvard University Press, 1992.

Friedman, Michelle. "Reckoning with Ghosts: Second Generation Holocaust Literature and the Labor of Remembrance." Diss., Bryn Mawr College, 2001.

Funk, Robert W. *Language, Hermeneutics, and the Word of God*. New York: Harper and Row, 1966.

——. "Jesus and Kafka." *University of Montana. CAS Faculty Journal* 1, 1 (1972): 25–32.

——. *Jesus as Precursor*. Philadelphia: Fortress Press, 1975.

Gadamer, Hans-Georg. *Truth and Method*. Trans. Joel Weisheimer and Donald G. Marshall. New York: Continuum, 1993.

Geisler, Michael E. "'Heimat' and the German Left: The Anamnesis of a Trauma." *New German Critique* 36 (1985): 25–66.

Gersdorff, Dagmar von. *Marie Luise Kaschnitz. Eine Biographie*. Frankfurt: Insel, 1992.

Geyer, Michael, and Miriam Hansen. "German-Jewish Memory and National Consciousness." In Hartmann, *Holocaust Remembrance*, 175–190.

Goldin, Leyb. "Chronicle of a Single Day." In *The Literature of Destruction*, ed. David Roskies. Philadelphia: Jewish Publication Society, 1989, 424–434.

Gordon, Avery F. *Ghostly Matters: Haunting and the Sociological Imagination*. Minneapolis: University of Minnesota Press, 1997.

Harnisch, Wolfgang. *Die Gleichniserzählungen Jesu. Eine hermeneutische Einführung*. Göttingen: Vandenhoeck und Ruprecht, 1985.

——. "Die Sprache des Möglichen. Die Gleichniserzählungen Jesu im Spannungsfeld von Rhetorik und Poetik." *Orientierung* 1 (1994): 23–32.

Hartman, Geoffrey, ed. *Holocaust Remembrance: The Shapes of Memory*. Oxford: Blackwell, 1994.

——. *The Longest Shadow: In the Aftermath of the Holocaust*. Bloomington: Indiana University Press, 1996.

Heschel, Susannah. *Abraham Geiger and the Jewish Jesus*. Chicago: Unviversity of Chicago Press, 1998.

Hezser, Catharine. *Lohnmetaphorik and Arbeitswelt in Mt 20.1–16: Das Gleichnis von den Arbeitern im Weinberg im Rahmen rabbinischer Lohngleichnisse*. Göttingen: Vandenhoeck und Ruprecht, 1990.

Hochhuth, Rolf. *The Deputy*. New York: Grove Press, 1964.

The Holy Bible: New Revised Standard Version. Nashville, Tenn.: Thomas Nelson, 1989.

Horowitz, Sara. "Memory and Testimony of Women Survivors of Nazi Genocide." In *Women of the Word*, ed. Judith Baskin. Detroit: Wayne State University Press, 1994, 258–282.

——. "Voices from the Killing Ground." In Hartman, *Holocaust Remembrance*, 42–58.

Hüppauf, Bernd. "Emptying the Gaze: Framing Violence through the Viewfinder." *New German Critique* 72 (1997): 3–44.

Hurley, G. T. "Buried Treasure Tales in America." *Western Folklore* 10(1951): 197–216.

Huyssen, Andreas. *After the Great Divide: Modernism, Mass Culture, Postmodernism*. Bloomington: Indiana University Press, 1986.

——. *Twilight Memories: Marking Time in a Culture of Amnesia*. New York: Routledge, 1994.

Jaspers, Karl. *Philosophical Faith and Revelation*. Trans. E. B. Ashton. New York: Harper and Row, 1967.

——. *Philosophy*. Vol 2. 1932. Reprint, Chicago: University of Chicago Press, 1970.

——. *The Question of German Guilt*. Trans. E. B. Ashton. 1948. Reprint, Westport, Conn.: Greenwood Press, 1978.

Jay, Martin. "The Uncanny Nineties." *Salmagundi* (fall 1995): 20–29.

Jeremias, Joachim. *Die Gleichnisse Jesu*. Zürich: Zwingli, 1947.

——. *Die Gleichnisse Jesu*. Göttingen: Vandenhoeck und Ruprecht, 1977.

——. *The Parables of Jesus*. New York: Scribner's, 1955.

——. *The Parables of Jesus*. New York: Scribner's, 1963.

Jobling, David. "Writing the Wrongs of the World: The Deconstruction of the Biblical Text in the Context of Liberation Theologies." *Semeia* 51 (1990): 81–109.

Jülicher, Adolf. *Die Gleichnisreden Jesu*. Vol. 1. Tübingen, 1910. Reprint, Wissenschaftliche Buchgesellschaft Darmstadt, 1969.

Kafka, Franz. "Give It Up!" In *The Complete Stories*. New York: Schocken Books, 1995.

——. *Letters to Milena*. Ed. Willi Haas. Trans. Tania and James Stern. London: Secker and Warburg, 1953.

Kaschnitz, Marie Luise, *Ein Wort weiter*. Hamburg: Claassen, 1965.

——. *Gedichte*. 1975. Frankfurt: Suhrkamp, 1993.

——. "Rauch und Nebel: I–IV" *Die neue Rundschau* (1964): 419–424.

——. "Wie man da stand." In *Exil, Widerstand, Innere Emigration. Badische Autoren zwischen 1933 und 1945*, ed. Hansgeorg Schmidt-Bergmann. Karlsruhe: Literarische Gesellschaft (Scheffelbund), 1993, 53–57.

Kingsbury, J. D. *The Parables of Jesus in Matthew 13*. Richmond, Va.: Knox, 1969.

Koenig, John. "In His Time and in History." *New York Times Book Review*, December 22, 1985.

Kritzman, Lawrence D., ed. *Auschwitz and After: Race, Culture, and "the Jewish Question" in France*. New York: Routledge, 1995.

Krondorfer, Björn. "Of Faith and Faces: Biblical Texts, Holocaust Testimony and German 'After Auschwitz' Theology." In Linafelt, 86–105.

——. *Remembrance and Reconciliation: Encounters between Young Jews and Germans*. New Haven, Conn.: Yale University Press, 1995.

LaCapra, Dominick. *Representing the Holocaust: History, Theory, Trauma*. Ithaca: Cornell University Press, 1994.

Langer, Lawrence. *Admitting the Holocaust: Collected Essays*. New York: Oxford University Press, 1995.

——. *The Age of Atrocity: Death in Modern Literature*. Boston: Beacon Press, 1978.

——. *The Holocaust and the Literary Imagination*. New Haven: Yale University Press, 1975.

Lektionar für evangelisch-lutherische Kirchen und Gemeinden mit Perikopenbuch. Hannover: Lutherisches Verlagshaus, 1985.

Levi, Primo. *The Drowned and the Saved*. Trans. Raymond Rosenthal. New York: Vintage Books, 1989.

——. *Survival in Auschwitz*. New York: Touchstone, 1996.

Levitt, Laura. *Jews and Feminism: The Ambivalent Search for Home*. New York: Routledge, 1997.

Linafelt, Tod, ed. *Strange Fire: Reading the Bible after the Holocaust*. New York: New York University Press, 2000.

Lyotard, Jean Fancois. *Heidegger and "the jews."* Trans. Andreas Michel and Mark Roberts. Minneapolis: University of Minnesota Press, 1990.

——. *The Postmodern Condition: A Report on Knowledge*. Trans. Geoff Bennington and Brian Massumi. Minneapolis: University of Minnesota Press, 1984.

Mack, Rudolf, and Dieter Volpert. *Der Mann aus Nazareth—Jesus Christus*. Stuttgart: Calwer, 1981.

Mailloux, Steven. *Rhetorical Power*. Ithaca: Cornell University Press, 1988.

Maurer, Herrmann-Josef. *Die Gleichnisse Jesu als Metaphern. Paul Ricoeurs Hermeneutik der Gleichniserzählungen Jesu im Horizont des Symbols Gottesherrschaft.* Bodenheim: Philo, 1997.

McFague TeSelle, Sallie. *Speaking in Parables: A Study in Metaphor and Theology.* Philadelphia: Fortress Press, 1975.

Meier, Horst, "Hitler zurücknehmen. Zum anti-nazistischen Imperativ bei Jean Améry." In Améry, 47–87.

Meyer, Ben F. "A Caricature of Joachim Jeremias and His Scholarly Work." *Journal of Biblical Literature* 110 (1991): 451–462.

Midrash Rabbah. Ed. H. Freedman and M. Simon. London: Soncino, 1939.

Milavec, Aaron. "A Fresh Analysis of the Parable of the Wicked Husbandmen in the Light of Jewish-Catholic Dialogue." In Thoma and Wyschogrod, 81–117.

Mitscherlich, Alexander and Margarete. *The Inability to Mourn: Principles of Collective Behavior.* New York: Grove Press, 1975.

Moeller, Robert G. "War Stories: The Search for a Usable Past in the Federal Republic of Germany." *American Historical Review* 101,4 (October 1996): 1008–1048.

Moore, Stephen D. *Literary Criticism and the Gospels: The Theoretical Challenge.* New Haven: Yale University Press, 1989.

——. "True Confessions and Weird Obsessions: Autobiographical Interventions in Literary and Biblical Studies." *Semeia* 72 (1995): 19–50.

Müller, Karlheinz. "Bedingungen einer Erzählkultur." In *Erzählter Glaube–Erzählende Kirche,* ed. Rolf Zerfass. Freiburg: Herder, 1988, 28–51.

Novick, Peter. *The Holocaust in American Life.* New York: Houghton Mifflin, 1999.

Oldenhage, Tania. "How to Read a Tainted Text? The Wicked Husbandmen in a Post-Holocaust Context." In *Postmodern Interpretations of the Bible,* ed. A. K. M. Adam. St. Louis Chalice Press, 2001, 165–176.

——. "Parables for Our Time? Post-Holocaust Interpretations of the Stories of Jesus." *Semeia* 77 (1998): 227–241.

Patte, Daniel. *Ethics of Biblical Interpretation: A Reevaluation.* Louisville, Ky.: Westminster, 1992.

——, ed. *Semiology and Parables: An Exploration of the Possibilities Offered by Structuralism for Exegesis.* Pittsburgh Theological Monograph Series 9. Pittsburgh: Pickwick Press, 1976.

Perrin, Norman. *Jesus and the Language of the Kingdom: Symbol and Metaphor in New Testament Interpretation.* Philadelphia: Fortress Press, 1976.

——. "The Parables of Jesus as Parables, as Metaphors, and as Aesthetic Objects: A Review Article." *Journal of Religion* 47 (1967): 340–347.

Phillips, Gary A. "Exegesis as Critical Praxis: Reclaiming History and Text from a Postmodern Perspective." *Semeia* 51 (1990): 7–49.

Poland, Lynn. *Literary Criticism and Biblical Hermeneutics: A Critique of Formalist Approaches.* Chico, Calif.: Scholars Press, 1985.

Politzer, Heinz. "Franz Kafka and Albert Camus: Parables for Our Time." *Chicago Review* 14 (1960): 47–67.

Pons Dictionary. London: Collins, 1987.

The Postmodern Bible. Ed. George Aichele et al. New Haven: Yale University Press, 1995.

Pratt, Minnie Bruce. "Identity: Skin Blood Heart." In *Yours in Struggle: Three Feminist Perspectives on Anti-Semitism and Racism.* (Elly Bulkin, Minnie Bruce Pratt, and Barbara Smith). Brooklyn: Long Haul Press, 1984, 11–63.

Prose, Francine. "Protecting the Dead." *Tikkun* 4,3 (1989): 48–51, 124–127.

Pulver, Elsbeth. *Marie Luise Kaschnitz.* München: Beck,1984.

——. " . . . eine Tänzerin aus dem Geschlechte Jubals, wie der hochmütige Kain." In *Marie Luise Kaschnitz,* ed. Uwe Schweikert. Frankfurt: Suhrkamp,1985, 93–117.

Rau, Eckhard. *Reden in Vollmacht: Hintergrund, Form und Anliegen der Gleichnisse Jesu.* Göttingen: Vandenhoeck und Ruprecht, 1990.

Ricoeur, Paul. "The Bible and the Imagination." In *Figuring the Sacred*, 144-166.

——. "Biblical Hermeneutics." *Semeia* 4 (1975): 29-145.

——. *Figuring the Sacred: Religion, Narrative and Imagination.* Trans. David Pellauer. Ed. Mark I. Wallace. Minneapolis: Fortress Press, 1995.

——. *Interpretation Theory: Discourse and the Surplus of Meaning.* Fort Worth: Texas Christian University Press, 1976.

——. "The Memory of Suffering." In *Figuring the Sacred*, 289-292.

——. *The Rule of Metaphor.* Trans. Robert Czerny. Toronto: University of Toronto Press, 1978.

——. *The Symbolism of Evil.* Trans. E. Buchanan. Boston: Beacon Press, 1967.

Ringelblum, Emanuel. *Notes from the Warsaw Ghetto: The Journal of Emanuel Ringelblum.* Ed. and trans. Jacob Sloan. New York: McGraw-Hill, 1958.

Robinson, James M. *A New Quest of the Historical Jesus.* Missoula, Mont.: Scholars Press, 1979.

Rosen, Alan. "'Familiarly Known as Kittel': The Moral Politics of the Theological Dictionary of the New Testament." In *Tainted Greatness: Antisemitism and Cultural Heroes*, ed. Nancy A. Harrowitz. Philadelphia: Temple University Press, 1994, 37-50.

Rosczak, Theodore. *Where the Wasteland Ends.* Garden City, N.Y.: Doubleday, 1972.

Ruether, Rosemary. *Faith and Fratricide: The Theological Roots of Anti-Semitism.* New York: Seabury Press, 1979, 95-116.

Sacks, Sheldon, ed. *On Metaphor.* Chicago: Chicago University Press, 1979.

Sanders, E. P. *Jesus and Judaism.* Philadelphia: Fortress Press, 1985.

——. "Jesus and the Kingdom: The Restoration of Israel and the New People of God." In *Jesus, the Gospels, and the Church: Essays in Honor of William R. Farmer*, ed. E. P. Sanders. Macon, Ga.: Mercer University Press, 1987, 225-239.

Santner, Eric. "History beyond the Pleasure Principle." In Friedlander, 143-154.

——. *Stranded Objects: Mourning, Memory, and Film in Postmodern Germany.* Ithaca: Cornell University Press, 1990.

Schippert, Claudia. "Ruining the Entire Afternoon: Memory in Bergen Belsen." Paper presented at Lehigh University, November 1994.

Schneider, Richard Chaim. *Fetisch Holocaust. Die Judenvernichtung–verdrängt und vermarktet.* München: Kindler, 1997.

Scholem, Gerschom G. *Major Trends in Jewish Mysticism.* New York: Schocken Books, 1954.

Schramm, Tim, and Kathrin Löwenstein. *Unmoralische Helden. Anstößige Gleichnisse Jesu.* Göttingen: Vandenhoeck und Ruprecht, 1986.

Schüssler Fiorenza, Elisabeth. *Bread Not Stone: The Challenge of Feminist Biblical Interpretation.* Boston: Beacon Press, 1984.

——. *But She Said: Feminist Practices of Biblical Interpretation.* Boston: Beacon Press, 1992.

——. "The Ethics of Biblical Interpretation: Decentering Biblical Scholarship." *Journal of Biblical Literature* 107 (1988): 3-17.

——. *In Memory of Her: A Feminist Theological Reconstruction of Christian Origins.* New York: Crossroad, 1983.

——. *Rhetoric and Ethic: The Politics of Biblical Studies.* Minneapolis: Fortress Press, 1999.

Schüssler Fiorenza, Elisabeth, and David Tracy, eds. "The Holocaust as Interruption and the Christian Return into History." *Concilium* 175 (1984): 83-86.

Schweitzer, Albert. *Von Reimarus zu Wrede. Eine Geschichte der Leben-Jesu-Forschung.* Tübingen: Mohr, 1906.

Sebald, W. G. *Unheimliche Heimat. Essays zur österreichischen Literatur.* Frankfurt: Fischer Taschenbuch, 1995.

Shandler, Jeffrey. *While America Watches: Televising the Holocaust.* New York: Oxford University Press, 1999.

Shapiro, Susan. *Recovering the Sacred: Hermeneutics and Theology after the Holocaust.* Manuscript (forthcoming).

Stern, David. "Jesus' Parables from the Perspective of Rabbinic Literature: The Example of the Wicked Husbandmen." In Thoma and Wyschogrod, 42–80.

Sypher, Wylie, ed. *Comedy.* Garden City, N.Y.: Doubleday, 1956.

Theissen, Gerd. "Theologie und Exegese in den neutestamentlichen Arbeiten von Günther Bornkamm" *Evangelische Theologie* 51 (1991): 308–332.

Theissen, Gerd, and Annette Merz. *The Historical Jesus: A Comprehensive Guide.* Minneapolis: Fortress Press, 1998.

Thoma, Clemens, and Michael Wyschogrod. *Parable and Story in Judaism and Christianity.* New York: Paulist Press, 1989.

Thränhardt, Dietrich. *Geschichte der Bundesrepublik Deutschland 1949–1990. Moderne Deutsche Geschichte.* Vol.12. Frankfurt: Suhrkamp, 1996.

Tracy, David. "Christian Witness and the Shoah." In Hartman, *Holocaust Remembrance,* 81–89.

United States Holocaust Memorial Council. *1945: The Year of Liberation.* Washington, DC: United States Holocaust Memorial Council, 1995.

Veeser, Aram H., ed. *Confessions of the Critics.* New York: Routledge, 1996.

Via, Dan O. *The Parables: Their Literary and Existential Dimension.* Philadelphia: Fortress Press, 1967.

Vonnegut, Kurt. *Cat's Cradle.* New York: Delacorte Press, 1973.

Weder, Hans. *Die Gleichnisse Jesu als Metaphern. Traditions–und redaktionsgeschichtliche Analysen und Interpretationen.* 1978. Göttingen: Vandenhoeck und Ruprecht, 1990.

——. *Neutestamentliche Hermeneutik.* 2nd ed. Zürich: Theologischer Verlag, 1989.

Wiesel, Elie. *The Gates of the Forest.* Trans. Frances Fenaye. New York: Holt, Rinehart and Winston, 1966.

Wilder, Amos N. *Early Christian Rhetoric: The Language of the Gospel.* Cambridge: Harvard University Press, 1971.

——. "*Semeia,* An Experimental Journal for Biblical Criticism: An Introduction." *Semeia* 1 (1974): 1–16.

Young, Brad H. *Jesus and His Jewish Parables: Rediscovering the Roots of Jewish Teaching.* New York: Paulist Press, 1989.

Young, James E. *The Texture of Memory: Holocaust Memorials and Meaning.* New Haven: Yale University Press, 1993.

——. *Writing and Rewriting the Holocaust: Narrative and the Consequences of Interpretation.* Bloomington: Indiana University Press, 1990.

Zelizer, Barbie. *Remembering to Forget: Holocaust Memory through the Camera's Eye.* Chicago: University of Chicago Press, 1998.

Index